A Timeless Place

The Ontario Cottage

Julia Harrison

D1527552

UBCPress · Vancouver · Toronto

21 20 19 18 17 16 15 14 13   5 4 3 2 1

Printed in Canada on FSC-certified ancient-forest-free paper
(100% post-consumer recycled) that is processed chlorine- and acid-free.

Library and Archives Canada Cataloguing in Publication

Harrison, Julia D. (Julia Diane), 1953-, author
A timeless place : the Ontario cottage / Julia Harrison.

Includes bibliographical references and index.
Issued in print and electronic formats.
ISBN 978-0-7748-2607-5 (bound). – ISBN 978-0-7748-2608-2 (pbk.)
ISBN 978-0-7748-2609-9 (pdf). – ISBN 978-0-7748-2610-5 (epub)

1. Vacation homes – Ontario – Haliburton Region. 2. Vacation homes – Social aspects – Ontario – Haliburton Region. 3. Country life – Ontario – Haliburton Region. 4. Haliburton Region (Ont.) – Social life and customs. I. Title.

GV191.46.O58H37 2013   333.78'0971361   C2013-903359-9
                                                   C2013-903360-2

Canada

UBC Press gratefully acknowledges the financial support for our publishing program of the Government of Canada (through the Canada Book Fund), the Canada Council for the Arts, and the British Columbia Arts Council.

This book has been published with the help of a grant from the Canadian Federation for the Humanities and Social Sciences, through the Awards to Scholarly Publications Program, using funds provided by the Social Sciences and Humanities Research Council of Canada.

Printed and bound in Canada by Friesens
Set in Rotis and Minion by Artegraphica Design Co. Ltd.
Copy editor: Stephanie VanderMeulen
Proofreader: Helen Godolphin
Indexer: Heather Ebbs
Cartographer: Eric Leinberger

UBC Press
The University of British Columbia
2029 West Mall
Vancouver, BC V6T 1Z2
www.ubcpress.ca

Dedicated to

Gladys Ethel Harrison (née Greaves)
1915-2012

and

John Henry Wadland
who first took me to the cottage

Contents

Acknowledgments

I would like to begin by expressing sincere gratitude to all of the Haliburton County cottagers who generously invited me to their cottages and shared their stories with me as I sought to understand what their cottages meant to them. Without their time, interest, hospitality, openness, and encouragement, this book would never have been possible. I must also recognize those cottagers from various corners of Ontario's cottage country who learned of my project and expressed sincere interest in it. To respect their privacy, I cannot mention any of these people by name but all of them deserve my thanks for their patience in waiting for the book to finally be published. I have also adjusted other details to further mask their identities.

Svitlana Gouin (Pcholkina), one of my graduate students, was also my research assistant. She contributed significantly to the research here and offered me valuable insights into the curiosities of the cottage experience. I owe a particular debt of gratitude to Betsy Struthers, a good friend and a passionate lover of her cottage who has believed in my project since I first mentioned it. Thank you for the encouragement, thoughtful commentary, and tidbits of information for my research. Your vote of confidence has meant a great deal to me. Susan Frohlick, David Picard, Mike Robinson, and Nelson Graburn have continued to encourage me in my forays into tourism research over several years now. Each of you has set high standards for me and kept me focused on the importance and richness of such work.

Joan McIlwain transcribed my interviews and took a sincere interest in my project. Lynda Mannik read the manuscript at a critical time and gave me insightful and valuable input. Cathy Schoel's hard work, professionalism, and moral support allowed me to find time and space to imagine that I could finalize the manuscript and see it published. Tracy Armstrong helped me navigate the Statistics Canada databases. Peter Gorman offered valuable editorial suggestions at an important point in the manuscript's development. Meaghan Beaton and Kristi Allain were excellent proofreaders in the final stages.

Emily Andrew, senior editor at UBC Press, has been a source of careful guidance and encouragement since we met several years ago. I deeply value her ongoing support and professionalism, and that of everyone else at the press. Thank you to production editor Ann Macklem for her patience. I also would like to thank the anonymous reviewers whose comments refined the manuscript in important ways. The Social Sciences and Humanities Research Council of Canada, the Symons Trust Fund for Canadian Studies, and the Frost Centre Research Fund generously supported the research for this book. The book has been published with the help of a grant from the Canadian Federation for the Humanities and Social Sciences, through the Awards to Scholarly Publications Program, using funds provided by the Social Sciences and Humanities Research Council of Canada.

Revised segments of Chapters 2, 3, and 7 are published here by permission of the publishers of "'I'm Sorry I Got Emotional': 'Real' Work and 'Real' Men at the Canadian Cottage" (J. Harrison 2012, 231-46); "Shifting Positions" (J. Harrison 2008b, 41-60); and "Belonging at the Cottage" (J. Harrison 2010, 71-92).

My family has come along with me in so many ways as I "went to the cottage." On their real visits to the cottage with me, my sisters Christine and Rosamund and my extended family – Derek, Bill, Morris, Miles, Ruchika, and tiny Norah – offered me profound and heartfelt insight into what the cottagers I interviewed told me about treasured memories of family nurtured in such places. My mother, who was never able to go with me, did not doubt that I would make the most of my excursions there. I only wish my father had known the joys of such moments.

John Wadland, whose knowledge of Haliburton County proved invaluable to my research and who knew the cottage experience well as a child, offered me an unimaginable wealth of insight, ideas, stories, and moments of laughter as we debated, reflected, and simply enjoyed together what lies at the heart of the Ontario cottage experience. Without you, John, I would never have ventured there. For that, and so many other things, I am immensely grateful.

A Timeless Place

1

An Introduction to the Cottage

I was grateful to encounter Caroline that afternoon. I had been feeling like an outsider at the crowded social gathering in an upscale Toronto neighbourhood. Our respective in-laws, two extended families whose connection went back fifty-five years, comprised the guest list at the party. These families had been neighbours for many years at their lakeside cottages. Caroline and I chatted at length about what had prompted the get-together. She observed:

> Canadians and summer. It is as if they have to make the most of it. It is a very precious time. Not a moment of it can be wasted. It is expected that everyone will make plans, and in Ontario that means making plans to go to the cottage. The whole country seems to anxiously await summer's arrival, expressing endless angst over whether it will deliver the promised days of warmth, sun and fun. Maybe it has something to do with the cold and snow of winter.

Caroline was an Australian who had come to Canada when she married her Canadian husband thirty years before. Since her move, she too had spent time at her in-laws' cottage. Both my relationship to my in-laws and my introduction to the cottage were much more limited, though, because I had only become a part of that collective a few years earlier. And my father-in-law had sold the family cottage years ago – thankfully, to my mind. It seemed as if Caroline and I were the only two people in the room who had not grown up with a cottage as a central part of our world; accordingly, we seemed to be the only ones who found the practice rather curious. We marvelled at how the memories of summers spent together many years before kept alive a special bond between the extended families, even though they had seen little of each other in recent decades. Caroline aptly concluded that Canadians saw these precious summer months as "an almost religious time," which was certainly reflected in the treasured memories of many in the room that day. Her astute and forthright observations intrigued me.

I had been living in Ontario for five years when I attended this gathering. Having spent the first four decades of my life in western Canada, I moved to Ontario to take up an academic position. My outsider status was somewhat more muted than that of my new Australian friend, but Canada's physical vastness and its regional, historical, and cultural differences still amplified the many subtle things about life in Ontario that were new to me. As the summer of my first year there approached, I was made aware of three assumptions about how I would spend this time: I would be going to my cottage at every opportunity, or negotiating as much time as I could at a relative's or friend's cottage, or, failing these two options, I would spend my summer lamenting the sad reality that I was not at a cottage on the shores of a nearby lake. Such presumptions initially struck me as mildly amusing, if not somewhat odd. I grew to take a more serious interest in what such expectations reflected about the cultural and social milieu of my new home, particularly when I realized that many of the lakes that were readily accessible to the city I now lived in were in essence private. I could access them by canoe if I could find the limited public access points, but if I wished to stop for a picnic on shore there was often little or no public land available. Cottagers seemed to own every inch of shoreline. In such an expansive country, I found it most troubling that the privilege of private ownership had taken precedence over what I had initially presumed were public recreational spaces. These realities were taken for granted it seemed by Ontarians. As a newcomer to the province I found them perplexing, if not troubling.

My desire to more fully understand the meaningfulness of the cottage experience was further prompted by the lively discussions I mediated among my undergraduate students in my Anthropology of Tourism courses at Trent University. My students were almost equally split between those who are cottagers – largely from the Greater Toronto Area (GTA) – and those who come from small towns in lake-filled regions of central/eastern Ontario, places that receive a summer influx of cottagers. When the class attempted to define who and what a tourist is, the question as to whether a cottager was a tourist inevitably emerged. Those who were cottagers insisted that they were something other than tourists, since they had a deep sentimental connection to, and often a multi-generational family history at, their cottage. Those from small towns who experienced the seasonal influxes of cottagers saw them otherwise, as non-locals or tourists who demanded special privileges and services and who brought much of the big city to the cottage. At the same time, cottagers were seen to resist economic development designed to benefit the local community, as it might disrupt the idylls of life at their cottage, on their lake (Pcholkina 2006).

Popular media reports at least since the mid-1990s, including repeated articles in all sections – news, lifestyle, business, and of course real estate – of local, regional, and national newspapers, fuelled the Ontario summer mentality that there was nothing more desirable than sitting on the dock at one's cottage, favourite beverage in hand and swathed in languid summer heat, surveying the calm and beauty of the lake as the sun slowly dipped below the tree-lined, rocky horizon.[1] All of this attention was rather surprising considering that, according to Statistics Canada data from the mid-1990s to the mid-2000s, only about 8 percent of Ontarians owned cottages.[2] Few commentators – or promoters of such notions – focused on what I, as a newcomer, felt were the less-than-enticing elements of this experience: the tensions and anxieties of the regular weekend trips on clogged highways to get to the cottage, the unrelenting investment of time and labour a cottage demanded, the financial burden of owning a cottage, and the realities of spending every weekend cooped up with family and perhaps not-so-much-loved friends and acquaintances. In this book, then, I examine what was – and is – seen to make life at the cottage so richly and passionately meaningful for those who own or regularly visit cottages in the Haliburton region of Ontario.[3]

Though a non-cottager might not understand the appeal of cottage life, many Ontario cottagers have profoundly strong ties to their cottage and actively seek to spend as much time there as possible. What I saw as the negative dimensions of cottage ownership were simply minor hurdles to cross or, in some cases endure, in order to indulge in all that made cottage life blissful. Sack (1992) has suggested that cottages are places "thick" with meaning (see also Chaplin 1999b; Cross 1992; Halseth 1998, 18-20ff; Jaakson 1986; Löfgren 1999, 139ff; Luka 2006, 171-76ff; Sack 1997; Williams and Kaltenborn 1999). This study supports this interpretation.

I developed a research project to try to grasp more fully why the experience of a second home – here called a cottage – generates such strong emotional attachment and commitment. This undertaking was a natural extension of my previous work, which sought to understand what made pleasure travel to international destinations meaningful to an inveterate group of middle- and upper-middle class Canadian tourists (see J. Harrison 2001, 2003). Cottagers, as I discuss below, have frequently been labelled in the academic literature as a type of domestic or second-home tourist (see, for example, Jaakson 1986).

I chose to focus my research on the loosely defined middle-class cottage experience of the Haliburton area of Ontario. This demographic paralleled that of my earlier work on Canadians who travelled internationally each year, which provided a basis for some comparison (see J. Harrison 2003, 2008b). Many of the cottages in the Haliburton region were developed in the two decades following World War II. I interviewed a few cottagers whose grandparents, often their grandfather, had a rustic hunting cabin in the area in the 1930s. A few others had spent their summers as children with their grandparents at cottages as early as the late 1920s and through to the 1940s.[4]

The 1950s-60s expansion of "cottaging" in the Haliburton region was positioned as a much more affordable experience relative to the adjacent Muskoka region.[5] The latter was one of the first areas in central Ontario developed for cottaging and summer residence, beginning largely with an influx of well-to-do Americans in the late nineteenth and early twentieth centuries. Jasen (1995, 117-24) notes that Muskoka's development as such a destination was due to the expansion of transportation technologies including railroads and steamships that operated on the large lakes in the region and to its more immediate proximity to large metropolitan centres (see also Luka 2006, 115-25). The latter initially brought wealthy Americans from midwestern cities and, close on their heels, Torontonians of similar status, seeking to avoid the stifling summer heat of crowded industrial urban centres. These arrivals prompted the development of resort hotels and, later, individually owned cottages. Throughout the first fifty years of the twentieth century, cottaging in Muskoka remained in very large measure the purview of the wealthy, if not the very wealthy. It also established for many the iconic status of the Ontario cottaging experience.[6]

Adjacent lake-filled areas, like Haliburton, steadily expanded in the last half of the twentieth century as more affordable cottage country, although Haliburton certainly had been an area of tourist interest since the early decades of the century (see Baker 1930; see Map 1 on following page). This area may lack the large lakes that are seen as the jewels of the Muskoka experience, but Haliburton does have many good-sized lakes that embody the aesthetic qualities – deep water, exposed rock and tree-lined shores – championed in Muskoka. Haliburton cottagers today would argue that "their" lakes have many more virtues than anything found in Muskoka. Post-World War II Haliburton developers aimed their sales campaigns at the newly emerging middle-class southern Ontario residents who had achieved a degree of sufficient prosperity that they could consider acquiring a summer cottage, even if quite modest.

Canada's population grew from nearly 14 million to over 21 million between 1950 and 1970.[7] Average annual wages almost doubled in this same period, with the cost of living annual increase remaining fairly stable at less than 5 percent.[8] Overall, Canada's population at this time was, in broad strokes, racially homogeneous. Until the late 1960s, 70 percent of the immigrants to Canada came from the United Kingdom and Europe; another 15 percent came from the United States. Immigration patterns began to change as Canada adopted a "colour-blind" policy in 1967. For the second half of the twentieth century, Ontario received the largest percentage of these new Canadians, regardless of their origins. Cultural differences between these populations should not be ignored, though the vast majority of immigrants in the decades immediately following World War II came from a Western European Judeo-Christian tradition. In contrast, the largest group (over 70 percent) of immigrants to Canada at the end of the first decade of the twenty-first century came from elsewhere, a topic I will return to in later discussions.[9]

In the chapters that follow, I reflect on the symbolic, aesthetic, social, cultural, personal, and, ultimately, moral levels of the deeply held meaning of a postwar Haliburton cottage. I explore the cottage as a place where people felt physically, emotionally, and, for some, spiritually grounded, as the place where they most wanted to *be*. The cottage is where treasured memories are carefully stored; where homogeneity across culture, class, and race, national identity, and tradition are presumed; where joy is found in much that is modern because it is integrally entwined with "timeless

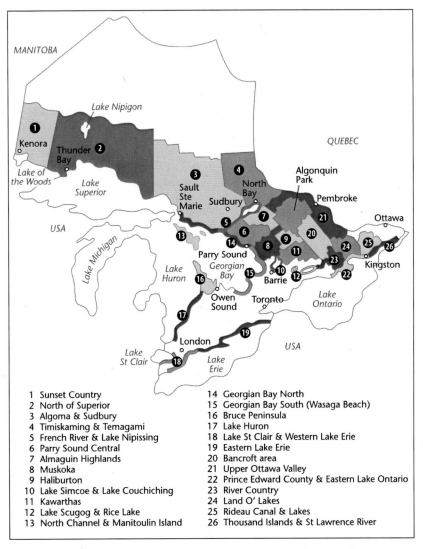

1   Sunset Country
2   North of Superior
3   Algoma & Sudbury
4   Timiskaming & Temagami
5   French River & Lake Nipissing
6   Parry Sound Central
7   Almaguin Highlands
8   Muskoka
9   Haliburton
10 Lake Simcoe & Lake Couchiching
11 Kawarthas
12 Lake Scugog & Rice Lake
13 North Channel & Manitoulin Island

14 Georgian Bay North
15 Georgian Bay South (Wasaga Beach)
16 Bruce Peninsula
17 Lake Huron
18 Lake St Clair & Western Lake Erie
19 Eastern Lake Erie
20 Bancroft area
21 Upper Ottawa Valley
22 Prince Edward County & Eastern Lake Ontario
23 River Country
24 Land O' Lakes
25 Rideau Canal & Lakes
26 Thousand Islands & St Lawrence River

Map 1 Ontario cottage country. Ontario's cottage country has no official designation, that is, it is not marked on provincial maps. However, it is a taken-for-granted place in the provincial landscape. Not a cohesive whole, it is understood to be divided into twenty-six distinct areas, each one understood to have its own character. Its representation here is based on a map originally drawn up by Tracey Wood/Reactor Art and Design that appeared in *Cottage Life* magazine (March 2006).

nature." It is a place where specific constraints of time are abandoned to be replaced by those deemed more pleasurable, lasting, and indulgent; where prescriptive regimes codify, desirably or not, the practice of life at the cottage. At the Haliburton cottage, I found that human bodies are specifically disciplined, measured, marked, and yet ironically imagined to be free. Intensely valued social relationships, be they those of 'family' or friends, are fostered and grounded there.[10] For many male cottagers, work became leisure, but often for women, leisure became work. I came to understand why the cottage is seen as a place where the "right" kind of behaviours, values, if not moral character, can be inculcated and re-warded. More succinctly, in this book, I explore what prompted and solid-ified the commitment and passion boldly expressed by those I interviewed about their cottage and what it meant to them. I also examine what I came to see as the ambiguities and contradictions of the cottage, a more trouble-some side inherent in all that it represented. Before I begin to explore these themes in more detail, I provide, first, some background on this much loved place, Haliburton County, and how it came to be part of Ontario's cottage country. I provide some background on those who bought cottages there in the latter half of the twentieth century, what others have said about such second-home domestic tourists, and how I conducted my research on those who cottage in this place of natural beauty.[11]

"Blessed with an Abundance of Natural Beauty": Haliburton County, Ontario

A tourism website for the province of Ontario describes Haliburton County as being "a pleasant two and a half hour drive [northeast of] Metropolitan Toronto ... [b]lessed with an abundance of natural beauty – crystal clear lakes, pristine forests and miles of ... wilderness trails."[12] Another source describes it as "a county of Ontario, Canada, known as a tourist and cottage area in Southern Ontario for its scenery."[13] A large county – 453,292 acres in size, the third largest county in the province (Barnes 2002, 1) – it is described in one popular guidebook as a "great elevated plateau" (locally known as the Haliburton Highlands) that gives way to "largely wooded [tracts] ... a skein of countless lakes and rivers, and a few farms in the southernmost corner" (Barnes 2002, 2).

Haliburton County lies at the southern edge of the Canadian Shield – the large outcropping of Precambrian rock that hangs like an apron around Hudson's Bay, spreading out to cover two-thirds of Ontario (see Map 2, p. 11). Glaciers scraped away much of the soil that once blanketed this massive outcrop when they moved through the area 12,000 years ago. Lakes formed in the depressions left by the receding ice and eventually a total of eight rivers carved their way through the granite and the isolated pockets of limestone. For millennia, Aboriginal peoples successfully tapped the wealth of resources that such geography offered them. By the seventeenth century, the British and French fur traders arrived seeking to exploit these assumedly endless riches; they were specifically in pursuit of the beaver. These waterways would later serve the rapacious industrial harvesting of vast timber stands of mixed deciduous and coniferous forests in support of the massive expansion of colonial regimes in the urban centres across the continent (Reynolds 1973).

Throughout the twentieth century, second-growth forests steadily reclaimed the rocky shores of the many picturesque lakes found in the county. In contrast to how earlier traders and industrialists perceived such topography, it progressively came to symbolize the rugged, if not sublime, beauty of the Canadian landscape, construed as a domain of leisure, a place of restorative and therapeutic nurturance, what Gunn (1997) called a "vacationscape" (see also Löfgren 1999, 93; Rojek 1993; Urry 1990). As such, it is seen to present an enticing alternative to life in the claustrophobic concrete and dehumanized reality of urban life. Such tropes fuelled what came to be the understanding of Haliburton County as the perfect place to have a recreational cottage, a place that offers a retreat from all things undesirable, and fosters, as one cottager told me, "just good times" for all who gather there (Barnes 2002, 1-3). Such benign imaginings, however, ignore the complex histories layered on the county.

Making an "Indian Canoeist ... a Novelty": A Historical Snapshot of Haliburton County

Haliburton County is the ancestral homeland of the Algonquian-speaking bands of Mississauga and Ojibwa who had sustained themselves for generations on the abundance of fish and game in the area.[14] By the mid-seventeenth century, the Iroquois, in search of ever-diminishing fur supplies, were pushing farther into the areas north of Lake Ontario, particularly the lakes and highlands of the Haliburton and Algonquin regions (see Map 3, p. 14). Always a fearful presence, the Iroquois gained control of the region by 1650. These incursions started the lengthy process of the displacement of Algonquian-speaking peoples from the area, which eventually culminated in their permanent resettlement on reserves at various places in the province by the early twentieth century.[15]

By 1818, Aboriginal bands who had slowly reclaimed parts of what is now Haliburton had surrendered their lands to the Crown in the Crawford Treaty in the face of ever more intrusive colonizing forces. Europeans and Canadians arriving in the area had brought disease, alcohol, and notions of property rights that limited access to land for hunting – all of which had devastating effects on the indigenous populations. By 1923, they had signed away the rest of their hunting territories in Haliburton, moving to reserves farther south and west and eventually making the presence of an "Indian canoeist ... a novelty" in the region (Reynolds 1973, 12). However, the legacy of the Indigenous history of the regions remains embedded in the landscape of Haliburton, as many of the lakes carry adapted versions of their original names – for example, Kennisis, Boshkung, Miskwabi, Kawagama, Kashagawigamog, and Kushog (see Map 2, p. 11).

At one time, the Haliburton region had been imagined to hold the secret of an easy and direct route to Georgian Bay and the waterways beyond. Military survey parties were sent by the Canadian government to the region in 1819, 1825, and 1827 to map the territory. In the face of the complex network of streams, rivers, and lakes and the unforgiving terrain that define the Haliburton landscape, the viability of such a route was eventually abandoned (Reynolds 1973, 21). But an even greater wealth captured the attention of private entrepreneurs as they observed the vast timber stands and the potential for mineral resources in the area. They also presumed that these lands had agricultural and homestead capacity, having noted the success of the Peter Robinson settlement in Peterborough to the south, which proved that "it was possible to tame the wilderness" (ibid.) (see Map 3, p. 14). In the early decades of the nineteenth century, small numbers of trappers had begun to live in the area over the winter "in small cabins and tending their traps" (Barnes 2002, 12-13). Like the early Aboriginal populations, they carried on the tradition of seasonal residence in the area.

The colony of Upper Canada, as Ontario was originally known, was positioned along the St. Lawrence River, a vital transportation route for the early colonies in the region.[16] It was to emerge as the dominant economic, social, and political force in the North American British colonies after 1776,[17] a role that deepened after Canadian Confederation in 1867. The first wave of British settlers to Upper Canada had arrived in the late 1700s from the United States. Known as the United Empire Loyalists, they were loyal subjects of the British Crown who fled following the American Revolution. These immigrants played a major role in shaping the identity of the province.

In the early nineteenth century, more immigrants arrived in large numbers from Ireland, England, and Scotland. The demand for homestead land steadily grew, but all the southern arable land had been taken up by earlier waves of settlers. Colonization roads – the Bobcaygeon, the Burleigh Falls Road, the Monck, and the Peterson – were painstakingly (and some never very successfully) carved out of the rock and boggy terrain to allow settlers more ready access to the Haliburton region. To entice settlers, free land grants were offered adjacent to a public road in 1853 (Cummings 1962, 4; Reynolds 1973, 25).

By 1859, the southern leg of the Bobcaygeon Road was completed as far as a small squatter settlement on the Gull River (see Map 2, p. 11). Following the government survey of the area and the arrival of the post office, this community was officially named Minden. It flourished until about 1929 as a somewhat prosperous yet "rough and tumble logging town" (S. Wilson 1997, 11) while agricultural settlement in the area floundered. The village would have to wait until the end of World War I before the first evidence of what would become its economic mainstay emerged. A small number of summer cottages were built close to Minden after World War I, their presence presaging the real boom in cottage development that would begin after World War II.

In 1860, the Canada Land and Immigration Company, an English company under the direction of Justice Thomas Chandler Haliburton, purchased 360,000 acres for fifty cents an acre "in the northern townships with the aim of reselling it to immigrant settlers" that they would bring to the area (Barnes 2002, 17-18). Model agricultural communities with schools, churches, roads, and, of course, arable land were promised to the new arrivals. However, the lands sold to settlers had often been previously leased by the Crown to lumber companies, and were, in many cases, either far too rocky or boggy for agriculture. The Crown was also dissatisfied with the Canada Land Company, as it claimed that the settlers were poorly prepared

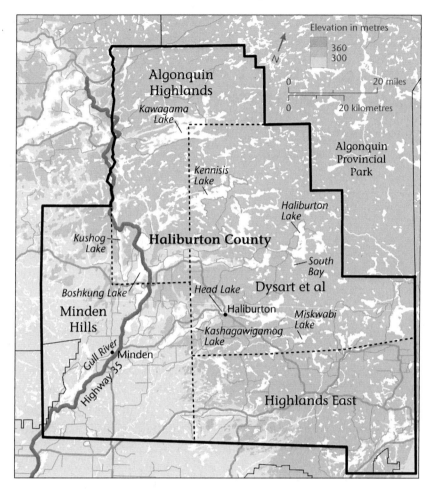

Map 2 Haliburton cottage country. The borders of Haliburton County encompass Haliburton cottage country.

for what they would face on arrival (Cummings 1962, 43). Eventually, a commercial and service centre for the struggling settlers in the area developed in Dysart Township on Head Lake. It was called Haliburton Village even though its namesake never set foot in the region[18] (see Map 2).

Most of those who came to Haliburton as either loggers or prospective farmers were of Irish, British, American, or Canadian ancestry. In fact, the greatest percentage of them was comprised of "the children and grandchildren of immigrants who first pioneered the Counties around the Great

Lakes. Included were descendants of United Empire Loyalists who fled the States following the American Revolution or the Whiskey Rebellion of 1791" (Reynolds 1973, 40). When settlement opened up on the western prairies, "many families moved [on] in search of more fruitful land and lives" (Baskerville 2002, 73). Others simply abandoned their farms and moved to burgeoning industrial centres such as Toronto. Those early settlers who managed to survive practised a subsistence pattern based on mixed farming, supplemented by hunting and fishing. Many also worked as wage labourers in an industry that made numerous lumber barons very wealthy. Yet, once the timber resources were depleted, the question remained as to how this land could be made productive in light of the challenges it presented to agriculture and the obvious limits of large-scale lumbering.[19]

In 1874, in response to requests from remaining local residents for more autonomy over their affairs to foster further colonial settlement and infrastructure development, the Legislative Assembly of Ontario created the Provisional County of Haliburton. The village of Minden was to become its administrative centre. It remained a provisional county, due to its small population, until its name was officially changed to Haliburton County in 1983. It still boasted a permanent residential population of only 17,026 in the 2011 census.[20] It took until 2001, as part of a provincially driven project of amalgamation of administrative and governing units, before Haliburton County was restructured into four larger municipalities, a dramatic reduction from its original constitution. The former townships included Algonquin Highlands,[21] Highlands East,[22] Minden Hills,[23] and Dysart et al. (see Map 2, p. 11).[24] By 2006, tourism and recreation, particularly that associated with those owning cottages in the county, was the cornerstone of the local economy. Small-scale forestry and limited mining and light manufacturing contributed in smaller ways to the region's viability. Reflecting a historical pattern of non-Aboriginals struggling to secure a viable livelihood in the region, in 2006 the unemployment rate among permanent residents in Haliburton remained higher than the provincial average. Such realities further determined an even greater reliance on cottagers and their demands for a service sector in the local economy.[25]

It Was "Very Muskoka": Cottaging Comes to Haliburton

A small number of tourists had begun to find their way to Haliburton in the late nineteenth and early twentieth centuries. Neighbouring Muskoka, which was much more accessible and was promoted in southern cities, had already begun to attract tourists. But Haliburton, "just as beautiful but much less accessible[,] did not receive its first tourist trip until 1865." One of the first references to tourists in the area offers little detail beyond noting that a group of young adventurers saw Haliburton as a diversionary route home from Muskoka, not a destination in itself (see Barnes 2002, 10).

In 1874, the Victoria Railway, originating in Lindsay and terminating in Haliburton Village, opened. Intended to service settlers to the area, it soon began to bring tourists. These early tourists came looking to stay in hotels, as the desire for summer homes, a tradition already emerging in Muskoka, would take some time to emerge in the Haliburton region.[26] This exposure to the area – "the charms of its scenic waters and rugged hills ... attracted camping and canoeing parties" – by the end of the century led a few to "purchase summer cottages and return annually" (Reynolds 1973, 178). The railway was never financially viable – the most it made in profit was $28, in 1880. By 1965, in operation for less than one hundred years, it reduced its service to only three trains a week. But even this limited service was well used by some post-World War II cottagers. In 1978, the year it terminated service, it was reduced to offering autumn colours recreational excursions (Barnes 2002, 28-33).

During the late nineteenth and early twentieth centuries, lumber companies moved rapidly through the region, felling the stands of magnificent white pine forests that blanketed it (Reynolds 1973). The need to protect the watershed of the many rivers of the Muskoka-Haliburton region, to temper the greed of the lumber barons, and to shelter some of the region's wildlife led to the creation of Algonquin Park in 1885 (see Map 3, p. 14). At the time, it was noted that such park lands were simply an extension of the region now encompassed by Haliburton County, and the former "would in all probability eventually become a health resort and tourist area for Ontarians" (Reynolds 1973, 75). In light of this, "holiday makers would be allowed to rent cottages on the shores of the lakes [in the park] and fishermen to fish in the waters" (Lambert and Pross 1967, 167).

By the end of the nineteenth century, a few local residents had started to build small cottages to rent out to summer visitors. These were usually located on lakes close to the small settlements in the area. By the 1920s, cottaging had established itself as a well-defined recreational practice in Ontario, even if it was practised only in a limited number of areas and by

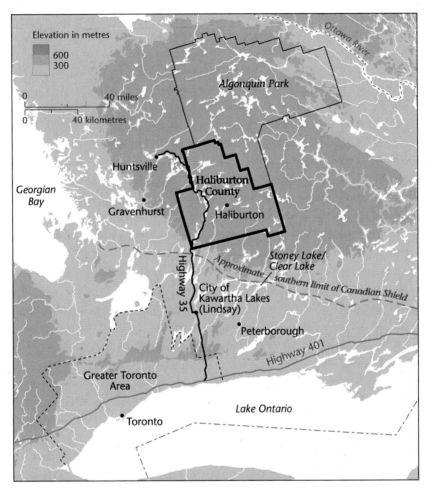

Map 3   Haliburton County and environs. To many cottagers, Haliburton is geographically and conceptually positioned between the imagined 'wilderness' of Algonquin Park and the densely populated Greater Toronto Area (GTA).

a small segment of the population (Luka 2006, 120). Haliburton had begun to imagine itself as a tourist destination, as evidenced by moves to organize the Highlands of Haliburton Tourist Association in 1935 (Rotary Club of Haliburton and Curry 1975, 43).[27]

The expansion of cottaging was both hit hard and yet eventually facilitated by the Great Depression of the 1930s. The financial constraints of the era limited much private capital investment in the practice but public infrastructure projects provided the labour to build "a majority of High-

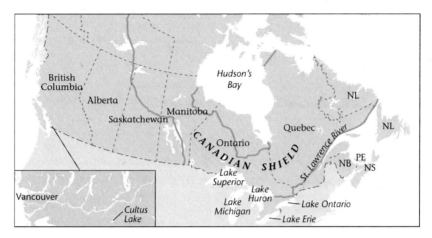

Map 4 Central Ontario and Cultus Lake, BC. The Canadian Shield, which shapes much of cottage country, is a dominant topographical feature in the central Canadian landscape.

ways 35 and 121" (Barnes 2002, 25). By the end of the 1940s, the improved condition of Highway 35, which followed much of the route of the original Bobcaygeon Road, facilitated access to lakes in the western end of the county (see Map 3, p. 14). And the economic woes of the Great Depression did not stop cottage development altogether. One cottager on Boshkung Lake reminisced about how his family worked intensely in the summer of 1932 to get a basic structure erected on their newly acquired cottage lot. Local farmers had begun to sell off lakeshore properties, often supplementing their unstable incomes by selling fresh provisions to cottagers during the summers (Boshkung Lake Millennium Book Committee 2001, 38, 43). Several cottagers I interviewed had early childhood memories of summers at their grandparents' cottages in the 1920s, 1930s, and 1940s on lakes adjacent to Highway 35. Still, these early experiences were those of a minority.

Cottaging grew exponentially in Haliburton during the immediate post-World War II period. Various factors fuelled this expansion: the two-day weekend became institutionalized for many in the labour force, standard periods of annual holidays were expanded, private automobile ownership rose, roads in cottage country were improved, guaranteed pensions became a reality, and disposable income increased. Waterfront Crown lands were released for private sale to encourage tourism and recreational development in regions such as Haliburton (Luka 2006, 127;

Stevens 2008a, 2008b). Such factors enabled the expanding urban and suburban middle-class population in southern Ontario to solidify its status and even imagine its extension upward as the people gained access to a recreational practice loosely conceived as the domain of wealthier classes, particularly in neighbouring Muskoka.

Reflecting on the practice of cottaging in the 1960s, Roy Wolfe (quoted in Luka 2006, 17; see also Wolfe 1962, 1965) posited that "the primary purpose of cottage life was status-seeking; the flaunting of wealth by lavishing splendour on unnecessary dwellings." Clayton Hodgson, a descendant of one of the early lumber barons and who, in the 1950s, sold some of the family property on South Bay on Haliburton Lake for a large cottage development project, explicitly summed up the sentiments of many who bought cottage lots in the county. His adolescent memories of an evening in 1945 spent at the cottage of family friends on Haliburton Lake led him to comment years later that he found the experience "very Muskoka" – he described the host, who "cut a very dashing figure on the lake"; he "was impeccably dressed; i.e.[,] white running shoes, white flannels and blue blazer" (Hodgson 1992, 127-28). Few cottagers that I interviewed would ever cut such a figure as they (or their parents) laboured long and hard in the 1950s and 1960s to make their roughly framed cottages and rugged lots habitable and functional for their families, but the symbolic referents of their labours would have resonated with such imagined elegance and status. Haliburton cottagers I spoke with, while on the one hand wanting to emulate what Muskoka was seen to represent, were on the other hand adamant that their cottage experience in Haliburton had matured over the last fifty years to be distinct from, and frankly better than, what Muskoka was held out to be.

By the early 1970s, the boom in cottage development had waned. A spike in oil and gas prices, the reality that many more women were entering the workforce full-time and were thus unable to spend extended periods of time over the summers at the cottage, the limits of desirable and easily accessible vacant waterfront properties, and the preoccupation of many baby boomers with solidifying their lives and careers all contributed to this lull. In the early 1980s, second-home properties became taxable assets in Canada, which altered the "fiscal context that had previously been quite supportive of cottaging" (Luka 2006, 132). But by the end of the decade, the baby boomers had gained greater financial stability, thereby stimulating a renaissance in cottaging. This shift is signalled by the launching of the magazine *Cottage Life* in 1988, a popular publication still in press today; for some it has become, as one cottager said, "the cottager's bible." At its heart, the magazine privileges what I call here the values and understanding of what it means to be a "real cottager" and to own a "real cottage" (Luka 2006, 132-34). For some of the people I interviewed, the magazine and the biannual trade shows it sponsors served as vehicles to champion what really mattered at the cottage (ibid.); for others, it commodified and trivialized the experience, which exemplifies just one of the contradictions that infused notions of the "real cottage/cottager" that emerged during my research.

What has happened over the last three decades in cottage country? Simply put, much. There has been a steady increase in the price of cottages in Ontario. Real estate reports suggest an increase in costs of as much as 25 percent, but regardless of the business interests that might favour such positive assessments for the purposes of demonstrating the efficacy of the cottage as an investment, by 2004 "the average cost of a waterfront second home property in Ontario exceeded the average cost of a dwelling in Toronto" (Luka 2006, 134). Following the global recession in the latter part of 2008, overall cottage sales in Ontario remained strong. By 2012, however, real estate prices in Ontario's cottage country were stalled. As one real estate agency said, "We have not seen cottage prices decline, but they haven't increased either" (Pigg 2012). Nevertheless, in 2012, waterfront property in Haliburton could not be acquired for much less than around $250,000; many properties were much more expensive (Royal LePage 2012; see also Archer 2010, 46). More and more people want their cottage to be a year-round property, which has led to the upgrading and expansion of many cottages into homes, or in many cases the building of entirely new, much larger, more "suburban-looking" structures. The cottage is becoming an ever more popular place for people to retire. One Haliburton cottager told me that on her lake over 50 percent of properties were occupied full-time by recently retired owners.

Condominium and fractional ownership properties can now be found in cottage country (Lorinc 2010). In 2012, one real estate agent suggested that "demand is booming for a different kind of 'cottage.' ... The maintenance-free waterfront condo for those looking for all the amenities of upscale lakefront living, minus the lawn-cutting and plumbing problems" (Pigg

2012). Such developments, which I did observe as present if not booming in Haliburton, bring a new clientele to cottage country, a group that in the eyes of some long-time cottagers has no understanding of the "culture of cottage country" (see J. Harrison 2010). Inheritance and succession issues loom large in many families as original owners of cottages die or simply become too elderly to manage the cottage. The dispersed nature of many families across the country and the globe further complicates who should or can take responsibility for the family cottage.[28] The luxury of a defined period of annual vacation has become more elusive as the neo-liberal pressures of often more precarious employment have taken hold in the first decades of the twenty-first century. Compounding the difficulties of escaping one's workplace has been the arrival of the technologies that allow cottagers to remain virtually connected to their place of employment even while at the cottage.

Change, or concern about change, at the cottage is a recurrent theme in what follows. Yet, for those I spoke with, the symbolic, aesthetic, cultural, and social values of the cottage and the experience that ownership/access was seen to offer remain undiminished. For those cottagers I came to know, their cottage remained, as a couple of them said, "the place where their heart is" and "where their soul resides." This sentiment resonated with what others who have written about this experience have found, wherever their studies have taken them.

What Has Been Written About the Cottage Experience

In Canada, the cottage has been a topic of interest for the popular press, but it has also attracted the attention of an array of academics including geographers, historians, and a limited number of sociologists and anthropologists. The trope of the cottage and the cottager has captured the imagination of Canadian fiction and creative non-fiction authors, poets, and filmmakers. This list includes some of the nation's most iconic literary figures. Many who have written about the cottage have grappled with what makes this experience a meaningful if not mythologized part of Canadian, specifically Ontarian, life.

It is important to note that there are several cottage country areas in Ontario, each with its own particular character and geography. Based on 2001 data, Luka (2006, 8n13) argued that 43 percent of all Canadian cottage owners were in Ontario, and based on my observations, the cottage experience is deeply embedded in the provincial zeitgeist. It is also a popular practice in Quebec and, drawing on census data, Halseth (1998, 23) concluded that the bulk of Canadian second-home owners are in these two provinces. Quebec *chalets,* as they are commonly called, were sometimes built with the singular intention of winter use, a tradition not common in Ontario, although many cottages are now being winterized for year-round use. There appears to be more limited scholarly study of the chalet experience in Quebec compared to what has been written by academics about cottaging in Ontario (see Bovet 1998; Martin-Roy 2007). However, the chalet experience does appear to garner many of the same expressions of strong emotional bonds and practical concerns that cottages do in Ontario. This adds even further irony to the assumption that the Ontario cottage exemplifies all that is "Canadian," with its "Canadianness" rooted in what is seen to be the cultures and traditions of all that comprised Upper Canadian – that is, Ontarian – history.

Recreational second-home ownership is also found in British Columbia, south-central Manitoba, northern Saskatchewan, and some regions of Atlantic Canada (see for example Barbour 2011, 58-96; Lehr, Selwood, and Badiuk 1991). In some of these regions, a cottage is variously called a cabin or a camp. My own memory from my childhood in Saskatchewan is that people spoke of "going to the lake" rather than identifying the structure they owned there. But beyond Halseth's (1998) study of cottaging in Cultus Lake, BC, and the Rideau Lakes in Ontario, little comparative work has been done of the second home experience in Canada (see Maps 1 and 4, p. 6 and p. 15). Allan Casey's (2009) book, *Lakeland: Journeys into the Soul of Canada,* offers a journalistic account of his travels to various cottaging and water recreational areas across the country. His work hints at the scope of more academic study yet to be done. It is important to note that other recreational practices have significant currency in various parts of the country. Skiing, hiking, and climbing in southern mountainous regions of Alberta and regions of British Columbia, sailing on both the east and west coast, and car camping in most other regions of the country are some examples of other popular recreational practices (see for example Dummitt 2007b; Harding 2010). However, it is beyond the scope of my research to comment on these practices and their predominance in regional zeitgeists.

The broader academic analysis of the second-home experience falls generally into two chronological blocks: the early work done in the 1950s to the mid-1980s, and a more recent body of work that emerged in the late 1990s and continued in a much greater flurry in the first years of the twenty-first century. Analysts who have turned their attention to this phenomenon demonstrated considerable interest in comparative reflection about the second-home experience in places such as the Nordic countries, the United Kingdom, Ireland, France, New Zealand, the United States, and Canada. Literary authors, journalists, creative non-fiction writers, and cottagers tend to concentrate their writing in a much more localized context. Well-known literary figures and journalists have waxed eloquently about, or at times probed the underbelly of, the cottage experience in Canada. Cottagers themselves often produce sentimental histories of life on "their lake."

Anyone interested in reading about the cottage experience in Canada, specifically that in Ontario, should begin with the work of geographer Roy Wolfe, whose contributions to the field began in 1951 and whose most significant early piece was his 1956 PhD thesis (see also Wolfe 1951, 1952, 1962, 1965, 1966, 1977). Grounding his analysis in postal lists to determine the location and density of cottages in Ontario, he reflected on what motivated people to pursue the cottage experience in Ontario. He posited themes of escape, being in nature, and status seeking. Despite the limitations of his methodologies, Wolfe offered some important insights and identified the experience as one worthy of intellectual scrutiny. In 1977, John Coppock edited *Second Homes: Curse or Blessing?* which brought together examples of international research from Norway, Sweden, France, the United States, and Canada. Its title alone highlights the complexities of the phenomenon. Were the economic benefits to local economies and the pleasures of life at the cottage worth the demands for massive infrastructure development, the threats to fragile physical environments, and the social tensions caused by the status differentiation between cottagers and locals?

In 1986, physical geographer Reiner Jaakson addressed his frustration at the lack of attention paid to the question of what is meaningful about the cottage experience in an article titled "Second Home Domestic Tourism." In this piece, he accurately identified the cottager as a form of tourist – much to the chagrin of many cottagers – and produced a laundry list of meanings attributed to the experience. The latter included things such as the tensions between routine and novelty, work and leisure, the desire for social and cultural inversion, the attraction of being in nature, and a search for identity, surety, status, continuity, and temporal and physical distance from life in the city. Jaakson's (1986) analysis was based on informal conversations and interviews he had done with cottagers throughout Canada over the previous twenty years. According to Plog (2001, 15), cottagers fall generally into a spectrum of "psychocentric" or "dependable" tourists who "try to make [as] much of their daily lives predictable and dependable." Annual, and in the summer weekly, returns to a well-known and much-treasured place offered such constancy. Two key characteristics of tourists in Plog's analysis resonated with many cottagers I interviewed: they "like structure and routine" and "prefer to be surrounded by friends and family" (2001, 16).

In the late 1990s and early 2000s, several geographers reinvigorated the study of second homes by examining the cottaging experience in locations such as the United States, Norway, Finland, and New Zealand, making important contributions to the field. The understanding of the second-home experience greatly benefitted in this latter period from the theoretical and analytical capacities brought to it by human, as opposed to physical, geographers. Drawing on comparative research in Norway and the United States and on the work of Anthony Giddens (1991), Daniel Williams and Bjorn Kaltenborn (1999, 215) argued that cottaging can play an important role in resolving the "identity dilemmas created by modernity and the phenomena of space-time compression." The cottage as a place for the construction or retrieval of self-identity has become a recurrent theme in the literature. But the specificity of what actually shapes that identity is something often glossed broadly.

Williams and Kaltenborn (1999, 226-27), in their research in Norway and regions of the United States, observed that cottaging could be seen to reflect distinctive nationalisms/regionalisms. Periäinen (2006, 109) noted that for Finns the "summer cottage is a set of nationalistic values, such as the belief that to be a Finn is to love nature and long for solitude" (see also J. Harrison 2010).

Halseth's (1998, 2004) comparative study of two different cottaging areas in Canada highlighted the tensions between selected rural communities and the development, and in some cases transition, of cottages to permanent residences. He established the links that these "elite" landscapes have to metropolitan areas, a theme Nik Luka (2006) later further developed. Drawing on the concept of "multiple residency" developed by Hall and Müller (2004) and Quinn (2004), Luka argues that cottage country has to be "built into the metropolitan housing equation" (2006, 292). To Luka, "the housing market of the Toronto metropolitan region effectively includes second-home settings in central Ontario cottage country" (ibid., 293). His discussion of the suburbanization of cottage country, the latter which he sees as a "generic category of landscape and urban form," and of the motivators of "the social practice of cottaging in central Ontario," sets a base to build on and refine. For example, I do not take his use of such notions as "pleasant place," "nature," and good "values" as neutral. I build on the work of Luka, Halseth, and others who argue that the Canadian cottage should be seen as an extension of the metropolitan space, examining how suburban social and cultural values play(ed) out at the cottage.[29]

Luka (2006, 38-39ff) surveyed the literature on second-home ownership to ascertain what others had said about the motivation and meaningfulness of owning and retaining a cottage (see also Pitkänen 2008; Vepsäläinen and Pitkänen 2010). Some elements of the meaningfulness of this experience highlighted in this literature include a cottage as presuming an implicit link to recreation and play; a place of family/childhood connection and memories; a return to nature as a primal/therapeutic/restorative space; a non-urban but not-quite-wilderness place; a place of community, belonging, and, for some, a place of spiritual connection; and a place of escape. Many of these themes and their complex entanglements as expressed by the Haliburton cottagers I interviewed shape much of what follows here.

Hall and Müller's (2004) *Tourism, Mobility and Second Homes: Between Elite Landscapes and Common Ground* is one of two relatively recent collections of papers based on international examples of second-home living. The essays in this volume give a central place to ideas of mobility, challenging at least in part the taken-for-granted assumption of the priority of the primary home over the second home, and highlighting the evolving "elite" nature of this experience. As Quinn (2004) suggests, multiple residency dwelling is a condition of many in the world today, be they elite second-home owners or immigrants and migrant workers who move regularly between two or more countries. Several authors further develop the tensions around the inequalities that are heightened when mobile populations or second-home tourists move in and make their presence felt in someone else's "home territory." Some attention is given to the question of the motivation of second-home tourism, but again this discussion glosses over key differences within this tourist group. Of particular note is Stephen Svenson's (2004) typology of the Canadian cottager. While useful, it is both homogenizing and particular at the same time, glossing gender, class and age differentials in cottaging behaviour and the nuanced understandings of this practice.

The chapters in *Multiple Dwelling and Tourism: Negotiating Place, Home and Identity*, edited by N. McIntyre, D. Williams, and K. McHugh (2006), further engage the topic of mobility in the life of the second-home owner, and the tensions that it sets up in relation to any simplified understandings of home and, by extension, place and identity. Such dwellings are far from being homes with an "inessential purpose," as Wolfe (1977) once called them. To many of the authors in this volume (and to those in Hall and Müller 2004; see also Williams and Kaltenborn 1999; Williams and McIntyre 2001), these dwellings comprise a phenomenon that needs to be seen in the context of modernity, globalization, a search for authenticity, a "thinning out" of place, and the resultant fragmentation of identity in the reality of the late modern world, something that cottagers proactively respond to by all that they invest in their cottages. As cogent and helpful as much of this analysis is, I am forced to query the assumptions of homogeneity and consistency across place, time, individual experience, gender, race, and class position that seem to underlie it.[30] Relatively little sustained attention has been paid to such factors. Lukà (2006, 124-25) notes that certain parts of Ontario's cottage country reflect ethnic/cultural divisions, and it is taken as a given that there are clear socioeconomic divisions between those who cottaged in Muskoka, for example, and those who cottaged in the Kawarthas (see also Wolfe 1951). But as Lehr, Selwood, and Badiuk (1991, 47) noted, looking at such developments in the Lake Winnipeg region, these divisions are "virtually ignored in the scholarly literature devoted to the study of recreational development in Canada." And while they made this claim some years ago, and in a period when there seemed to be little interest in the study of cottaging, there has been no significant attention to these social and cultural factors in much of the current literature. Alluding to this very oversight, sociologists Perkins and Thorns (2006, 76-78) recently noted that there is a "conspicuous lack of critique" in the research on second homes; rather, it is characterized by "its positive inclinations of leisure, escape, and meaningful experience." I concur with this observation, though with no intention of dismissing the important work done by many on the second-home experience. Instead, I seek to build on it.

The researchers in much of this more recent work use a variety of methodologies. Surveys, questionnaires, and statistical information provided through government surveys and censuses are common. Highly directive and structured data collection techniques aimed at selected recreational activities and the subjects' response to doing them is another methodology recommended by Williams and McIntyre (2001). Luka (2006) supplemented his detailed online survey with a wealth of material gleaned from cottagers in semi-structured interviews about their experiences. While he quotes extensively from these interviews, there is much more to be teased out of such material. But his main priority, as is fitting of his field, was situating cottaging in the socially constructed place of central Ontario. I have discussed elsewhere (J. Harrison 2008a) the distinctive strengths that the more open-ended qualitative methodologies of ethnography can offer a study of cottagers, something that I see as complementing these other strategies while directly and strongly privileging the voice of the cottagers and what they say and do. The role of the researcher in my fieldwork is critical, and I make no assumptions or attempts to eliminate that presence. I see this as extremely beneficial to the depth, character, and scope of analysis I am able to offer.

Regional historians have discussed the development of seasonal tourism/cottaging in particular areas (for example, in Ontario, Hodgins and Benidickson 1989 on Temagami; C. Campbell 2004 on Georgian Bay) and as part of a broader analysis of recreational and environmental history in Canada (Jasen 1995; Loo 2006). Peter Stevens's (2008a, 2008b, 2010) work is focused on the development of cottaging in the immediate post-World War II era in Ontario; one theme he covers is the role of the automobile and highway development in shaping the Ontario cottage experience – a point made in some of Wolfe's early writings – and cottagers' views of nature and the environment of the era. Stevens's demonstration of how modern technological developments greatly expanded the potential access to the cottage experience is very relevant to my work.

Michael Ondaatje (1987), Margaret Atwood (1991), David MacFarlane (2000), Mordecai Richler (1997), and Janice Kulyk Keefer (2007) are just a few of the well-known Canadian fiction authors who have found the cottage and cottage country a fruitful setting. Even renowned American authors take their heroes to a Canadian cottage, as John Irving (1989) did Owen Meany. The cottage has been a recurrent theme in Atwood's poetry and that of other Canadian poets (see for example Purdy 1974; B. Struthers 1996, 2005, 2008). Life at the cottage, or the cottage as a place of important life transitions, figures in a range of Canadian films – *The Barbarian Invasions, Five of Us, Away from Her,* and *Who Loves the Sun* are just some examples. An abundance of creative non-fiction has been written by individuals such as Roy MacGregor (2002, 2005), Charles Gordon (1989, 2006), Lawrence Scanlan (2004), Allan Casey (2009), and Amy Willard Cross (1992). There is even a one-time hit song, "You Sold the Cottage," by the 1970s-'80s Canadian pop group Martha and the Muffins about what the sale of the family cottage meant to an angst-ridden teenager.[31] Some of this writing is intended to be comedic, while other pieces are quite black. But at its heart, this work expresses a desire to capture some of what the cottage represents to Ontarians, who in much of this material are taken to be the "generic Canadian." In the first decade of the twenty-first century, the appeal of the cottage as a setting for popular novels continued. Kit Pearson set her children's story *Looking at the Moon* (1991) at the cottage; John Ibbitson's *The Landing* (2008) and Dorothy Palmer's *When Fenelon Falls* (2010) are examples of this genre written for an adolescent audience; Robert Rea's *The Earth, The Stars, and Whisper* (2003) and Gregor Robinson's *Providence Island* (2011) are other examples of novels about the cottage, best read there to pass lazy summer afternoons.

Anthropologists say very little on the topic. Swedish anthropologist Orvar Löfgren includes a chapter titled "Cottage Cultures" in his 1999 monograph *On Holiday: A History of Vacationing.* His discussion is topically and geographically wide ranging, chronicling the historical experiences on both sides of the Atlantic. He highlights many relevant themes – familial continuity, local/cottager tensions, nostalgia, gender tensions – but offers little detail and no in-depth analysis. Shiho Satsuka's 1997 master's thesis, "Re-creation through Landscape: Subject Production in Canadian Cottage Country," was a pioneering anthropological work in this field. Satsuka situated her research in Georgian Bay, Ontario, and spent time talking with and observing cottagers' daily lives. As a Japanese national, she found this an ideal location for examining Western notions of individualism and how they were inculcated and reinforced through cottaging behaviour. I draw on many themes that have historically shaped anthropology: kinship, gendered divisions of labour, status markers, belief systems, and ideologies. Such discussions are complemented by some of the more contemporary preoccupations of anthropology, themes that augment these traditional pillars of analysis: memory, belonging, place, and embodiment.

Studying the Haliburton Cottager

Making generalizations about those who own a second home in a particular geographic region of Ontario is challenging. One could compile an array of statistical profiles that in some measure would expose the broadest parameters about who owns and uses Haliburton cottages, and likely one would find significant variation among that group, particularly as the social and economic positioning of some Haliburton cottage families has shifted dramatically in the last fifty years. Such "facts" speak only in the most limited way to my curiosity about the meaningfulness of this experience.

It was difficult to do traditional participant observation fieldwork with cottagers.[32] Many lakes in Haliburton, as in many other areas of Ontario's cottage country, are completely surrounded by cottage properties, thus defining the lakeshore as private property and eliminating any obvious access for the general public. To avoid the dilemma of trying to turn friendships into research relationships, I avoided bartering the goodwill of my friends who own cottages. I needed to figure out a strategy to make contact with cottagers beyond meandering down private laneways hoping that it was a weekend the owners were in residence and that they would take the time to talk to me. Such a strategy could likely have triggered police attention and accusations of trespassing, particularly as greater concern about security and crime prevention has blossomed recently in cottage country.

Many cottage owners on Ontario lakes organize themselves into cottage associations or, as they are called today, property owners or ratepayers associations that act as networking, lobbying, and advocacy groups for cottagers' interests with various levels of government.[33] Most communicate with their members through newsletters, annual meetings, and seasonal social events. When I began my research in 2004, a few had websites.[34] For those that did, I used links to executive members and eventually received offers to put a small ad in their upcoming newsletter or obtained invitations to speak at association meetings. I also attended Haliburton community events in the county to meet people and talk about my research. At one such event, I met a reporter from a local newspaper who subsequently wrote a story about my research project. His article generated a large number of contacts for me. I also placed ads in the two local papers. In a limited number of cases, I followed up on personal contacts who, in turn, had contact with cottagers on lakes in Haliburton. To further contextualize what those I interviewed were telling me, I drew on the magazine *Cottage Life,* beginning with its first issues in the late 1980s and continuing to the present, and on the steady stream of articles about the Ontario cottage experience that appeared yearly from 2003 to 2009 in early spring in the real estate, lifestyle, business, and news sections of national newspapers such as the *Globe and Mail,* the *National Post,* and smaller newspapers in Haliburton and surrounding counties. Only in limited measure did these former sources speak specifically to the Haliburton experience, but where they did, I drew directly on them. In dealing with the cottage experience more broadly, they allowed me to situate the experience both comparatively and contrastively to the wider Ontario/national experience.

All but two of my meetings with cottagers were conducted on-site – that is, at the cottage. These interviews and informal conversations lasted anywhere from two to eight hours, and were with one family member, a husband-and-wife couple, a family including parents, adult children, and, in some cases, their spouses. I often stayed for lunch and/or dinner, was given a tour of the cottage, and frequently received a boat tour around the lake. I remain in ongoing email contact with several of these cottagers, and often returned more than once to visit them at their cottages. My research assistant did some of the interviews I draw on here, using a parallel protocol of questions and format.[35] Thus, my discussion and interpretations here are based on the semi-structured interviews, informal conversations, and some ongoing extended communications over email and follow-up visits with fifty-four Haliburton cottagers.[36]

The cottagers interviewed either owned or shared ownership of cottages on both large and small lakes; some have lengthy familial histories of cottaging in Haliburton, while others only recently acquired their cottage. Three-quarters of them had lived for significant periods of their lives in the GTA (see Map 3, p. 14). Many still considered that region home when

I met them; others had moved to smaller communities closer to cottage country to facilitate easier access to their cottage in retirement. Some lived in other large or mid-size Ontario urban centres or had permanent residences much farther afield, either in western Canada or, in a couple of cases, the United States.[37] A very few had grown up their entire lives in small towns or spent their very early years on farms. A very large portion of the cottagers interviewed were middle-aged and older, hardly an un-expected age range considering the cost of owning a cottage today. Additionally, this was likely the demographic most interested in talking to me as they had a significant financial, personal, and emotional invest-ment in the experience.[38] Only in a few cases did individuals under forty own their cottage; most frequently I met them at a property owned by their parents, other family members, or close friends. In one case, several siblings had come together to jointly acquire a cottage.

Some of those interviewed would never consider living permanently at the cottage; others were contemplating such a move in the future; only a very few had made it. What they all shared was a passionate commitment to the idea and experience of life at the cottage, whether they had known it for five, fifteen, or forty years, or even if a few had sacrificed some of what it represented by moving permanently to cottage country. Nearly half had owned or their family had owned the cottage where I met them for more than thirty years. A few had had their cottage property in their family for considerably longer, and there were a couple of individuals whose grandfathers had owned some form of modest recreational property in Haliburton as early as the 1920s.

At the other end of the spectrum, just 30 percent had owned the cottage where they were interviewed for less than fifteen years; some had just bought their first cottage less than five years before I met them. It is im-portant to note, however, that some of these more recent owners had owned another cottage elsewhere, usually on another lake in Haliburton, prior to purchasing their current one. These families demonstrated a passionate commitment to the experience of cottaging in Haliburton – many had been cottaging there for at least twenty years and some much longer – if not to a particular cottage. The remainder, however, could not be considered new to the Haliburton cottage experience, as they had owned their prop-erties for at least fifteen years.

As for their educational backgrounds, almost three-quarters of them had at least some post-secondary education, resulting in employment histories that covered a wide range of professions and occupations in the fields of education, finance, law, public service, arts, television, engineering, health services, administration and management, business, law enforcement, manufacturing, sales, and marketing. There were very few who worked (or had worked) outside of such "middle-class sectors," as postal workers, secretaries, and office support staff. These cottagers in particular had purchased modest cottages in the immediate postwar period, when such things were relatively more affordable. Approximately half were retired or semi-retired. Very few had annual incomes of over $150,000 a year. The vast majority made less than that amount; many declared incomes of less than $75,000 a year, an income base that for some was quite stretched in an effort to keep their cottage. Most were frequent newspaper and magazine readers; the *Globe and Mail,* the *Toronto Star, National Geographic,* and *Cottage Life* – the latter definitely the most popular – were common favourites. As for their hobbies, a wide range of sports, reading, gardening, arts and crafts, and home (that is, mainly cottage) repairs were most commonly noted.

The demographics of age, occupation, income, education, length of cottage ownership, and other objective markers capture some characteristics of who these people are. There was an equal number of men and women, even if it was initially men who more frequently contacted me about wanting to be part of my research. With the exception of two people who had married someone with a familial history of cottaging, everyone could be classed as Caucasian. In keeping with such backgrounds, many were from families that had roots in Canada extending back for more than three generations on at least one side of the family; almost all (98 percent) traced their ancestry to Western Europe, the United States, or Central Canada. For those whose sexuality could be assumed based on their identification of their partners (current or in the past), with the exception of one couple, all were heterosexual. I have changed all names to pseudonyms in what follows.

Being in "Poor Man's Muskoka"

When I attended the annual general meeting of one cottage association to inform them of my research, I began by saying that I had chosen to focus my research in Haliburton, not Muskoka or even Georgian Bay, the places that are generally taken to be the iconic cottage locations in Ontario. My statement, to my surprise, was greeted with a round of applause. I was told, "We are not Muskoka; it is better here in Haliburton. Muskoka has been spoiled." For these cottagers, my decision validated what they assumed had prompted me to base my research there: Haliburton was where "real cottagers" would be found. Cottages in Muskoka and Georgian Bay, in particular, were seen to belong to the wealthy, if not the very wealthy. Company presidents, politicians, lawyers, stock exchange "high rollers," even movie stars and "other Americans" had cottages there, as one cottager told me. According to her, "mansions of old money, not cottages," dominated the lakeshores there, structures that were definitely not the product of the sweat, labour, energy, and frugalities of the "ordinary" families who cottaged in Haliburton. With big cottages went big lakes and big boats, things many of those I spoke with said would detract from any real sense of community at the cottage. These other cottagers were not part of the "do-it-yourself/we can do it too" ethos of the cottage in Haliburton.[39]

Simply put, Muskoka cottagers were perceived to be ostentatious in their demonstration of wealth.[40] Haliburton did not have the dance halls,[41] sailing clubs, and large marinas that Muskoka did and, in fact, many of the Haliburton cottages were quite isolated before the improved road access in the latter decades of the twentieth century; others still are. These things prompted both a self-reliance and a mutual dependency on others on the same lake, something several commented was particularly strong when they were first building their cottages or among women who had spent their entire summers with their children at the cottage, a pattern characteristic of the 1960s and 1970s. The towns of Minden and Haliburton – as opposed to Gravenhurst and Huntsville in Muskoka – were, in the minds of those I spoke with, "real towns." As Neil said, "You can still buy the essentials of life on the main streets of these places, and not only the 'tourist trinkets' found in [Huntsville]." And if comparisons were made in the other direction, Haliburton fared well relative to places such as Wasaga Beach and much of the Kawarthas where the working class went to cottage, with the exception of Stoney and Clear Lakes in the Kawarthas, as they had cottages as expensive and elegant as any found in Muskoka (see Maps 1 and 3, p. 6 and p. 14). These places were, as Marnie noted, "cottage, next to cottage, next to cottage, laid out like a suburb."

Even if Haliburton is "poor man's Muskoka" (this phrase has also been used for cottaging in the Kawarthas), as one cottager suggested, it is more appealing to cottagers I interviewed. It has a landscape that parallels that of Muskoka – albeit on a smaller scale – but without its perceived social snobbery. "Haliburton cottagers just would not fit in Muskoka," Marianne observed. Several cottagers noted that there are different access routes to Haliburton, something that allows them to escape the horrors of driving up only one major exodus route out of the GTA on a Friday night in the summer, what those I spoke with saw as the fate of those heading for Muskoka. As Becky summed it up, Haliburton has the rustic traits of "real cottage country: the trees, the bonfire, the rocks, the clear water, the peace, the quiet, even the bears at the dump, the work ... [unlike Muskoka where,] heavens, they even have garbage pickup!"

Haliburton was also one area where those deemed to be outside of an elite class were able to afford a cottage in the massive postwar expansion. In 1953, $2,500 (paid in instalments) would buy you a small cottage and a lot on Haliburton Lake.[42] Those who bought cottages throughout the second half of the twentieth century in Haliburton included teachers, ministers, accountants, salesmen, small entrepreneurs – those who can be seen as generally representative of the middle class in Canada. Such accessibility could be changing, as most cottages in Haliburton at the end of the first decade of the twenty-first century were priced between $250,000 and over $1,000,000. Such cottages, no matter what their purchase price, require sufficiently deep pockets to carry the burden of a mortgage (for most), property taxes, and utilities, in addition to the travel costs to get there and ongoing maintenance costs.[43] And many of those who currently own relatively modest cottages through purchase or inheritance are finding themselves struggling with significant increases in property taxes or, if they choose to sell the property, the requirement to pay capital gains taxes. Advocacy groups such as the Federation of Ontario Cottage Associations (FOCA) and the Waterfront Ratepayers after Fair Taxations (WRAFT) have been at the forefront of the struggle to raise awareness with all levels of government about how problematic recent increases in property taxes have been for many Ontario cottagers, threatening (and in many cases succeeding) to force individuals or families, particularly those who do not fall into the category of the wealthy or the elite class, to sell much-loved properties.[44]

Canada has a history of discomfort with the idea of being a society divided by class hierarchies, even if, as John Porter (1965) affirmed, such blindness is a "self-delusion." To Porter, Canada was "a vertical mosaic ... best understood as ... a fixed hierarchy of distinct and unequal classes" (Helmes-Hayes and Curtis 1998, 8). As the second decade of the twenty-first century approached, however, anxiety around the life of the middle class was grounded in questions not so much of its existence as its continuance. Such uncertainty about the future would appear to be nothing new to the American middle class. Barbara Ehrenreich's (1989) *Fear of Falling: The Inner Life of the Middle Class,* Katherine Newman's (1988) *Falling from Grace: The Experience of Downward Mobility in the American Middle Class,* and Robert Frank's (2007) *Falling Behind: How Rising Inequality Harms the Middle Class* all imply that the American middle class has a sense of collective consciousness, a central element of which would seem to be a nagging fear of losing or "falling from" this social position. Dyck (2000) would argue that such concerns are also characteristic of the Canadian middle class in the twenty-first century (see also Curry-Stevens 2008).[45]

There is a certain irony in this latter reality, since the middle class as it took shape in the nineteenth century, certainly as it emerged in Ontario, "held aloft the 'vertical vision': that social mobility was achievable ... and that everyone should pursue social mobility [upwards]" (Holman 2000, 98; see also Newman 1991, 113). The middle class strove to maintain its position by accruing social, cultural, and economic capital through education, sufficient income to facilitate a certain lifestyle, and the expression of particular tastes, demonstrating as Dunk (1991, 3) did for a cohort of working-class Canadian men that culture is "intimately related to a sense of class." Owning, maintaining, and, for many, upgrading a cottage flagged multivalent capital accumulation, a particular lifestyle, and a distinctive taste and aesthetic of the middle class. Those who became cottagers in the immediate post-World War II era were carving out a new identity, something that brought them significant cultural and social capital, drawing on only a relatively modest amount of economic capital.[46] Ownership of a cottage, no matter how basic, became a sought-after marker in the post-World War II status hierarchies of Ontario (Wolfe 1965; 1977). Such cultural practices, in Sider's (1986, 10) terms, came to matter, among many who could be identified as middle class, a group that, at the time, was largely comprised of the descendants of the Western European and American immigrants who arrived in the province in the first half of the twentieth century.

The Canadian middle class, as Curry-Stevens (2008, 385) argues, "has both similar and dissimilar interests to those below and above them." It has a sense of a desired lifestyle to inhabit, even if there is significant range in what defines it. Regardless of such flexibility, or maybe because of it, many in the middle class remain vulnerable, needing continually to be "authorized and asserted, continually struggling to be taken seriously, and seen as worthy of moral authority ... [wanting their] entitlements ... to be taken seriously, [their] perspectives authorized, and [their] property legitimated" (Skeggs 2004, 154). They seek to secure a diversified "asset base" or capital that is economic, cultural, social, political, and, I would argue, moral (Curry-Stevens 2008, 385). Such is the angst of the middle class – and angst it is, for as Curry-Stevens demonstrates, since the 1980s the "money-flows" for Canadian middle-class families have been in decline; only those in the highest income levels experience continued growth (381-83). This trend undermines the "intergenerational transmission of capitals" needed to secure the position of the middle class (Sayer 2005, 948; see also Dyck 2000).

Middle-class identity is not only denoted by a socioeconomic category that facilitates the possession of "an array of consumer goods" (Stuber 2006, 288). It is a category shaped by "*symbolic boundaries* and cultural constructions" (ibid., italics in original). The former are "conceptual distinctions made by actors to categorize objects, people and practices, and even time and space" (Lamont and Molnar 2002, 168; see also Stuber 2006, 288). As such, these symbolic boundaries of class function to draw lines between "us" and "them." To those I spoke with, it was the middle class who owned Haliburton cottages and knew the culture of life there. This distinction excluded those who lacked the knowledge and lineage to understand what a "real" cottage was all about. Euphemistically, this could be read to mean the lower/working classes. As Sayer (2005, 948) would argue, this latter group is seen to lack "access to the practices and ways of living [in this case, being at the cottage] that are valued." Those who rented cottages were often deemed to be of a different – that is, lower – class. But the distinction also implicated the upper classes, such as those who cottaged in places such as Muskoka. The latter were seen to live in a world where the virtues of the cottage experience were something purchased as opposed to lived;

where the experience was somehow less authentic because it was an experience mediated by a service class who attended to all the labours of maintaining a cottage; and where the cottage experience was marred by the peer pressure for obvious demonstration of one's financial worth.

Equally distant to many of the cottagers I met are the "nouveau riche" – those who have benefitted from the unprecedented wealth accumulation experienced by some sectors of the former middle class in Canada in the 1990s and first decades of the twenty-first century. This group is moving into Haliburton and often tearing down the more modest cottages of an earlier era and building much larger and grander – to some, "monster," or as Svenson (2004, 74) would call them, "trophy" – cottages (Gordon 2006).[47] Other concomitant, and to some, offensive, developments undertaken by these either new or "born-again" cottagers include elaborate landscaping, docks, road development, and walkways, all heavily lit, blocking out the marvels of the night sky and making the lakeshore look like a suburban streetscape. Such "improvements" have often required extensive deforestation of the cottage lot (see also Luka 2006, 176-85). These cottages have the latest amenities of any upscale urban dwelling. The ostentatiousness of such structures and the lack of consideration to the impact of development on one's neighbours were deeply troubling to those I interviewed, who considered themselves "real" cottagers.[48] And while owning a cottage has always been a statement about one's social status, it was one that in the true Protestant middle-class cultural ethos of Ontario of many of those I interviewed, was most respected if it was acknowledged but, at the same time, quietly understated.

I would argue that being a Haliburton cottager carries a certain moral signification (see Sayer 2005a, 948; 2005b). The cottagers I spoke with (or their immediate ancestors) had accrued sufficient "external goods" – economic, temporal, and social resources or confidences – to acquire/retain/maintain a cottage, which those who had even greater access to these resources (such as those in Muskoka) had earlier established as a valued practice. For cottagers with such external goods, their Haliburton cottage expressed a distinctive set of "internal goods" (see MacIntyre, quoted in Sayer 2005a, 957-60). These latter "satisfactions, achievements, and skills" are qualities that define what life at a Haliburton cottage is all about.

I am most interested in cohesion around status markers, assumed rights, and moral values, things that both draw on and cultivate the social and cultural capital class identity (Bourdieu 1984). As Dudley (1999, 4, emphasis in original) clarifies, "Membership in the middle class is not ... a matter of achieving a certain standard of material success and, once having done so, resting on one's laurels: it requires the unremitting performance of a distinctive *moral character* – one which is ... culturally-defined as [much as] it is economically-based " (see also Lamont 1992, 181). Such moral character presumes taken-for-granted reasonableness, rationality, resourcefulness, self-reliance, hard work, and dependability, qualities that reinforce and ideally enhance one's "deservedness" to retain one's place in society and, in this case, have a cottage in Haliburton.

Thus, life at the Haliburton cottage is rewarding, at least in part, as it enhances and nurtures such confidence in one's social position and demonstrates one's right as a good citizen to such pleasures (see Bellah et al. 1985, 6). John Urry (1995, 130) observed that as ideas of "modern citizenship" evolved beginning in the nineteenth century they presumed a right to "not be at work," to have time for leisure. Progressively, such ideas became "embodied into people's thinking about health and well being." The Haliburton cottagers I interviewed saw their cottages as symbolic of these rights and values. As one cottager said, "I've paid taxes and worked hard all my life [to have] ... my prized possession, my cottage." Many cottagers had invested significant economic, social, and symbolic capital, and emotional energies in the anticipation of passing their cottage on to the next generation of their family. Such a legacy would progressively secure the cumulative wealth and status of one's descendants. The government was seen to be operating outside of understandings of reasonableness, rationality, and dependability – for example, when a new property assessment scheme came into practice in Ontario in the late 1990s. As one cottager said when faced with a dramatic increase in his property taxes, "I believe that it is unfair to have to sell the [cottage] to pay the ... taxes thereby depriving my grandchildren of the cottage," a statement that implies that it was his rightful legacy to pass it on to his progeny. Many cottagers saw, or wanted to see, their cottages as "inalienable possessions," things that "objectify their ideal of a stable identity [and] in [that] sense ... come to constitute the materiality of [their] social identity" (Weiner quoted in Miller 1998, 129).

The cottagers I interviewed understood "capitalism as the natural order of things; economic competition was an essential part of the human order and private property as an inviolable right" (Holman 2000, 98). Home ownership as a status marker thus became among the middle class, in Hirsch's terms, a "positional good ... an obvious example of social status in a competitive society" (quoted in Walter 1982). From the 1920s to the end of the 1940s, however, housing in Canada was in a state of crisis. Few new houses were being built, and many inner-city dwellings were over-crowded and in a state of disrepair (Owram 1996, 11-12). But by the postwar boom of the 1950s and 1960s, a house had shifted to a "material good ... which ... with proper organization of resources, everyone can have" (quoted in Walter 1982, 296; see also S.D. Clark 1966, 52-53).[49]

Particularly with the emergence and massive expansion of the suburbs in the same period, something greatly aided and abetted by the automobile and attendant road development, the middle class achieved what had at one time been the privilege of only the wealthier upper classes. Continuing in this direction, "the small cottage ... by the lake ... represent[ed] ... a more democratized form of the desire to capture and be part of the panache, style, and status of the early [upper class] resorts" – in other words, a "positional good" (Halseth and Rosenberg 1995, 149; see also Coppock 1977; J. Harrison 2003, 11, 20-24; Urry 1995, 213). As Stevens (2008a, 49) has argued, "[By the 1960s] many people in Ontario began to view [their] cottage ownership not as a privilege, but as a birthright" (see also Miller 1998, 138; Urry 1995, 130). Such possessions were understood as a treasured "scarce resource," not something accessible to everyone. The ownership of even a modest structure defined the "symbolic boundaries" of a privil-eged yet deserving group (Lawler 2005, 801).

Regardless, some of those who are passionate about their current cottage could still imagine owning something "better" – not to be interpreted as necessarily grander. Richard, for example, acknowledged that the north end of his lake was somewhat nicer and, in an ideal world, he would like to own a cottage there. Fred had always wanted to own a cottage on an island on his beloved lake for the sense of privacy and independence it would give him. These cottagers proudly saw their often modest cottages as standing in contrast to the opulence, size, and expanded amenities of the "monster" cottages that were starting to appear on some lakeshores in Haliburton, and were seen to predominate in Muskoka. Those who are building these grander cottages are likely a diverse group, worthy of separate study. In an example I discuss in Chapter 2, such a cottage was built by someone who had spent many childhood and adolescent summers on a Haliburton lake, in a much more modest cottage. Real estate reports (Royal LePage 2007, 2008, 2009) suggest that young professionals are one group buying such "trophy" cottages, those who require that their purchases have pristine waterfront, are low maintenance, are adjacent to amenities of interest, and have a number of bedrooms, a large kitchen, a great room, and a wine cellar – the latter for certain not something typically found in a modest cottage. Cottagers countered this list to me with priorities such as great sunsets, closeness to nature, relaxed atmosphere, good times with family and friends, hearing the call of the loon, watching a beautiful sunrise, endless conversations, walks with your family, and sitting down to rest with no guilt feelings. Such things could be experienced at a "real" cottage and for those I spoke with, this was a Haliburton cottage.

Between 1949 and the early 1970s, optimism and assumptions of increasing affluence characterized the ethos of the Canadian middle class, particularly the youth, or baby boomers, who were a driving force behind it (Owram 1996; B. Palmer 2009, 185). In this period, the standard of living of the "average Canadian" doubled (Owram 1996, 310). While this group never dropped the moral vigilance needed to keep its fortunes, there was a confidence that their efforts would continue to be incrementally successful. Such buoyancy fostered the idea that a cottage in Haliburton was relatively affordable and, for some, a desirable marker of their status, identity, and financial stability. But no matter how treasured such cottages were, some "got away" (Teitel 2009); family cottages were sold in response to a wide variety of life circumstances. Thus, in the early years of the twenty-first century, some members of the middle class who grew up as children at the family cottage were driven to acquire their own in an effort to replace the lost material, social, and cultural capital that had been accumulated, as well as all that was symbolic of life at the cottage.

But whether this latter group will be able to acquire such trappings, and whether others will be able to retain them, is uncertain. In 2000, Dyck (145) wrote that "increasing economic and social unpredictability ... in recent decades [has been] at odds with traditional [middle class] expectations" (see also Newman 1991). Even prior to the major economic crisis of 2008-09, the ability of youth to find secure employment and to set themselves on the path towards the same economic and social trajectory as their parents was uncertain at best. A "deindustrialized" North American economy and the loss "of what were once seen as being 'good' (and continuing) jobs" of the late twentieth and early twenty-first century challenged the optimism earlier postwar generations had assumed (Dyck 2000, 145). Furthermore, "remaining in the middle class mandate[d] husbands and wives [both] have to work [outside the home], coping as best they can with the task of raising children" (Newman 1991, 113; see also Frank 2007). Simply buying a home, never mind a second home, became an increasing struggle for many children of the middle class.[50] As cottage prices have continued to rise in recent years, young members of the middle class do not buy a cottage without careful long-term planning and frugality.[51] The fact remains that in the early years of the twenty-first century, the average age of cottage owners was fifty-two, they did not have children living at home, their income was in the top two quintiles, and they had 60 percent greater household wealth than those who do not have cottages (Kremarik 2002). Owning a cottage is fast becoming a privilege of those who only questionably could be called middle class (Halseth 1998, 2004; Halseth and Rosenberg 1995; Luka 2006, 11).

It is important to emphasize that the decision to own or retain ownership of a recreational cottage such as those I came to know in Haliburton is shaped by much more than the broad and slippery parameters of class hierarchies. Personal and collective historic trajectories, social and cultural values, expectations and aesthetic sensibilities, and past and present lived realities shaped by racial, gendered, sexual, ableist, and ideological imaginings of just what might be possible all have a profound influence here.

I begin in Chapter 2 by highlighting what it means to be at the cottage. Being at the cottage is nurtured by a sense of what makes life ultimately pleasing and desirable there, what I call the "cottage aesthetic"; it is nurtured by its role as a "keeping place of memory" and, for many, its spiritual connections. Chapter 3 continues to explore this layering of meaning, probing the cottage as a place of community; as a place where nature is tamed and rendered therapeutic, in the process making the cottage experience resolutely and quite comfortably "modern"; and as a place that is understood to be at its core "Canadian." Chapter 4 discusses the regimes, new and old, that discipline and, some would say, distill to a mere product for consumption the practice of life at the cottage. I discuss in Chapter 5 the disciplined, durable, fearful, unconsciously racialized and thus beautiful human body at the cottage. Chapter 6 explores the cottage as a nurturer of 'family' and as a generational treasure-house of familial legacies and belonging. Gender roles and their relationship to ideas of work and leisure at the cottage are the subject of Chapter 7. In the final chapter, returning to the interrogation of the meaningfulness of the cottage experience as expressed by the cottagers I interviewed, I reflect on what I see as the tensions that are embedded in what Kimmel (1990, 94) would suggest is the "painlessness of the presumptions of privilege" of life at a Haliburton cottage. Such a frame prompts reflection on the future of life at a Haliburton if not a "Canadian" cottage.

2

The Cottage: A Special Place

Many cottagers I interviewed repeatedly described cottage life using words such as *beautiful, fulfilling, happy, fun, deeply satisfying, peaceful, free*. It linked them to the past, held them secure in the present, and ideally promised much for the future. They understood such responses physically, emotionally, and, some, spiritually. Aaron called his cottage experience "a meditation." He elaborated,

> You look forward to coming here because you know you're going to feel good ... [it] is a spiritual feeling. It's getting close to yourself ... not in a religious way, but in a personal, feeling way, in your mind ... that's part of what happens when I am up here. You know you are going to feel good.

Such responses confirmed what Ava said, that being at her Haliburton cottage was "being in a special place." It was a place that was layered with, if not haunted by, memories – national, familial, personal. Kevin said cottages "do not just absorb dust, they absorb memories." As such, talking about one's cottage and time spent there was not something anyone did with disinterest or detachment. Rather, such conversations exuded passionate and intense responses, regularly spawning exuberant and joyful laughter and, at times, heartfelt tears. As Elaine said, "[These powerful sentiments] make my cottage the only place I want to be." In this chapter, I probe understandings of this place, the cottage, and what it meant to be there for those Haliburton cottagers I came to know. I suggest that, for the cottagers I interviewed, being in this place was shaped, in part, by the cottage aesthetic, the layering of memories captured there, a honed "sense of place," and the awareness that one's ties to the cottage transcended mere earthly realms, manifesting, as one cottager said, in a "karmic connection." Those who understood such things shared the tacit knowledge that they were "real cottagers." They recognized the intangible yet powerful essence that emanated from their special or even sacred place. They knew intuitively what was meant by "the cottage feeling," that integral element that made life at the cottage something rich and desirable.

The Cottage Aesthetic

What do I mean by the cottage aesthetic?[1] If the word *aesthetic* means something that prompts "a positive emotional response" and can be understood to express "perfect functional utility ... simplicity ... [and/or] elegance" (Morphy 1992, 181), then the cottage aesthetic captures the notion that the cottage is a fundamentally functional place in the shelter and facilities that it provides and also nurtures all that makes one feel good – embodying, despite its often modest character, the epitome of perfection, simplicity, and elegance. If an aesthetic is also about being able to discern what such perfection is, then it implies the development of taste, "the art of *discrimination* ... [the] making of *judgments*" (Porteous 1996, 21, italics in original). The Haliburton cottagers I spoke with saw themselves as having an "ability to notice or discern" what made the cottage experience meaningful and thus beautiful. Such taste, Sibley (1959, 423) argues, has been nurtured by the historical, social, cultural, and political influences of the world in which they live.

As such, both the cottages I visited and the cottagers I interviewed expressed an aesthetic, something grounded in a collective Western (if not Canadian, even Ontarian) aesthetic (Howes 1991). What is seen to make the cottage a desirable experience is influenced by class, race, gender, particular notions of nationalism, and related social, economic, and political perceptions, ideologies, and values. In the cottage aesthetic the "sensory ... bodily pleasures" (Featherstone 1996, 275) are complementary to and not in isolation from the "cognitive appreciation, distantiation, and the controlled cultivation of pure taste" of the more traditional Kantian aesthetic.[2] The cottage aesthetic is generated in an immersive, sensuous, and emotional bodily experience *and* has resonances with a more distanced engagement.[3] It is grounded in the simple, the mundane, the everyday lived dimensions of cottage life, along with the larger, the awe-inspiring, and ultimately what are taken to be the sublime dimensions of the experience (Featherstone

1996, 268, 270; Leddy 1995). The cottage aesthetic is seen from afar but can also be something in which the cottager is deeply immersed; it is both conspicuous and subtle; both concrete and abstract (see also J. Harrison 2003, 97). The values I discuss here presume a swath of moral values – the cottage aesthetic as I define it is "intimately related" to moral values (Hospers 1972, 50). Such moral values mean knowing how to be at the cottage. But first, one has to get to the cottage, beginning with a known and predictable physical journey, a pragmatic, psychological, anticipatory, if not tantalizing transitional passage to a special place.

"Are We There Yet?"

Adrian captured the sentiments of many when she said going to the cottage "is more than a physical move. It's not moving your life to the cottage. It's travelling to your other life, your preferred life." As such, descriptions of the anxiousness and anticipation to get there was a recurrent theme in my conversations with Haliburton cottagers. After we had been chatting for much of the afternoon, Garry laughingly asserted that he had the perfect title for my book. "You have to call it, 'Are we there yet?'" I had indeed heard that this phrase was a frequent and somewhat tedious children's lament from the back seat of the car on the drive to the cottage. But it clearly expressed a sentiment that, for many, stretched well beyond childhood. The beauty of life at the cottage was the enticing reward that awaited one's arrival there, if only one would get there already! Garry's quip spoke to my quest to try and understand just what "there" was, and why it was so appealing.

The journey to the cottage both tracks a physical move to another place and marks a social, emotional, and psychological transition. As a liminal space between cottagers' permanent residences and their cottages, it shaped, structured, and ultimately helped make pleasurable the cottage experience – even if, as I suggest below, there was often carsickness, tedium, and exhaustion experienced along the way.[4] Ingold (2000, 204; see also Heidegger 1977, 356) would argue that physical mapping of routes to places brings them into being; in Michael Haldrup's (2004, 447) terms, such mapping is "navigating" travel to a place, "at which arrival is anticipated." In my conversations with cottagers, I discovered that the actual journey to the cottage was suffused with such concepts.

A car was needed to physically get to the cottage in the postwar era.[5] And since "between 1945 and 1971 ... the number of cars [in Canada] increased an astounding 577 percent" (Anastakis 2008, 55), many Ontarians would have had this basic requirement in hand. The car was a powerful force in cottage country: Stevens (2008a, 29) argues that the automobile "determined not only the social and geographic scope of cottaging, but also the flavour and layout of Ontario's cottage communities" (see also Halseth 1998; Luka 2006). But at a most basic level, an expanded road system opened up many more points of access for cottages in Haliburton and elsewhere in the province.

Access to Haliburton cottages was typically one of three types: from a primary highway, by a series of more minor and private roads, or seasonally by boat or, in more recent decades, snowmobile, for those lacking direct land access. Central to being a cottager is being mobile, and so a car and the attendant road system remain a vital part of the fabric of cottage life, even for water-access cottages, as one still has to drive to the marina where the boat is docked. Stevens (2008a, 55) has suggested that the need for this kind of mobility "might become an impediment to [cottage] culture" if one considers the limited capacity of "global oil reserves and the long-term prospects for North American automobility." This may someday prove true, but it does not seem to have happened just yet.

Before the trip to the cottage could even begin, the packing for the journey had to be completed. Several cottagers told me of their memories of the days when their parents would, as Trevor said, "pack everything they could think of, whether they needed it or not" to take to the cottage for the summer. This process began weeks ahead of the departure date. In the final stages of preparation, it was "Dad's job" to accomplish the impossible and get everything into the car – whose space was often expanded with a roof rack or small trailer, or by stowing things in the boat – and still leave room for "Mom and the kids." Then, on departure day, somehow everyone squeezed in and set off – as Trevor remembered, with "the back bumper dragging on the asphalt as you [got] out of the driveway." Alice remembered insisting that her children got to bring only one toy and one book with them – "there was simply no more room." Garry recalled that once they were out of the city, he and his brothers began plaintively asking, "Are we there yet?"

In recent decades, such expedition-style planning has been somewhat ameliorated, as rarely is there only one journey to the cottage for the summer. Fewer families spend the entire summer at the cottage, and with improved access even those who do spend extended times there often make periodic trips back to the city to attend to myriad commitments. Michael said that he was involved in so much in the city that it was impossible to leave for extended periods of time. And as more cottages are used throughout the year, major summer moves fade to distant memories. Trevor, who now has a fully winterized cottage, takes only his briefcase and a small cooler with him on his trips up every Friday. As he noted, "Everything else is there."

The time it took to travel to the cottage largely determined the frequency and pattern of visitation. The driving time for those I interviewed ranged from a maximum of forty hours[6] to thirty-five minutes.[7] Between these two extremes, travel times fell into three broad categories: one to one and a half hours; two to four hours; and six to thirteen hours.[8] Most travel times fell in the middle range of two to four hours. The time it would normally take was a determining factor for some as to where they purchased their cottage; a few others were prompted to move their permanent residence to allow readier access to their cottage. Particularly for those who lived in the Greater Toronto Area (GTA) or points beyond, the journey was an important part of the transition to being at the cottage. Quite simply, the intensely urban, congested environment of the GTA and the freeway system that many travelled on for at least some of their journey, with its multiple lanes of traffic at some points, looks, sounds, and feels very different from anything that is found in Haliburton. The journey to the cottage often began on multilane highways in the GTA that eventually gave way to two-lane roads.[9] The final leg of the journey was usually on a privately maintained road, sometimes nothing more than a one-lane track, that led to the cottage. For those without road access, the last leg of the journey could be made by boat, once all the contents of the car were loaded into it. With each stage of the journey between home and the cottage came greater psychological and emotional distance.

Cottagers strategized their journeys, often varying their day and time of departure, as well as their route. Every departure was structured around personal and professional commitments, something that seemed to increase exponentially as children grew into adolescence, and as the schedules of two working parents had to be accommodated. Those who had the flexibility started work early on a Friday to ensure that they could be on the road by mid-afternoon to avoid rush hour traffic; others left later on, around 8:00 or 9:00 p.m. to avoid the traffic; others planned their business calls in the northeast corner of the GTA for Friday afternoon so they could leave straight from there. And if cottagers were self-employed or retired, they travelled to the cottage outside of peak periods and days. Routes were selected carefully, depending on the time of year, the day and time of travel, and the local traffic reports and conditions. The first segment of the journey could and would vary depending on these factors, as cottagers often tried to avoid as many of the GTA's major egress routes as possible. Isabelle's job on her family's trip to the cottage was to act as a sort of scout, to access as best as she could from various vantage points what the traffic backlog was, thus allowing her husband to modify their routes accordingly. Others sought back routes intending both to avoid traffic and to find a "nice drive." As Vicky and Dwayne said,

> *Dwayne:* We do not go near [Highway] 400. We vary our routes ... but right now we're stuck on a route ... that is almost second nature to drive now. You get in the car and you go ... the car could almost drive itself. You get used to it.
> *Vicky:* We have a two-hour drive home, but it's a nice drive. We go onto Highway 35, then on to some side roads, across country ... it's pleasant, and it's good still time-wise.

But it took more than safely and efficiently manoeuvring one's car along the chosen route. Garry remembered that the trip to the cottage as a child in the 1950s was very long:

> The old road was very curvy and kind of slow. To drive up here it used to take us about three and a half hours each way. There were four young children to keep entertained in the car. It wasn't easy. But we would sing songs and do everything we could to keep ourselves occupied. It seem[s] such a long drive when you are child. And I used to get carsick, so I had my head between my knees all the way. It was awful!! But it was worth it when we got here.

The forty-hour journey that Rhonda and her family make every year from Alberta needs to be highly organized:

> Everyone has their own pillow ... the kids listen to their own music and watch DVDs. We've got soft drinks and everything in the van with us. When we stop to get gas, we go to the washroom, get another drink, take the dog for a walk, or eat something.

Their journey was truly a liminal space between home and the cottage. Rhonda continued:

> We are just driving. There are only one or two roads that go to Alberta [from here]. We are not sightseeing. We are just travelling through. We can do the trip in two days straight ... If we drive just eight or nine hours then go to a motel, we lose that night sleeping. Sleeping is important, but our prime objective is to get to the cottage.

For some, the experience associated with the cottage begins well before one arrives there. Becky said, "For me, the minute I get in the car and I start driving to the cottage, I am already there ... just knowing we are coming here, I feel good." Brigita observed of her husband on Friday nights in the summer as they started the drive to the cottage, "We were only five minutes in the car and I could tell by his face ... it was changing. He got in a much better mood. It was really noticeable." For Isabelle, it took until she drove over the last hill on the road to her cottage:

> I don't know what it is but all of a sudden it just felt like the whole weight would be lifted off me. It's a weird feeling, it's just like ... and the fresh air would come whoosh ... and I'd just leave everything behind.

Leon literally used the trip to and from the cottage as a transition zone. On the way to the cottage he planned all the things he wanted to do over the weekend, and on the return journey he sorted out his business commitments and calls for the upcoming week.

Of course, for many cottagers, even in the days when it was generally only Dad who came back, there had to be a return journey to the city on Sunday, starting sometimes as late as midnight, or possibly very early

Monday morning. As with all cottage departures, this was not remembered as one that inspired much anticipation and excitement. As Isabelle remarked, on Sunday

> you get into some of the traffic and it's annoying because you've had a great weekend, you're relaxed, you've had a good time, and then all of a sudden you're into bumper to bumper and you get stressed out.

This journey signalled, for some, a return to all that the cottage was not: paid work, demanding schedules, competing demands for time, and noise, people, congestion, and pollution. For others, it was simply a realistic return to "their other life," the one, as Anna acknowledged, "that makes the money so [the cottage] is possible." The journey between these places was one of significant importance, oscillating between anticipation and impatience, excitement and frustration. But in the end, such travels from home took cottagers to the place where they wanted more than anything else "to be."

A Place to Be

What it actually means to be a cottager and to be at a Haliburton cottage is a recurrent theme throughout much of this book. It was clear that there are different ways of *being* at the cottage, not all of which are necessarily either compatible or considered legitimate by fellow cottagers. I suggest that there are, broadly speaking, three loose categories of cottagers, two of which were represented in my research. All three of these groups have somewhat divergent notions of what it means to *be* at the cottage. In suggesting these three groups, I recognize that I run the risk of glossing contradictions, ambiguities, and outright exceptions in such generalizations. It is nevertheless helpful to synthesize some of the commonalities into ideal types while acknowledging that within any one group there will be significant variation and a host of inconsistencies. These groups broadly reflected cottagers' expressed concerns over how competing aesthetics, values, and priorities were going to be able to coexist harmoniously in Haliburton in the future. For the sake of simplicity, I will call these three groups the traditionalists, the socialites, and the transients.[10]

A traditionalist sees the cottage as a modest dwelling, making an assumedly limited impact on the environment, demanding little in the way of landscaping and tree clearance, requiring minimal technologies beyond electricity and a septic system – amenities some cottagers, albeit few, actually shunned. It is a place where "cottage toys" are kept to a minimum; one may have a canoe, a small motor boat, a paddleboat, or possibly a sailboat. Higher-powered boats are certainly common, but are generally used as a form of transportation, or, at times, for limited water sports activity. Whether such boats are the fastest and the newest is of no concern.

A traditionalist's cottage is rife with "the cottage feeling." The building could be something that was built from scratch by a grandparent, parent, other relatives, or oneself. Alternatively, at its core it might be an early prefab structure, possibly in some cases ordered originally from the Eaton's catalogue (Long 2000). The original structure has usually been improved and moderately expanded, typically as a do-it-yourself project by family members. Some of these cottages have been upgraded for winter use, but without dramatically altering the integrity of a desired understatedness. It might include a new structure if it was modest in size and captured or retained the requisite "cottage feeling."

Time spent at the cottage is imagined to be pleasurable, peaceful, and restorative.[11] Many traditionalists have long histories as cottagers, and the longer your history on a lake is, the more you are understood to be a true cottager. Others, however, are much more recent arrivals, but they desire the experience of life at the cottage as suggested by media representations and popular discourses – tranquility, natural beauty, and restorative experiences.

To traditionalists, those who know how to be at a cottage appreciate what Urry (1995, 197) called "quiet recreation." Swimming, canoeing, games, reading, puttering, and socializing with family and friends are popular summer pastimes. Cross-country skiing, snowshoeing, skating, and snowmobiling are winter activities. Traditionalists, in Urry's (31) terms, adopt a variant of the tourists' "romantic gaze" while at the cottage. The latter emphasizes a "private and personal, and a semi-spiritual relationship" with what they gaze upon. Cottagers generally do not "gaze" in solitude as do the "romantic" tourists Urry describes, but they prefer a social context that consists of people they know well or are closely related to.

If these cottagers have ever read Martin Heidegger's much quoted essay, "Building Dwelling Thinking" (1977), they might claim his interpretation of what it means to dwell is not unlike what they experienced at the cottage.[12] For Heidegger (1977, 349), to *be* is "to dwell," and more than one cottager passionately expressed that everything about their *being* – at a physical, emotional, psychological, intellectual, and spiritual level – was positively nurtured by, and centred on, their dwelling at the cottage. In Heidegger's terms, dwelling means to "stay in one place"; "to be at peace"; to be "safeguarded"; to "spare," and, thus, to not disrupt, change, or damage (ibid., 351). It assumes a "*primal* oneness [with the] earth, sky, divinities and mortals" (ibid., emphasis in the original; see also Ingold 2000, 185).[13] For cottagers, if they could not truly dwell all the time, at least they could do so at the cottage. Those who saw themselves as dwelling at the cottage would identify with those Heidegger (1977, 361-62) perceived as "capable of dwelling," such as those he wistfully describes as having built the peasant farmhouse in the Black Forest.[14]

Heidegger (ibid., 350) affirmed that "we do not dwell because we have built, but we build ... because we are dwellers" (see also Ingold 2000). Cottages are thus built, "cultivated and cared for" in Heidegger's terms (ibid.) and, ultimately, blissfully inhabited by cottagers because of all that such structures are imagined to be. They become what Ingold (2000, 185) calls "the homeland of [the cottagers'] thoughts," a theme that resonates with the expressions of nostalgic nationalism that abound at the cottage. In tension with this assumption stand the views of those I call the socialites, who also consider themselves "real cottagers," because many of them have long family histories of cottaging, but simply wish to live in a place, as Lenora said, "where everything works."

The socialites, who ironically would not necessarily feel alienated by Heidegger's notions of dwelling even if their cottage experience manifests little of what he described, prefer a cottage renovated to include many urban comforts – including dishwashers, washers, and dryers, air conditioning, hot tubs, Jacuzzis, big barbecues, high speed internet connections, granite countertops, fully equipped entertainment centres, etc. – if not a new structure altogether that functions as an intensely social place, what some might call a "party place," with fast boats, all the latest motorized water toys, and accommodation for lots of visitors.[15] Such a cottage is fully winterized, thereby serving as a base for snowmobiling and skiing. It is important to note that acquiring *all* of these amenities was the dream of only some Haliburton socialites, but such things constituted their ideal cottage.

Pcholkina (2006) suggested that such cottagers have a "modernizing approach to nature," often working to modify, if not upgrade, its natural beauty with lawns, gardens, artificial lighting, elaborate walkways, docks, and decks. Some are relatively new arrivals on the lake; others are younger generations of traditionalist cottagers. The friends they have at the lake are increasingly weekend visitors from the city, as they feel little connection with their neighbours on the lake, many of whom could also be recent arrivals themselves. Pleasure at the cottage is derived from play that is oriented to speed and athleticism, with high-powered boats, water skis, wakeboards, and personal watercrafts (PWCs), and an intensely social environment with both friends and family. The socialites exemplify a version of Urry's (1990, 31) "collective gaze," where the tourist, in this case the domestic tourist, prefers a place where there are many others like them, and where the social atmosphere generated by such a group is what makes the experience enjoyable.

The third group is made up of what I call transients. They include both those who rent cottages and, more recently, those who own a condominium or time-share in cottage country.[16] Both traditionalist and socialite values and attitudes are found among transients. Some renters have long-standing relationships with particular cottages, lakes, and communities – many would self-identify as traditionalists. Other renters, even if they cannot afford their ideal socialite cottage, value their time at a cottage for its capacity as a "party place." They have no vested interest in how the neighbours respond to their loud music and antics on the water, never mind the impact that the latter has on shoreline degradation and other water and environmental issues.

In her editorial in the October 2006 issue of *Cottage Life*, editor-in-chief Penny Caldwell (2006, 11) observed, "According to the letters we have received, this was the summer of disrespect." It was the summer that renters appeared in larger numbers throughout cottage country, as many people found themselves forced to let their cottage to help pay increased property taxes. The renter, the short-term visitor, the owner new to cottaging – this person, "real" cottagers argue, fails to understand what one cottager called proper "cottage etiquette" (ibid., 17). These transient populations are not aware of the unspoken rules about fast boats, loud music, and understandings of privacy that "real" cottagers intuit, the latter based on what is presumed to be primordial knowledge. In the eyes of many, they do not understand what it means to quietly contemplate the landscape or to gaze at the stars from a canoe at midnight, and they do not know or appreciate how much physical labour (and resultant sense of accomplishment) comes with just keeping the cottage useable. They do not understand the layering of history, personal and otherwise, that is embedded in the cottage. In brief, they are ignorant of what some see as the essence of cottage culture. If they had a cottage aesthetic, it was understood to differ greatly from that of the cottagers I interviewed.

Condominium owners and fractional time-share owners represent another kind of tourist in cottage country. Some could almost be seen as voyeurs to the cottage experience. They may or may not have any previous experience at a cottage, and while they have opportunities to rent water-craft, they do not necessarily have the skills to use them. Still, they have some sense of the cottage's apparent appeal. I did not interview or engage in conversation with any of these tourists, so I offer no comment on their perceptions of their experience. I mention them only because their actual – albeit somewhat limited – presence was a concern to some Haliburton cottagers. These individuals were, in general, seen not to demonstrate any long-term commitment to, or understanding of, the practice of cottaging; and they troublingly increased the density of people in the area and on any one lake. To those I interviewed, they would not know how 'to be' at the cottage; they would understand little of the "cottage feeling" and the cor-porate or mass-produced spaces of a condominium or time-share were seen to be structures that could never nurture such a feeling.

The Cottage Feeling

What was this phenomenon that several of those I spoke to called the "cottage feeling"? What did it mean for a residential building on a lakeshore to "feel like a cottage"? Whatever it was, it was pleasing and treasured. It was not something that could be defined by a rigid list of criteria but rather, for all of those who valued such a notion, was central to their cottage aes-thetic. The cottage feeling was found in both the physical attributes of the building and the area around the cottage; but it was also an attitude and a sensitivity – for some almost an intuition. For traditionalists, it captured much of what McCracken (1989) called "homeyness,"[17] a richly symbolic value that privileges the "diminutive" over the "monumental and brutish" and "eschews uniformity and consistency;" it has an "embracing aspect" that "demonstrates a descending pattern of enclosure," which, at the cottage, begins at the boundaries of the property and the waterfront and ends in the family memorabilia crammed into the cottage's every corner; it is "open" to guests and greets them "with generosity and warmth"; it has a "mnemonic aspect"; it has an "authentic property"; it has an "informal property"; and, most importantly, the occupant, in this case the cottager, is "an integral part of it." Homeyness, in McCracken's distillation, "is for many people the adhesive that attaches them to family, time and place" (1989, 175). It "is an unalloyed good, difficult to achieve, challenging to sustain, but always unambiguously desirable ... [it] is one of the great objectives of family life." It is also a buffer against the "cold and unforgiving" character of modernity (ibid., 177-78). And in the minds of those I spoke with, it was eminently achievable at the cottage.

For some, the cottage feeling was "nostalgia for a simple past" (Pcholkina 2006, 75). Darcy and Rhonda characterized it as "going back to the basics." To the traditionalists, the cottage feeling was nurtured by "keeping life at the cottage," a place "a little more rustic ... a little more natural," a place "not citified," a "little place in the woods."

These things, Roberta emphatically stated, were what made "a real cottage" and these places where the cottage feeling flourished. Luka (2006, 291) called those who held such views "cottage purists." The cottage feeling for them often began with keeping one's privacy protected from the lake. Part of such reserve was, as Aaron said,

> not really wanting people to see in. So, we've given up the view of the lake to keep our privacy. And when you are out on the water, you really cannot see in. Nobody really knows what's up here, until you get out of the boat. And then when you want to get the feeling of the lake, you just go down to the dock ... There you are floating on the water. And it's quite nice.

Cottages that were fully exposed to the lake, something usually accomplished by cutting down most of the trees on the shoreline property, were an affront to what some saw as the essence of the cottage experience. These cottages challenged any sense of intimacy and closeness, qualities seen to characterize ideal social relations at the cottage but also imagined to describe physical spaces.

The bedrooms in Frances's cottage were not big enough to fit both a bed and a dresser. As such, they were emblematic of what cottage spaces should be. She and her husband thus slept in one room and had their clothes in another, an accommodation she felt one should simply accept at a cottage. Elaine admitted, "The cottage beds are not as comfortable as those at home, but that is what you expect." As Brigita observed, "You have everything in a home. And that's convenient, but that's not a cottage." Keeping the cottage feeling alive meant being prepared to make compromises in creature comforts; everything else pleasurable about the cottage makes up for such modest adjustments.

To some, retaining a reticent character meant that one neither painted a "real" cottage with garish colours nor used anything as tacky or suburban as aluminum siding. For some, that meant only staining, not painting. For instance, Charles wanted to "eliminate the red, white and blue colour schemes that jump out at you," and to find acceptable understated colour schemes of white, grey, and forest green.

Many cottagers were proud of the fact that at the heart of their cottage was an original structure, something likely first erected in the 1950s or 1960s. Some such cores were log buildings erected by the original cottagers, but many were prefabricated structures that had been provided by the developer or acquired from the Eaton's catalogue. Others were small structures built from scratch by a parent or grandparent. A unique one had originally been the Santa Claus house used in the Toronto Eaton's store for many years.

The retention of elements of the foundational spaces kept alive the founding spirit of the cottage experience. In the case of the Santa Claus house, the spirit of magic and make-believe could be imagined as embedded in its transformation into a cottage. However, the cottages of very few people I met with had remained as these original structures. The vast majority had undergone significant renovation, and many had had extensions added. Such expansion had to be done to accommodate the next generation of family who wanted to be at the cottage – a motivation that some would sanction as the only acceptable reason to increase the size of a cottage. Metaphorically, modest additions were superimposed layers that cocooned and held safe the original heart of the cottage. Expansion and improvement were also prompted by the reality that many of the original cottages were built by amateurs on limited budgets: sometimes the structures just started to fall apart because of poor craftsmanship and the use of inexpensive materials. But in their rebuilding, the cottage feeling would not be lost. As Lisa and Henry said,

> *Lisa:* We have great memories from when we first acquired this place ... it was completely falling in ... but those were the most fun times we had up here. The mice were running rampant through the whole place ... the floors were rotten ... But it was fun ... our children were very little ... life could not have been better. And the place was a wreck. But we would sit here ... and look at the moon ... and drink wine and talk.
> *Henry:* ... and it was terrific. All our friends and relatives came to help ... to rebuild ... but not destroy ... what was there.

All but three of the cottages I encountered had at least the modern conveniences of indoor plumbing, and all but two had electricity. Visiting the outhouse was now a curiosity, for some an adventure. Such improvement meant to Charles – one of those who chose not to have indoor plumbing – that

> cottaging is becoming much more complicated ... [where some want] everything just like home with dishwashers and garburators and big boats and fast this and fast that ... Why go to all this trouble of creating another home? As far as we're concerned, this isn't like home. This is a different place. It's a cottage. It feels like a cottage.

With electricity came the potential to have a TV at the cottage. But Brigita dismissed such things as "being like you are at home ... we are not going to have a TV ... we don't want a TV," just as Roberta could not understand why "anyone would want a dishwasher at the cottage." Both she and Isabelle said they had their best conversations with their family while doing the dishes at the cottage. Such experiences fostered the cottage feeling.

In keeping with the notion that cottages were places that should be modest, or "not fancy," as Susan said, and should demonstrate at least a nod to a legacy or past, many furnished their cottages with castoffs from their own homes in the city or those of their friends and relatives. Nobody cared, and some even preferred, if things were mismatched. Roberta said of her parents' cottage she inherited, "It looked cottagey or, you know, sort of thrown together." Castoffs included practical things like furniture, dishes, pots, pans, kitchen utensils, and bedding, but also art works and other decorative items that did not seem to fit anywhere else.

Deborah appreciated the value of such recycling not only from a monetary point of view but also from what it represented at an aesthetic level. When she and her husband built a new structure to serve as their cottage, she did not want to lose all of the essence of "what a cottage really should be," something she had experienced growing up at her parents' cottage. She did not want everything to be new and so opted to have her "somewhat tired kitchen" from their home in the city moved to the cottage, and have a new one installed at home. Alice and Leonard took their old record player to the cottage when they decided that they would enjoy some music there. They never considered acquiring a new CD player for such purposes. In a similar vein, Sarah refused to buy anything new for their cottage and took great pleasure for many years haunting second-hand and antique shops for things that they could purchase cheaply, refinish, and use at the cottage. There was a certain sense that stepping into a "real cottage" should feel vaguely like slipping on a comfortable and not-too-fashionable pair of slippers. It should feel safe, secure, and inviting, a place layered with stories and memories.

The "cottage feeling," I came to understand, was like a patina. The Oxford English Dictionary (OED) defines "patina" as "a pleasing surface sheen acquired with age or frequent handling." This definition suggests something handled often and carefully; something marked but never scarred; something treasured and held dear; something that could be layered on as time passed; it accrued in "glacial time," which I discuss further in Chapter 4. Such a patina would build up at the cottage, as Elaine said, "because we have come here for so many years." Or, Aaron said, what made the cottage feel good was just that "over the years ... *everything* kind of adds up ... even if [one's time here] is fragmented." "Everything" includes all of the metaphorical and symbolic meanings attached to the actual structure and place, as well as the social and personal experiences and memories associated with that place. It meant, for Elaine, knowing that you should not "act like arrogant urban people, and be part of where you are." But as Ava learned, it seemed that some cottagers had, in fact, forgotten where they were and lacked any appreciation of the virtues of the cottage feeling.

There is a second meaning offered by the OED for patina: "any thin or superficial layer on something." Such a gloss is what some cottagers told me that magazines like *Cottage Life,* trade fairs like the *Cottage Life Shows,* and any shop that advertised "cottage décor" were trying to sell.[18] A real cottage feeling is not something that can be packaged and marketed. For many of those I interviewed, it was something that was lived, but it was also incredibly fragile. Many saw the cottage feeling as under threat. Behaviours around PWCs and other high-powered water toys, and the arrival of cellphones and the internet at the cottage were symptomatic of this challenge. But one of the things that contested the cottage feeling most was what many of those I interviewed called "monster cottages" or, even more insultingly, "large suburban homes," being built on lots where "real cottages" had once stood.[19]

The new cottage that went up beside Ava exemplified all that many felt was inappropriate and fundamentally wrong with such developments. She and her husband had at one time owned the empty lot beside them. They had been forced to sell when they needed money to put a roof on their home in the city, but they felt comfortable when they sold it to the son of someone who used to live down the lake. The buyer was well known to them as he had helped them build their cottage when he was a teenager. Ava and her husband had built their cottage using poplar logs from their own property. They had hewn and stripped the logs themselves, and then erected a small A-frame structure with a small extension at the back, in total about 700 square feet. Periodically, they had hired a couple of young men on the lake to help with the construction. They figured this experience had attuned the person who bought their extra lot to what a "real cottage" should feel like. As it turns out, they could not have been more wrong. What had been erected beside them was, in their minds, the exact opposite of a "real cottage."

Their new neighbour was an established professional in Victoria. He now had his own family. As Ava concluded, he had clearly "adopted a West Coast aesthetic" and, in the process, lost any appreciation for what a Haliburton cottage aesthetic was all about. He told Ava that he had never forgotten his childhood and adolescence spent on the lake, and purchased

the lot to ensure that he did not lose his connection to it, as his parents
had sold the family cottage when he was a young adult. He then proceeded
to build a 3000-square-foot, three-storey mountain chalet constructed
with logs imported from British Columbia and designed to sit well on an
alpine slope, despite the fact that the lot was basically flat. It had multiple
bedrooms and three bathrooms, at least one of which had a Jacuzzi tub.
He had the lot entirely restructured to facilitate the construction and design.
The removal of many of the trees on his lot caused serious drainage problems for Ava's neighbouring lot each spring and during heavy summer
rains. Granite countertops, a dishwasher, a washer and dryer, expensive
carpeting, hardwood floors, and a three-car garage were other characteristics that Ava felt were completely inappropriate to a cottage. Moreover,
she wondered what impact such a structure would have on the lake. It
completely towered over Ava's cottage, blocking the sun for a good part of
most summer afternoons. The only saving grace was that he and his family
came only once or twice a summer for very short visits, so at least they
did not have to engage with them personally very often. Yet such limited
usage only made the construction of such a "monster cottage" all the more
tragic in Ava's mind: a cottage feeling would never become the patina of
such a structure. Was it possible to retain or generate the cottage feeling
without an almost religious commitment to rusticity and a charming hap-
hazardness? Some cottagers were actively engaged in demonstrating that
it was.

Drew and Lenora were building a new 1200-square-foot cottage on a
small private lake in Haliburton. They had rented for years and Lenora
confessed,

> Given our age we want our creature comforts. At the cottage [we rented]
> we roughed it a fair bit and that was great then. And now we're saying,
> okay, we want plumbing and power and sinks and stoves and fridges ...
> we want everything that works.

Lenora found the "quaintness of age" rather tiresome. While Ava's neighbour's chalet offered an especially egregious affront to the feeling of a
cottage, some cottagers felt that it would be impossible for any new cottage
to capture this essence. Darcy and Rhonda said that they would never move
to the cottage permanently, otherwise they would have to build anew.

They felt that they would lose the cottage feeling if they built a much different structure than the one they had.

Yet several had built new cottages, and they argued that what their cottages captured could be a cottage feeling, possibly one for the twenty-first century. Joan, like Lenora, was not terribly nostalgic about a rustic cottage feeling. To her, it meant the smell of mould and the assault of stale air on one's nostrils, combined with the accumulation of grime and dirt. It suggested anything but the treasured patina of loving use, a far cry from the scents and tactile sensations that some cottagers fondly associate with their cottage.[20] A somewhat reluctant convert to the cottage experience, Joan insisted that any cottage she would own would not have any hints of these sensorial memories. If Sam got to pick the place – the lake where he had spent most of his childhood summers – where they would be spending extended periods of time in their retirement, she insisted on control over what the actual structure would look like. So they built a modest one-storey structure, well hidden by trees, with a small dock, all in the tradition of a "real cottage." But that is where the similarities ended. The interior of their cottage had been designed by an American architect known for his fashionable urban lofts, and decorated to look like an upscale apartment in New York: lime green and dark navy was the dominant colour scheme, spot-lit by halogen lights; they had stainless steel appliances and trendy minimalist furniture. Its newness sparkled. Contemporary abstract art hung on the walls. There was no sheen of repeated use here. No colonial style furniture covered in garish plaids, no mismatched dishes, and no pictured or stuffed loons, moose, bears, or fish to be found.

But it was the warm, congenial spirit of Sam and Joan's family and their passion for the cottage experience that overwhelmed me as I walked in the door. It seemed that the cottage feeling could transcend décor and design. The lake out front and the trees surrounding their cottage made a rather ironic backdrop to this transplanted urban space, but this disconnect did not seem to have any impact on the positive dynamics of the sociality generated there. They were preparing for a large family gathering when I first spoke to them, and, more immediately, were poised to greet close friends who lived down the lake. The cottage, it appeared, could be "naturally social," even if it appeared to be misplaced in nature. What really lay at the core of the cottage feeling was, as Trevor said, the "one thing that cottagers valued the most, a sense of place."

A Sense of Place

Just what did Trevor mean by the phrase "a sense of place"? Ideas of place are grounded in various understandings, representations, and material forms in the contemporary world. They carry with them multiple and sometimes pejorative notions of geographic location, fundamental phenomenological debates about the human experience, and volatile tensions centred on inclusions and exclusions, as determined by the social, cultural, and economic forces and discursive representations that have played out globally and locally over the past millennium (for example, see Bender 1993; Crang and Thrift 2000; Cresswell 2004; Harvey 1993, 4; 1996; Massey 1991, 1993; Mitchell 2002).

In his book *Landscape and Power*, Timothy Mitchell (2002, ix-x) sees space/place/landscape as a "dialectical triad." He draws on Henri Lefebvre's ([1974] 1993) notions of "perceived, conceived and lived space," including his argument that such concepts need to be triangulated rather than understood separately. In brief, Mitchell (2002, ix-x) interprets Lefebvre as follows: perceived space – "the everyday practices and performances that 'secrete' space" or Lefebvre's "spatial practices"; conceived space – "the planned, administered, and consciously constructed terrain" or Lefebvre's "representations of space"; and lived space – "space mediated through images and symbols" or Lefebvre's "spaces of representation" (see also Urry 1995, 25). For David Harvey (1993, 23), the potency of this matrix lies in the fact that it "denies the particular privileging of any one realm over the other, while simultaneously insisting that it is only ... social practices" that produce place both "in the mind as well as on the ground." As such, place is a social, cultural, and, ultimately, political construction, something that cannot be seen outside of the realm of money, commodity, capital, and exchange (ibid., 13; 1996, 212; see also Mitchell 2002).[21]

Place is therefore shaped by history, by the forces of imperialism, by the entrenched social hierarchies of colonial states, and by the global market system. In concurrence, Tim Cresswell (2004, 26-27, 29) observes that inequities grounded in class, race, sexuality, gender, and myriad other social processes do not happen "on the head of a pin," but rather in "space and place" (see also Massey 1993); or, as for Timothy Mitchell (2002), such forces become "naturalized" onto landscape. Mitchell (2002, 1-2) sees the notion of landscape as an "instrument of cultural power, perhaps even an agent of power" (see also Bender 1993).

With a nod to phenomenology, Yi-fu Tuan (1974, 1977) and Tim Relph (1976) conceive of place as something experienced, created by the everyday and the mundane as it is performed on a regular basis, resulting in an intimate knowing of a place (see also Cresswell 2004, 21-23). Following Heidegger ([1977] 1994), an intimate knowing of one's place is vital to "being in the world" (Cresswell 2004, 21) and for many cottagers I interviewed, their favourite place to be in the world was their cottage. Unlike scholars such as Harvey (1989, 13), who suggests that these notions of place reject "any sense of moral responsibility beyond the world of immediate sensuous and contemplative experience," many cottagers would not have any problems with Heidegger's rather idealized vision of a dwelling place. Regardless, social, cultural, and ultimately political practices produced the cottage in its material, representational, symbolic, and, I would argue, aesthetic forms as the locus for all that is experienced there.

Trevor's and other cottagers' "sense of place" was something actively created by their intimate knowing of their cottage. In keeping with Harvey, Mitchell, and Cresswell, those I interviewed knew that their cottage could not be readily distilled to a simplistic notion of place,[22] even if their understandings did not necessarily overtly encapsulate the complex social, political, and cultural, if not moral, dimensions that these scholars insist must be acknowledged. Many cottagers did see their cottage as a place strongly linked to a Canadian historical meta-narrative and concomitantly a certain set of moral values. What I saw as the tensions between the cottage as a place of "dwelling" and the cottage as a place that swirled in the political, social, cultural, and historical context of the wider world was grist for the passion for life at the Haliburton cottage.

It was clear to the cottagers I spoke with that the cottage was a complex place; it was, as Sack (1997, 8) suggested, a place "thick with meaning."[23] Physically, it incorporated more than the lakeside house-like structure and all of its internal furnishings that provided shelter, sleeping quarters, food preparation, and storage facilities, and, in almost all of those I visited, human waste disposal capacities.[24] It also included the docks, decks, diving rafts, patios, gazebos, saunas, outhouses – even if the latter were unused in recent years – and other constructed sites such as lawns and artificial beaches – as well as myriad cottage "toys," including canoes, paddleboats, PWCs, wakeboards, sailboats, tubes, and pontoon and power boats. It included the privately owned property and its trees, rocks, and wildlife.

The lake, particularly that area immediately adjacent, was part of the cottage, as were the roads, lanes, or routes tracked on the water from the marina to the cottage (for water-access cottages) and other pathways and connecting links on the property. Frequently, the cottages and cottage properties of neighbours and relatives and even, for some, the local community and favoured shops, vendors, and sites of recreation were understood to be encompassed by the idea of the cottage.[25] These various locations were woven together by the physical paths, journeys, and ultimately the social relations that connected them.

For cottagers, repeated return to this place densely layered it with memories and a nostalgia for the past, the anticipation and indulgence of the lived moment of the present, and hope for stasis and continuance in the future – the latter being, some might argue, the most tenuous imagining if time and space at the cottage are only, as Tuan (1977, 6) suggests, a "pause" in the "work in progress" (see also Relph 1976, 33).

A Keeping Place of Memory

For cottagers, Haliburton's "texture," as Ingold (2000, 193, 198-99) would say, is at its purest a composite of mythic elements of larger national narratives of settlement and wilderness – the stuff of history – and more personalized stories of how individual families came and continued to be cottagers in that place – the stuff of memories.[26]

Robyn and Megan said of their cottage, "We have so many good memories here." Jay Teitel (2009, 87) noted that the cottage is "the ideal mechanism for memories" for cottagers. Just like the all too common cobwebs of spiders found at the cottage, tangled webs of memories lurked in every nook and cranny of the cottages I visited. For some, the cottage was a place richly swathed with such webs. Richard eloquently captured the layering and entanglement of memories at his cottage, which in this case is the cottage his parents first acquired when he was a young child:

> Sometimes I sit on the beach and look out and think that [our cottage]
> is really a timeless place because it's been so steady in my life. I could
> turn around and be sixteen and see my Camaro sitting in the back; or I
> could be twenty-six and see my first-born in a crib; or I could be forty-
> two and it would be today; or I could be ten years old and turn around
> and see my pail and shovel there. I think that's the most precious thing

about it, when you turn around and you see your family or your parents
are there and you realize what year it is and what time it is. That's what
makes this place so sacred.

In Pierre Nora's words, Richard's memories are in fact "in permanent
evolution" (1989, 8-9, emphasis added). Nora accurately described memory
– as opposed to history – in much the same way as I came to understand
it from the cottagers I met, as something dynamic.[27] History was of little
interest to many cottagers, while memory remained

> open to the dialectic of remembering and forgetting, unconscious in
> [its] successive deformations, vulnerable to manipulation and appro-
> priation, susceptible to being long dormant and periodically revived
> ... [it is] a bond tying [those who hold it] to an eternal present ... [it is]
> affective and magical, only accommodat[ing] those facts that suit ... [it]
> nourishes ... recollection that may be out of focus or telescopic, global
> or detached, particular or symbolic ... responsive to every censorship or
> projection ... [it] installs remembrance within the sacred; [it is] blind to
> all but the group [it] binds ... [it is] collective, plural, and yet individual
> ... [it] takes root in the concrete, in spaces, gestures, images and objects
> ... [it is] absolute. (ibid.)

There was no questioning in Richard's mind about the absoluteness, the
reality of the memories that he held so dear of his times spent at the family
cottage. It was why, he told me, he wanted to be at the cottage as often as
he could, and definitely every weekend in the summer, even if his wife and
adolescent daughters indicated that they would like to spend more time
in the city. Re-visiting the cottage kept the sacredness of his memories
alive, even if his brother, who found the family cottage a somewhat less
compelling place to visit, queried much of their veracity.[28] Losing the
meaning of these memories by never returning to the cottage would be
like falling into a "black hole," Richard said. Despite some pressure from
his wife and children, Richard strongly resisted any changes to the physical
structure and ritualized practices of the cottage.

Because they had a strong desire to talk about their memories, my
discussions with cottagers were mostly about what had happened in the

past, whether the previous month or thirty years ago. What was hoped and planned for in the future filled up much of the remainder of the conversations. The present was the often tenuous bridge between all that had gone and the future, charged with hope and fraught with anxiety.

Childhood and adolescent memories consistently acted as natural starting points for many of my conversations, and were often revisited as context to later discussions. For those who began their cottage experience as adults, their childhood memories of family recreational experiences – such as car camping – were compared almost always negatively to experiences at the cottage. Those who were parents and grandparents talked about their efforts in the past and their desire in the future to create opportunities for "the stuff of memories" of their children and grandchildren at the cottage.

According to Maurice Halbwachs (quoted in Connerton 1989, 35), individuals "acquire, localize and recall their memories" through membership in kin networks and in groups defined by class, race, gender, and nationality. Such groups shaped much of who cottagers understood themselves to be, and how and why they valued their experiences at the cottage. Identification as a cottager was, for many, grounded in the stories they told about their life on the lake or the early years of cottaging in Haliburton. And it is in such stories that memories find "a context" (Kenny 1999, 421), ensuring that they do not become lost.

A "socially specific spatial framework" is essential for any collective memory to exist, as "memories are [always] located within the mental and material spaces of the group" (Halbwachs quoted in Connerton 1989, 37). Places are thus "archives of memory" (Wynn 2007, xvii; see also Turkel 2007), one of the "cultural vehicles" required for "its expression" (Antze and Lambek 1996, xvii). In this case, the "spatial framework," the "archives," or what Pierre Nora calls "milieux de mémoire" (1989, 7), were the cottages of those I interviewed. As materialized places of memory, all of their meaning was externalized and objectified, making real a range of deeply held social and cultural values (see Antze and Lambek 1996; Kenny 1999; Nora 1989; Turkel 2007).

Nora (1989, 7, 12) contrasts "milieux de mémoire" with sites of memory, or "lieux de mémoire." The latter are the structured, formalized, determined, "devotional" edifices of history that capture "moments of history ... [that are] no longer life, not yet death, like shells on the shore when the sea [lake?]or living memory has receded."[29] And with the anxiety expressed by many cottagers about the future of the cottage experience, the commodification and simulations of the experience that have emerged in cottage country, and the vagaries of the policies of the state, it could be argued that the Haliburton cottage, despite what some cottagers might say, has passed from a "milieux de mémoire" to a "lieux de mémoire." The cottage has become a place where memory is reified and commodified by what it is imagined to be, rather than what it was in the last part of the twentieth century (Antze and Lambek 1996, xvii). Recognizing such tensions, I argue that the cottage has elements of Bordo's (2003, 174, 176) "keeping place[s]."[30] Keeping places are

> a special kind of *lieu de mémoire* ... that [is] episodic, ephemeral, and unstable; they are subject to relapses and rebirths ... they may contain nothing ... valuable in the sense that museums and safety deposit boxes carry valuables .. At their most fragile (and powerful) they are [not] held together ... by institutional structures ... [they are] passed on by word of mouth over generations ... [they] give dominance to living witnesses.

I argue that such keeping places capture the tension between memory that is "intentional, conscious, collective, habitual, and willful," what Nora called "memory secured by memorization," and what Bergson called "true memory that is unwilled, occasional, uncontrollable, and individual" (as quoted in Bordo 2003, 172) or what Lowenthal (1985, 194) described as "wholly and intensely personal."

A great deal of recent writing about memory is centred on its traumatic, implicitly negative, disruptive, and troubling character (see for example Antze and Lambek 1996; Kenny 1999). Memories that are predominantly, but not exclusively, associated with the cottage are, however, quite the opposite. Many are about the positive, the ecstatic, or the "peak" experiences that happen there (Maslow 1964; see also Csikszentmihalyi 1990). They are also about the everyday, understood to be extracted from the mundane. Such "everydayness" is seen to capture simplicity, honesty, the authentic. As Jessica reflected, "Thinking about all of those memories is good for your soul." Treasured memories are thus a central part of what makes the cottage a beautiful and, for many, spiritual place – a place of "karmic connection."

A Place of "Karmic Connection"

Sam explained to me how he had never understood why his parents sold the family cottage. When they made this decision, he was just starting his medical practice and, also having a young family, had not been able to buy it from them. They had said they needed the money, yet when sorting out their estates after their deaths years later, he discovered that monies from the sale had remained untouched in a bank account. Sam's central objective was to acquire property on this lake in the same bay as his parent's cottage had been located, as he said, "to reclaim his place there." He wanted to extend to his children "the gift of memories" that he carried with him of times spent there as a child. Since he lived no less than a thirteen-hour drive away, a cottage somewhere closer to home might have seemed like a good idea. Nevertheless, Sam was not interested in such reasonable options (see also Pitkänen 2008, 170). He eventually succeeded in achieving his goal – buying a cottage lot where he wanted and eventually building a new cottage there.

Shortly after his purchase, a neighbour on the lake gave Sam a series of photographs that he had taken of Sam as a young child with his mother on the exact property that Sam had just acquired. He had no memory of standing on the beach of the property he now owned, but he did remember that his mother liked to canoe over to the west side of the bay to enjoy the afternoon sun. To Sam, this suggested that he had some sort of "karmic connection" to this place, something that he felt had drawn him to this exact location.

Others articulated this idea in various ways. Their cottage was the place they "belonged"; it was where "my heart is"; it was their "spiritual home"; it was where "my roots are"; it was where their "soul belonged." In fact, many cottagers used "home" and "cottage" interchangeably. Some called the cottage their "real home"; others labelled it their "family home," or characterized "coming to the cottage [as] coming home" (see also Löfgren 1999, 139; Luka 2006, 171-74). Home, security, family, comfort, and place are also linked together by theorists and academics. Quinn (2004, 129) argues that recreational second homes challenge the notion that an urban-based home is "the main source of place-based identity," while the cottage is a place that, in Sack's (1992, 4) terms, "[makes] feelings real." Some feminists have argued that the blanket positive assumptions at work in this connection should not be so lightly glossed over, as home can also have negative connotations, including those of a carceral and overwhelming patriarchal power. This theme arises even in connection to the cottage.

After he and his wife had looked at countless cottages in the area, Neil eventually bought one two doors down from the one his mother had owned when he was a child. As he put it, this purchase "just seemed right." This sentiment echoes what I heard from others: the place in cottage country to which cottagers felt they belonged was most often a very specific one. In the cases of Sam and Neil, it was a particular bay on a lake; for others it was even more specific, to a particular lot on a lake. Roberta could not imagine anything but the exact cottage and location she had known all her life; she simply would never consider owning any place else. She was just one of many cottagers I met who knew very little about other parts of their lake, particularly if it was a bigger lake. A large number knew nothing at all about neighbouring lakes.

Most cottagers valued their cottage as a place of stability; it was, as Jordan said, the "one thing that has remained constant" in life. Bill noted, "The thing about cottages is that the friendships made up here seem to last a lot longer. People seem to change their houses, but they seldom sell their cottages casually." Many of those I interviewed had lived in different countries, various parts of Canada, in several communities in Ontario, or just in more than one house in one city. Richard, whose minister father was moved regularly by the church, came to understand the family cottage as his "anchor" in his "nomadic life." It was always a base to return to and it became his permanent address when he was leading the peripatetic life of a student. Following her husband's death and concerned about her family's financial future, Marianne contemplated selling the family cottage. Her pre-adolescent children resoundingly convinced her that if anything had to be sold, it should be their house in the city. They were far less attached to it than they were to the cottage, even if they visited there only a few weekends and a couple of weeks each summer. They felt, as Aaron did, that he wanted his cottage "to be in my life for the rest of my life." Harry, in his eighties, knew that he and his wife were going to have to sell their house in the city, but he emphatically said, "We won't sell the cottage ... that is the one place that is home."

A different group of tourists I previously interviewed had ideas of home as a place of memory, identity, security, permanence, belonging, and comfort, but also as a place of nation – in this case, the Canadian nation-state (J. Harrison 2003). I quickly learned when I ventured to the cottage in Haliburton that this duality was delightfully and pleasingly repeated there. The cottage is entangled with community, at both a very local and a national level, the latter in many ways unlike any other place I had experienced before. It carried a particular set of understandings about what it meant to be Canadian. Ironically, it was also a very modern place, despite imaginings of it as intimately tied to nature. Understandings of the Canadian/Ontarian landscape and history, and of the country's place and that of its citizens in the modern world, shape what the Haliburton cottage experience defines as Canadian, and how cottage experiences are remembered at personal, familial, community, and larger social and cultural levels.

3

Community, Nature, Modernity, and Nationalism at the Cottage

During my research, I came to learn that valuing the Haliburton cottage experience meant valuing what it meant to be Canadian, even if that was understood from a particularly Ontarian perspective. It also meant experiencing the cottage as a resolutely modern place tied intimately to the urban space, while being firmly grounded in the opposite – nature. Such shared notions about all that the cottage was seen to symbolize, and the common experience of bringing into reality such referents, forged strong bonds of community among cottaging neighbours throughout the second half of the twentieth century. But in the first decade of the twenty-first century, the connections began to falter, for some, as local dynamics changed through generational shifts. The ambiguities, contradictions, and shifts reflect what Clifford Geertz (1973) would understand as the messiness of social life. In this chapter, I explore how understandings of community, modernity, nature, and nation added layers to what made the Haliburton cottage experience a densely meaningful if not in many ways a messy and contradictory one.

"Can We Come Over and Help?"

To Olive, the cottage was a place where people were willing to lend a helping hand, to reach out to others, to see everyone as part of a community. She said,

> the people that you meet here are always in a good mood ... everybody is happy and nobody is bickering about this or that. Everyone just wants to know what you are doing over at your place. "Can we come over and help?" You'd never get that in the city.

The Sandersons saw their cottage as a gathering place for friends around the lake. Jacob likened the smoke from their regular Saturday night bonfires to "sending up smoke signals, calling people to come down." Friends brought friends to these gatherings. Laura never worried about how many people showed up – in the practice of cottaging, "nobody ever comes empty-handed." In a similar vein, Hannah made sure that anyone who did visit them at the cottage knew that she was not going to play hostess: at the cottage they were all on the same footing. She concluded, "We are fortunate that the friends that we have, everybody is very agreeable to that concept." Good friends know how to be at the cottage. They know the etiquette. They know what is expected and willingly comply. Delores saw the cottage as place where people learned the fundamentals of what it took to function in a group or of simply "getting along." She said, "You can go and spend thousands and thousands of dollars on team-building exercises at work, or you can just learn what you need to know at the cottage."

Social relationships outside of the family sorted themselves into two groups at the cottage: those formed, nurtured, maintained and generally kept at the cottage – "cottage friends and family" – and those brought from the city. Second- or third-generation cottagers had long-standing relationships with many of their neighbours on the lake. There was great comfort in these strong bonds.

To Lorne, life at the cottage was about these relationships. He had no desire to be at the cottage when his neighbours there had left for the season. He said, "It would be lonely, socially isolated." Trevor appreciatively observed, "Everybody up here is the same." They felt as though they were members of a very tight community. Several had gotten to know their neighbours as their families built their cottages, often helping each other along the way.

Many cottage relationships did not extend beyond the cottage, as permanent residences were scattered widely across Ontario and in other parts of Canada and the United States. Sally, who had only ever come to her grandparents' cottage for two weeks each summer growing up, declared that her best friends were those she saw every year there. The bonds between her and two other young women cottagers were so firm that they had all been part of each other's wedding parties, even though their permanent homes were scattered across the North American continent.

Contrarily, Alice observed that her daughter always brought friends from the city with her to the cottage, even though she, too, had grown up on the lake. Alice noted that as she matured, her daughter seemed to have less and less in common with those who had been her close friends at the cottage throughout her childhood and adolescence. This pattern saddened Alice; she saw it as representing the loss of the deep connection to all that the cottage could be.

Of those I interviewed, some who grew up at the cottage began to find their social networks shrinking, as many of the families that had had cottages on the lake had sold them over the years as family dynamics changed, people died, marriages collapsed, or, more disturbingly for some, the next generation was not interested in keeping the cottage. And for some new owners, the time they spent at the cottage might not match that of their neighbours, as fewer people now stayed for extended periods at the cottage on predictable schedules. The diminishing strength of social contact on the lake was brought home very clearly by a couple of cottagers. They and their families had always been very involved in their local cottagers' association, serving in various capacities on the executive or organizing social events throughout the summer. But many of these organizations were struggling now to fill their executive positions as younger generations had neither the time nor the commitment to the lake that their parents had. Those who one cottager called "the weekend warriors," those more concerned with "partying and having a good time," did not know what it really meant to be part of a cottaging community. Those who came less frequently to the cottage also tended to do much of their shopping in the city and did not regularly patronize local Haliburton businesses.

These shopping practices and the sheer reduction in time that people spend at their cottages have led to the demise of many small stores and marinas on Haliburton lakes (K. Barker 2010). Such businesses had been at one time central to the sense of community on some lakes. Some noted their passing with sadness and as symbolic of the loss of something important; others felt simply that since they could no longer serve the supply needs of cottagers, their closures were inevitable.

Some who were more recent arrivals to cottage country had fewer deeply rooted friendships there, as they often found the existing social networks exclusively entrenched. Moreover, they were usually more interested in sharing their recently discovered cottage pleasures with those they knew from the city. Bringing city friends to the cottage could, however, be either a joy or a burden,[1] as Abigail found out when she invited her school friend to the cottage. She said of her friend, "She did not know how to be at the cottage. She kept asking me what we were going to be doing next. She did not know what a cottage was. She was really annoying all weekend." Abigail was not alone in her frustration; others commented that when inviting friends from the city, you had to be sure that they knew how to be at the cottage. Still others enjoyed introducing friends to the cottage because they saw it as their mission to proselytize its pleasures and virtues. But Susan told me that they had stopped inviting many friends from the city a long time ago; their guests often brought "too much of the city" with them. She and her family did not want such influences invading their cottage, so their social world was centred on their neighbours on the lake. These were people who knew what cottaging was about. Darcy and Rhonda admitted that they did not invite many friends over. Their cottage was "too small" and, besides, "it was always full of family." Regardless, everyone I spoke with agreed that a web of social relationships at the cottage, whether with a few select individuals or cast much more widely, stood in contrast to the experience they knew in the city. In reality, however, all that was the modern city was never very far from, and in some cases was perhaps even central to, life at the cottage.

A Modern Place

Despite what many cottagers imagine, cottaging has always been a modern experience and is now a postmodern one – even if it was originally, in many ways, an anti-modernist undertaking. The move to summer recreational properties in places such as Muskoka and Georgian Bay beginning in the 1890s – coined "the cottage syndrome" by Altmeyer (1976, 25, 23) – was prompted by a desire to escape the artificiality of the city, a place of "stone and mortar ... rattlin' roarin' streets ... clanging telephones ... [that produced] jaded minds" (see also Williams 1973, 62-63). This syndrome was part of what Ian McKay (1994, 9, 31) has called the "aesthetic colonization of the country by the city" as part of an anti-modernist "recoil from an 'overcivilized' modern existence to more intense forms of physical or spiritual existence."[2] Raymond Williams (1973, 62) describes the desire to escape the city – which in the Western world has a long-standing history – as being "in direct reaction to the internal corruption of the city, the rise of the lawyer, merchant, general, pimp and procurer; the stink of place and of profit; and the noise and danger of being crowded together." Those who seek "the cool country ... [as a] fortunate resident" are looking to escape the claustrophobia found in the "kind of hell" of the modern city. Haliburton cottagers, it seemed, were Williams's "fortunate resident[s]."

If consumption became the "locus of modernity" (Sack 1992, 5) in the twentieth century, acquiring a cottage can be seen to capture the social relations – including those shaped by economic, scientific, technological forces, and personal and collective values, attitudes, and beliefs – of modernity. A prerequisite for those who wished to become cottagers was a confidence and optimism in their own personal, as well as the national and global economic rationality, stability, and future. Somewhat contradictorily, a belief in the virtues of such a purchase reinforced the values of "the local community ... as the natural basis for moral order ... in which [one] can become rooted" (ibid.). These two positions capture what Dummitt (2007a, 14) describes as "the deep ambivalence ... [that characterized] many Canadians' response to high modernism" (see also Kuffert 2003). They were at the same time optimistic and nostalgic, global and local, laying, as Sack (1992, 6-8) would argue, the groundwork for the emergence of the even more unstable and fragmentary "condition of postmodernity," the other "modernity" that soon showed up at the cottage.

It is worth repeating that the desire to own a cottage, no matter what its internal tensions, could only be realized by the technologies of modernity. The "well ordered ... landscapes of transportation and settlement" were required to get to the "more traditional, local and concrete sense of place" – the cottage – and had first been accomplished by survey systems, Crown land disposal, and railroads and steamboats, the latter quickly replaced in the postwar era by the automobile and highways (Sack 1992, 9; Stevens 2008a, 2008b, 2010; Urry 1995, 130).

Beginning in the mid-1930s and right up until the mid-1970s, through the catalogue shopping services offered by department stores such as Eaton's and aided by the post office and local delivery systems, the modern cottage consumer could be completely outfitted for the summer with food staples, hammocks, lanterns, fishing tackle, boat motors, and even a prefabricated cottage (Long 2000). Orders could be placed in bulk before leaving for the cottage and delivered dockside over the summer months, or they could be placed at local post offices for next planned delivery over the summer.

The original cottages of several of those I spoke with had been delivered in just a manner and methodically erected by family members, and a few were still in use decades later. The presence of such modern and efficient retail networks delivering such fundamental goods and services to cottagers – symbols of all that the urban world was assumed to herald – were deemed acceptable, even necessary, to fully enjoy the cottage experience (see Belisle 2001).

Ironically, however, any links to the urban world were seen as recent developments, opposed by many cottagers who witnessed the increasing urbanization of their lake with the appearance of permanent vinyl-sided homes, cellphone towers, deforested and landscaped shorelines, and an increase in density as the twentieth century rolled into the twenty-first. But both conceptually and in very material ways, the urban world had been present at Haliburton cottages since their earliest days, fuelled most basically by postwar cottagers' desire for indoor plumbing, electricity, and properly maintained and upgraded access routes.

But acceptance has its limits. The twenty-first century brought a different urbanized landscape of technology to the cottage, best symbolized by cellphone towers and high speed internet. Such arrivals progressively challenged any imagining that urban and nature were presumed opposite, and unquestioningly nature was increasingly becoming even more mediated at the cottage. Such entanglement only adds to the complexity and, for some, the meaningfulness of the place. For others, it sowed the seeds of anxiety about the future of life at the Haliburton cottage.

In 1966, Canadian sociologist S.D. Clark posited that "people cannot move from the city to the country without bringing with them at least some of the equipment necessary for building an urban society" (12). And while Clark made these comments in reference to the development of Canadian suburbs, particularly those that developed in the postwar period around the city of Toronto, the same could be said to characterize the move of those who extended their exodus past the suburbs to a seasonal cottage in Haliburton.[3] Luka (2006) convincingly argues that the cottage must be seen as an "urban form," even more specifically as a "(sub)urban form" (see also Halseth and Rosenberg 1995; Mathieson and Wall 1982; Priddle and Kreutzwiser 1977; Stevens 2008a, 29; Svenson 2004). For Luka (2006, 93), "water-oriented second-home settings in central Ontario cottage country are part of the Toronto metropolitan region ... [something made real] through the principal links of recurrent, often ritualized individual and household practice of multiple residency" (see also Quinn 2004). Sharon Wall (2009, 25) noted that "in liberal capitalist societies and under certain conditions of modernity, the seemingly innocuous realm of leisure is shaped by the same relations of power, and problems of identity, authenticity, and meaning, that we are lead to believe are left far behind when we pack up our bags, head out of the city, and get 'back to nature.'"

Mobility between these two places reinforces their connectedness, two places linked by "corridors and/or stepping stones" (Dramstad, Olson, and Forman quoted in Luka 2006, 294). The early 1950s South Bay, Haliburton Lake development, for instance, while a standard cottage country single-tier necklace settlement (Halseth 1998), was developed in the same manner that suburban developments were – standard-sized lots, with a choice of four standard cottages all sold at once and positioned in parallel locations on their lots.[4] In 2012, it looked very much like a large-lot suburban development that just happened to have a few more trees and to circle a natural body of water in the county of Haliburton. For most of the Haliburton cottagers, such claims would be heretical – the cottage to them is the "anti-city" (Cross 1992; Pcholkina 2006; Williams 1973).

Nature at the Cottage

Nature at the cottage is complex and at times contradictory.[5] It can be benign or fearsome. But whatever it is to cottagers, it is also a socially constructed reality, defined by its link to the city. It could be characterized as "metropolitan nature" (Urry 1995, 199), that which Green (1990, 76) identifies as being "located relatively distant from the city and turned into a place to be viewed for leisure and recreation through an individualized rejuvenating experience."[6] Long-term cottagers admitted that their attitudes to nature had shifted dramatically over recent decades. As Stevens (2008b, 42) points out, cottagers in the 1950s and 1960s saw the lake as both a "dump" and a "sewer," often making little "distinction between landscape and landfill." Garry suggested that if one could drain some of the Haliburton lakes one would find countless cars, fridges, stoves, boats, motors, and all manner of things that early cottagers had tossed. Household garbage was disposed of in pits at the back of a property, or regularly burned in incinerators. Laundry, including diapers, was done in the lake, as well as bathing with soap and shampoo (see Stevens 2008b, 42-48).

The list of environmental concerns that many cottagers now think threaten life at the cottage include: leaching septic systems affecting water quality; noise pollution caused by bigger boats, PWCs, and lawn mowers; light pollution at night from floodlights and walkway lights on cottages; a proliferation of lawns and gardens requiring fertilizers and pesticides; shoreline degradation due to wakes from larger boats and increased water traffic; the construction of "monster" cottages or suburban year-round homes at the lake that has resulted in the elimination of vegetation interfering with the natural balance of the shoreline; and simply too many people on the lake, disturbing the peace and quiet of life at the cottage.

Many cottagers told me that protecting water quality was a priority. Some cottage associations have "lake stewards," who monitor water quality as part of the Lake Partner Program of the Ontario Ministry of the Environment. Cottagers also told me about trying to politely inform their neighbours that using non-biodegradable, chemical shampoo in the lake was not a good idea, and reporting to their cottage association what they perceived to be algae blooms as a result of a faulty septic system. Concern about the increased impact that cottagers were having on nature and the quality of life at the cottage – at a time when there has been a dramatic reduction in the capacity of the provincial Ministries of Natural Resources and the Environment to monitor watershed and land use planning in cottage country – prompted several cottage associations in Haliburton to undertake developing a "lake plan" with the aid of a consultant to guide the process and the volunteer labour of association members.[7] These plans are intended to "provide a process to identify and protect important natural, physical, and social values on individual lakes," to "identify land use policy to recommend to private and Crown land use planning," and to lay out "a series of stewardship approaches" to be undertaken by those who have cottages on the lake.[8] These could be seen as another of many attempts to regulate cottage life, no matter how noble their stated intention.

Cottagers I spoke with felt a direct connection to nature or the natural world; they voiced this as, "being with nature," "getting back to nature," "feeling closer to nature," and "reconnecting with nature."[9] Becky said,

The reason people come here, whether they realize it or not is because it's nature ... that's what draws them ... that's what makes them feel good, that's what makes them feel at peace. And they get to enjoy the wonders of nature, the rocks, the trees, the lake, the clean air.

Several cottagers expressed concern about the fragility of nature as they understood it at the cottage.[10] Don stated, "I feel responsible for this place. I feel dedicated to it, as I just feel good here." Robyn was troubled by her observation that they "don't see the baby loons like we used to ... the water gets chewed up [by high speed boats] ... A few years ago, we had a loon that got washed up on the shore and it was all entangled in fishing line and it was so sad." Leon was willing to be the steward for the lake where his cottage was, testing water samples regularly in accordance with a Ministry of the Environment lake partnership program to monitor water quality.[11] Jordan noted that "the size, number, and health of the trout that they're catching is diminishing every year and the lake is being taken over by rock bass." Susan worried that "with so many cottages along the lake there is no abundance of wildlife left." Brigita confessed, "We try not to disturb the shoreline too much, but just being here we do change things a bit." As someone who had immigrated as a young adult to Canada in the 1960s from central Europe, she attributed much of her love of the cottage to an almost primordial sense that she "always had a feeling that [she] was close to nature. [She] always felt pretty good [at the cottage]." It had been an easy transition for her to come to love life at the cottage as a place of nature. Like Frances, she tried to act as a caretaker for nature. Frances laboured to nurture the shoreline near her cottage, "thinning out the trees so the big ones can continue getting bigger and stronger." She was also involved in her cottagers' association:

[We work hard to] do our best to demonstrate acceptable behaviour and development around the lake. We try to educate the people on the lake and those coming here as to how important it is to all of us that there are beautiful big fish in [our lake]. There are incredible things that we want to preserve and maintain for future generations.

She was not alone in seeing the relationship "between humans and nature [as] long-term." This relationship burdened those who recognized it with "a special responsibility for its preservation [which] entails ... the taking of a very long-term perspective, certainly one extending ... beyond the lifetime of anyone presently living" (Lash and Urry 1994, 242, 246-47). For many, thinking about future generations at the cottage was of vital importance. Such preoccupations did not always prompt cottagers to be as attentive to their long-term impact on the natural environment as some, like Frances, wanted all cottagers to be.[12] Heartfelt sentiments did not necessarily prompt interrogation of the impacts of their own continued presence on the lake.

Lorne and Bill had each owned cottages on the same Haliburton lake for over forty years. They wanted their cottages to be places to which their children and grandchildren would always want to return. To encourage this, they thought it important to improve on or beautify what nature offered. When they built their cottages, the regulations about what could be done to shorelines were considerably more relaxed than they are today. Both men removed many of the trees from the water's edge and brought sand to create beaches for their offspring to play on. In reality, their impact on the shoreline was dramatic, and they were forced to spend considerable energy each year – and soon their sons/sons-in-law would be obliged to do the same – to keep their beaches from being washed away. In their minds, their "improvements" only increased their cottages' pleasure factor, and they interpreted them as minimal adjustments to their properties, even though they knew that such "re-development" would not be allowed today. Lorne would have agreed with Steven, another cottager, when Steven asserted that "the lake is the way it ha[s] always been, and the shoreline has not really been touched." Kuhn (1995) has noted that violence and domination are not to be overlooked as elements of any aesthetic. Lorne's and Steven's cottage aesthetic was seen by some to be "violent," as the men sought to overtly dominate and manipulate nature.

It would be wrong to imagine that what Frances and Brigita are concerned about preserving, or what Lorne and Steven "improved," was any kind of pristine environment. Haliburton is best understood as an industrial landscape: it is in very large measure an area of second growth from having been heavily logged in the late nineteenth and early twentieth centuries, and there has been significant mining done in the region. Little of this mattered to cottagers, however. Their comparative framework was across space, not through time. Still, it is important to note that the nature in which their Haliburton cottage was located was not wilderness, a dominant trope in the discourse of Canadian identity. Nature was something more cultural than wilderness was understood to be.

Trevor distinguished between his fully winterized cottage with the waterfront land around it and a piece of "bush" that he had just purchased. The former was

> not a city-like property by a long shot, it [still was] only a little over an acre and it's quite well manicured. If you want to see wilderness, we can walk across the highway and there's a bush lot that I have over there. It is about sixty-five acres ... that's not touched ... that's wilderness. There's a beaver pond and stream where there might be some fish, and you might snag a deer back in there.

Wilderness is untamed, rife with wildlife, without road access, and much more expansive in scale. This understanding of wilderness prompted several cottagers to make an annual visit to Algonquin Park, just north of the Haliburton region, an opportunity, as one said, to "be in the wilderness."[13]

Wilderness and nature, while related, were clearly not one and the same to those Haliburton cottagers with whom I spoke.[14] Nature at the cottage was wilderness on a smaller, more manageable scale, in some contexts very friendly. It was something, as Luka noted (2006, 278-79), with which cottagers sought to have a "symbolic and/or aesthetic interaction." Wilderness, on the other hand, was something "adjacent to the cottage environment, but removed from it by some buffer." Nature was, as Aaron said, "the beautiful surroundings ... the lake, and the woods and the wildlife." To Tony, "it was the water, it had to be the water that was the lure." For Becky, too, "it was all about the water." Exploring these beautiful surroundings could even be made into a game. Anna organized scavenger hunts for her children to "help them learn to identify things." The children had to find things like "a maple leaf, a piece of birch bark, a particular flower."[15] Such activities, she said, led to "a neat kind of interaction with nature." A more playful, not to mention thrill-seeking, interaction with nature was demonstrated in the acrobatics of the water skiers, wakeboarders, PWC riders, and snowmobile drivers; something Satsuka (1997) would suggest was just another way of "taming nature."

Beaver, chipmunks, squirrels, deer, loons, ducks, herons, blue jays, hummingbirds, raccoons, muskrats, rabbits, groundhogs, foxes, turtles, frogs, mink, trout, minnows, and even skunks and porcupines – "cottagers' nature" – brought fun and pleasure to life at the cottage, as long as most of them did not get too close.[16] Like many things about nature, these creatures were delightful if they did not transgress the accepted terms of engagement as set by the cottager.

One of Alice's great pleasures was watching the chipmunks scurry through the leaves as they prepared for winter. Lisa described a memorable afternoon:

> We saw a beaver so we called everyone to see it. Then there was a loon nearby. Then we went down the lake to a friend's cottage and there were six ducks sitting on their dock, and a heron sitting on a rock. It was all very quiet, [and we were] just watching them. It was really cool.

Susan boasted, "By the end of the summer [the chipmunks] actually eat out of my hand, because they are so used to me feeding them peanuts. So, it is that kind of nature at the cottage." These creatures as "nature at the cottage" suggest that nature is basically benign, at times awe-inspiring, and enjoyable. The animals can be cute, charming, even cartoon-like. They can be artificially represented, as in the plastic loons, squirrels, chipmunks, deer, bear cubs, and skunks that adorned some cottagers' properties, or displayed in hooked rugs, prints, or wooden sculptures found on the walls and interior spaces of some cottages (Pcholkina 2006, 61-66, 70). They can be anthropomorphized. In his account of the story of a mother raccoon moving her young ones from one tree to another, Conrad attributed her scolding and frustration with those that lagged behind to emotions similar to those a human mother would express.

Nature gives pleasure whether observed at a distance or more directly experienced. Not everyone I spoke with agreed as to which animals were sources of pleasure and enjoyment. Susan thought that the fox she often saw was "a little cute" animal, whereas Robyn and Megan worried that it would attack their cat, which they bring with them from the city (Pcholkina 2006, 98).

Larger animals such as bears, moose, or wolves were another matter. Knowing that bears in particular might be around their cottage was a source of fear and apprehension for cottagers. Their presence linked the place too directly to wilderness. But "bears in nature," almost a form of domesticated wildlife like those found at the garbage dump, were another matter. Landfill sites in cottage country have always attracted bears, and are therefore important destinations for cottagers, incidentally for their practical purposes, but more often for the thrill and excitement they offer as places to view such wildlife. For Jacob, such encounters were a highlight of his childhood at the cottage. Being able to get close, but not too close, made seeing the bears even more titillating. The dump provided a "zoo in the wild" – a domesticated space where potentially dangerous animals were openly on view but kept safely at a distance. Another way that such larger animals were thoroughly domesticated was in the stuffed animal heads that adorned a couple of the cottages I visited. And so these creatures prompt a "positive emotional response" (Morphy 1992, 181) without crossing the threshold of an intense negative sensorial reaction – they pose no direct threat.

Nature is not always as apparently and heavily mediated as the bear blithely sitting at the dump was imagined to be.[17] The personage of Mother Nature, in particular, has "rules" that, as Alice observed, "you have to bend to." Cottagers have to accept that in May and June the blackflies will be out in unimaginable numbers, the mosquitoes will soon swarm in, and, by the end of the summer, wasps will be everywhere. Staying away from the cottage during peak bug season, building screened porches and being vigilant about their maintenance, or simply, as Vicky said, "slathering on the repellent and covering as much as your body as you can," are various strategies that cottagers adopted to adjust to such "rules" of nature. Such strategies are followed with increased vigilance now that mosquitoes carrying the West Nile virus have arrived in cottage country.

Conrad eventually realized that Mother Nature did not need his help and that he should not try to impose his own aesthetic standards on her but rather let her take care of the waterfront:

> There's lots of cedar there and of course the cedars grow out and then eventually they fall in. And so you had all these skeleton cedars. My first instinct was to clean it all up. I created this huge brush pile. A few years later, I realized, "what was that all about?" Now they fall in and well, that's where they belong. Mother Nature's going to take care of that.

Coming to the cottage allowed Anna and her children to learn to "appreciate the stars, the moon, the rain, the sun, and not to worry about whether it's too hot or too wet ... as these were things we could not change."

After the beds of annuals she planted died prematurely, Susan accepted that "what grows, grows," and that is not likely going to include plants brought in from the greenhouse in the city. Aaron took pleasure in the power of storms that moved up the lake, especially when he watched them from the safety of his cottage. The winds, the waves, the trees that bend, the lightning and thunder – he loved the "sheer fury of it all."

Mother Nature embodies the rhythm of the seasons and the changing colours and moods of each. She also makes more startling and unexpected changes, just to remind everyone of her power. Don did not lament the destruction of the three large pine trees at the entrance to his property after they were hit by lightning one summer. As he described it, there were "large pieces of pine tree scattered all over the bush. It now all looks different. Things change. And that's part of the attractiveness of it."

But being completely accepting of nature has its hazards. Many cottagers exerted significant time and energy throughout the winter to ensure that the snow did not accumulate on the roof and threaten the structural support of the cottage. Those who did not frequent their cottages in the winter hired local individuals to keep an eye out for such concerns. But nature could enter the cottage in others ways, beyond the all-too-common invasion of mice, bats, and squirrels. Norman and Marnie found an uninvited guest in their cottage one spring when they arrived:

> *Norman:* Doesn't matter what you paid for the cottage, you can still have a green heron come down the chimney.
> *Marnie:* Our son [found it].
> *Norman:* He came up a day ahead of us, thank goodness, and got the place cleaned up.
> *Marnie:* It came down the chimney...
> *Norman:* ... and of course it cleaned the flue as it came down ... And flew around in here and every time it hit every wall or the ceiling, it left black soot everywhere, and eventually it died.
> *Marnie:* ... the poor bird.

"We're the interlopers ... we just come and borrow [nature] for a while," Norman and Marnie said, but in this case they felt that the heron had taken unacceptable liberties with their generosity. Nature was something best kept outside the cottage. Yet the tragic – at least for the heron – intrusion of nature into the cottage symbolized the unruliness of nature in cultured spaces. Many cottagers admitted that they expended significant amounts of energy each year to push back nature's efforts to reclaim the cottage. Despite this, as Pcholkina (2006, 61) and I argue, cottagers see nature overall as generally accommodating, if not malleable, a force (if not a source) of strength but not necessarily threatening.

How much nature was "let be" at the cottage was clearly a matter of personal taste and aesthetic preference. Completely letting nature be in charge suggested that a cottage should be allowed to fall into ruin and eventually disintegrate. Naturally, no one was willing to go to that length or frankly even imagine it. With a little bit of management and negotiation, their place in nature could be maintained, if not improved. Alice and Leonard struggled with this as they debated whether or not to have some trees cut down on their property. They wanted their cottage to be filled with natural light, as it had been originally, but over the forty years they had had their cottage, the trees had grown significantly. Even more problematic, the forest composition had changed. In the 1990s, tent caterpillars, in combination with a drought, killed many of the birch trees on their property – nature, it seemed here, was not on their side. White pines now dominated. They felt forced to cut some of them down because they blocked the light and harboured mosquitoes. Some of the larger trees had also become a potential threat to the cottage in heavy windstorms. Nature needed to be moulded to suit their cottage aesthetic and, ultimately, their sense of security.

The topic of lawns at the cottage highlighted the differences between cottagers regarding how far one should go with letting nature be or "improving" or "managing" it. Lawns need open space to grow, so trees have to be cut down; they need fertilizer and even pesticides to thrive; and they need to be mowed regularly. For some cottagers, lawns have a significant negative impact on micro-environments; substances that are designed to assist their growth have detrimental impacts on marine environments; and lawnmowers are simply one more contribution to noise pollution.[18] Lawns are not part of "nature" and hence are environmentally and aesthetically problematic. And as Sam said, "Even the weeds up here are beautiful, so why would you need to plant a lawn?"

However, those cottagers who had lawns argued that they let light in, prevent dirt from being tracked inside, keep the bugs down, and suit their aesthetic. One cottager maintained that his lawn makes his cottage "look tidy." Cottagers who had lawns claimed to have stopped using any kind of chemicals that would be detrimental to the lake, but resolutely had no intention of letting the lawns return to their natural state. Robyn said, "I like the lawn. I know that environmentally I should let it go back to natural. But I don't want to. I don't fertilize. And I am trying to let it grow back on the shoreline ... for me my lawn is aesthetically pleasing."

Other points of tension that divided cottagers about how much nature should be interfered with or modified were what Brigita called the "floodlights across the lake [that] made it look like the city" and blocked the wonders of the night sky, and the elaborate decks, docks, and walkways around properties, which she felt made their cottages look like a "maze of urban freeways." Frances wondered why "people came to the cottage if they were going to try to impose all that came from the city." It is important to remember, though, that such things were all a matter of degree. Some cottagers seemed to be working in opposition to what it meant to dwell at the cottage but they would challenge the categorization of "non-dweller," saying they were just "improving" on Mother Nature. Both positions are highly relative, and in the end potentially contentious.

Many cottagers I spoke with had a finely honed sense of what they felt made nature beautiful and acceptable. Yet others saw it as merely a distant backdrop. Howard and Emily had bought and sold four cottages in search of one that captured their aesthetic sense of what was important in a cottage, specifically, direction and water access. Their current cottage was a newly constructed 1,600 square-foot structure (they were still finishing it when I first met them), with a dishwasher, washer and dryer, air conditioning, high speed internet, and a large deck. These were things Emily thought she would "never have at a cottage, but now she did, she liked it." Ironically enough, they still remained somewhat dissatisfied with their latest acquisition, even if it met many of their aesthetic criteria. These upgraded technologies did not challenge what they saw as ultimately important at the cottage. What really mattered was their ability to access the "right kind of nature." As they told me,

> *Emily:* One thing we're lacking on our property is pine. That is something we really like. Our neighbours all have pine trees, but I don't think we have any. We like birches, too, though. The last three places, we've had

a nice clump of birches ... that was nice. We really like the birches but it would be nice to have pine trees. We've got lots of, what we would term, ugly hemlock here ... they aren't very attractive.

Howard: They do provide protection in the winter, however. What is most important to us is direction.

Emily: We face southeast here ... If it wasn't for the slope ... and the trees of course ... we'd be getting sun all day long. When we were on [the last lake] we faced southwest and that's absolutely the best; well, in our way of thinking, it's the best direction. But the summer we've had this year, I think we would have really been baking in that sun. So this is good.

Howard: Direction is very important, very important.

Emily: It was our number one criteria. When we bought originally, we knew nothing, we just knew we wanted to have a cottage.

Howard: But then we bought a cottage facing north, *the* wrong direction.

Emily: A lot of people are happy with north because sometimes they get some west sun. But we got sun all day long in the back in the morning, and then it came down to the dock finally, but too late. Other people don't think it's such a big deal. For us, it's probably the most important thing, that and fairly accessible water.

Howard: That's second for us.

It seemed in very large measure that cottagers took it for granted that nature at the cottage was there for their enjoyment (Pcholkina 2006; Satsuka 1997; Stevens 2008a, 2008b). For many, it was a landscape that they moved through or simply sat back and observed. Not everyone felt connected to it. In fact, Henry was quite frank, saying, "I don't have a great attachment to nature." His cottage simply provided him a "beautiful place to run or ride his bike." Nature functioned as a backdrop to his activities, and the pleasure was derived from the non-natural infrastructure of the highways and roadways, allowing him to move easily *through* nature but not *in* nature.

Ida had a similarly distanced response to nature at the cottage. Growing up abroad, she had learned to see the outdoors as an arena for the pleasures of physical activities and enjoying scenic vistas. Nature was, in some ways, almost a "generic space," something that simply stood in broad contrast to the urban world (Luka 2006). Ida said, "I [always] enjoyed the outdoors [growing up at home] so it was natural for me to enjoy it up here."

For some cottagers, nature was something that should be "on show," admired from a distance, something like a stage set. Deidre and Roger liked to take their pontoon boat out with their friends late on summer afternoons. Roger said the scenery served as a backdrop and the lake as a venue for the conversation and cocktails they enjoyed with their friends. In fact, everyone sat on the boat with their back to the lake, a positioning that facilitated their social interaction. These cottagers experience nature much as Macnaghten and Urry (1998) suggest tourists look out the window of a train or car.

Becky, who found the power and dynamic force of nature a little overwhelming at times, also found it pleasurable to simply admire nature from a distance. She told me,

> I am not a big fan of storms. But here I like watching them. A couple of weekends ago we had some storms. I put the chairs near the window. The kids [and I] sat there and they thought it was like the coolest thing. Instead of having the TV on, they listened to the thunder and the lightning.

Conrad felt the same way watching a mother raccoon move her young ones to a new location: "I felt like I was watching a Walt Disney movie!" Lorne and Olive enjoyed watching sunsets from their respective cottage docks. It was a perfect way to end a day at the cottage, and they did not let anything interfere with their panoramic view. When the trees on their cottage properties became intrusive, they simply cut them down. From such a distantiated perspective, nature was something readily manicured, managed, and reimagined.

To some, nature was simply a muted, almost absent context for all that was social at the cottage. As I noted in my field notes after my visit with Marianne and her parents, whose cottages were located in one of the more suburban-like developments on a large lake in Haliburton, no one spoke about the natural environment of the cottage when I asked what they liked about being there. The conversation highlighted events and memories about people, past and present. The only reference to any elements of the natural world that came out in our conversations was mention of the lake as a venue for water skiing.

One thing I did learn from all those I spoke with was that, no matter how they perceived its place at their Haliburton cottage, nature and wilderness fundamentally defined that place as Canadian, and prompted what seemed to me uncharacteristic expressions of nationalism.

"You Just Have to Fly the Flag"

What struck me on my first visits to Haliburton was the large number of Canadian flags that were flying on cottage properties. When I asked Jacob why there was a flag flying at his family cottage, he said, "You just have to fly the flag." Similarly, Jack said, "You just fly one at the cottage." Some of these standards were rather tattered and worn and hung on roughly hewn poles of varying heights and stability; others were startling in the brilliance of their red and white, mounted on erect and firmly fixed proper flagpoles. All were visible from the lakeshore, the veritable "front entrance" of the cottage. These standards at Haliburton cottages suggested to me a literal expression of Billig's (1995, 6) "banal nationalism," where repeatedly and without fanfare, "the nation is indicated, or 'flagged' in the lives of its citizenry." I wondered what this uncharacteristic expression of Canadian nationalist sentiment said about life at the cottage.[19]

I quickly learned that the cottage was understood to be a fundamentally Canadian place, capturing what it meant to be Canadian (see also Luka 2006, 168-70). As one Haliburton cottager said, "real Canadians want to be in the woods," a sentiment that resonated with others. Spending time at the cottage was what Canadians did, season and weather permitting. When I pointed out to one cottager that in some parts of the country, specifically some parts of western Canada, centring one's leisure time at the cottage was not as ubiquitous as it was in Ontario, he asked me, "What, then, do people in the West do on the weekends if they do not go to the cottage?" He simply could not imagine life without such a practice. To him, as he elaborated, such people were somehow denied the experience of something quintessentially Canadian.

It is crucial to note that Canadians by character seem forever ridden by ambivalent – some would say conflicting – images of themselves as distinct national citizens. Challenging Canadians to clearly articulate what comprises our national identity, beyond asserting that it is not American and listing the stereotypical icons such as hockey, maple syrup, the RCMP, and beaver, can prompt a moment of anxiety (C. Campbell 2003, 83; 2004).

However, among cottagers I spoke with, there was a certainty that life at an Ontario cottage captured what it meant to be Canadian. I make my comments here with exclusive reference to a sense of national identity in Anglo-Canada. The situation is much different in francophone Canada, specifically in Quebec, and among many Canadian Aboriginal peoples.

I would argue that these expressions reflect a nostalgic nationalism, something that hearkens to a generic past, an idealized time of simpler and clearer understandings about what was implied if you labelled yourself Canadian. The assuredness of these feelings is rooted in the fact that so many cottages, including those in Haliburton, are in the province of Ontario.

A relatively recent article in a Canadian national newspaper about the struggle Ontario faces in developing a strong regional identity was titled, "The province that thinks it's Canada" (M. Campbell 2008, A15; see also C. Campbell 2004, 6). The article analyzed the changing position of the province in the social, political, and economic topography of the nation in the first decade of the twenty-first century. The Canadian federation is fraught with regional tensions and the ever-growing financial clout of oil-rich provinces such as Alberta, Saskatchewan, and Newfoundland. In addition, with the collapse of the Ontario-based manufacturing industry in the first decade of the twenty-first century, it has been clear that the once-dominant economic position of the province is changing. But unlike other parts of the country that have strong regional – and, in the case of Quebec, nationalist – identities, historically Ontarians have seen themselves as Canadians first, Ontarians second (M. Campbell 2008, A15).

Several factors fuel this perception, the origins of which can be traced to the arrival of the United Empire Loyalists, some of Ontario's first immigrants, in the late eighteenth century. Loyal subjects of the British Crown, they sowed the seeds of the strong Anglo identity or Britishness that took root in Ontario, reinforced by the subsequent waves of immigrants from England, Scotland, and Ireland throughout the nineteenth and twentieth centuries. This character stood in stark contrast to the tenacity of the francophone identity in Quebec.[20] Any overriding Britishness as an emerging regional identity was dissipated in western Canada by the large number of central European, Ukrainian, and other non-Anglophone immigrants who arrived as agricultural settlers on the Prairies in the first half of the twentieth century.

Ontario's Britishness masked the identities of the thousands of non-Anglo immigrants who settled in the province during the last 150 years; these waves of immigrants from all parts of Europe, the Caribbean, South Asia, and China failed to challenge the trenchant British colonial character of much of south and central Ontario. It would be many years before the names of those who held the reins of the economic, political, and social power in the province could trace their original ancestry elsewhere than to British, Scottish, or Irish immigrants, and some would still question to what degree that has even happened as yet. Such Anglo ancestry became part of what it meant to be Canadian in the province.[21] Second, in the immediate post-World War II era, when Canada's economy modernized and diversified, Ontario was at the forefront. National policies were all set with reference to Ontario (Courchene 2008). This reality enhanced Ontario's historically established strength as the political and social force of the nation. To Ontarians, Canada was Ontario. They had little sense of the province as simply a region of Canada.

Third, Ontario is geographically the second-largest province (Quebec is the first) and it is the most populous in the country. Toronto, the capital of Ontario, remains the nation's largest city, with a population of 5.5 million in its metropolitan area.[22] It continues to grow at a rapid rate, much of the increase due to the number of immigrants who settle there.[23]

Lastly, it is the rocky, lake-filled, windswept Canadian Shield that shapes much of cottage country. This landscape occupies as much as two-thirds of Ontario's land mass. For many Ontarians, by accident of history and geography, it is *the* iconic Canadian landscape (see C. Campbell 2005). It was also the subject of the first recognized group of artists to record on canvas the distinctiveness of the Canadian landscape as they understood it.

Beginning in the 1920s, a group of Toronto-based artists – soon to be known as the Group of Seven – began exhibiting their work locally and later at the fledgling National Gallery in Ottawa. They travelled primarily in the Shield regions of Ontario, painting in what came to be known as the first distinctly Canadian style the rocks, water, and windswept trees of the areas around Georgian Bay, Haliburton, and Algonquin Park (C. Campbell 2003, 73-75, 80; Osborne 1992; Whitelaw 2000).[24]

Cottagers said of this same landscape: "All of this is quintessentially Ontario, and therefore quintessentially Canadian" (Luka 2006, 168). The rugged Canadian Shield setting came to hold an "exalted position ... in the national symbolic" (ibid., 276; Whitelaw 2000, 130). Claire Campbell (2003, 81) acknowledged that the "sweeping expanse of the Canadian Shield and its boreal wilderness have long been thought of as the nation's physical and spiritual foundation, at least in central Canada ... [in fact] many believed that a pure, rugged unsettled northland would produce a superior Canadian race."[25] These latter sentiments had a long history in Canada.[26] The adjective *northern* "was equated with toughness, strength, and hardihood," something that would be only strengthened by the harsh climate found in Canada (Berger 1970, 53). These characteristics would come to describe those who were "real Canadians." For many of the cottagers I met in Haliburton, these "real Canadian" characteristics represented an ethos that reverberated with their own efforts to secure a place in this exalted land for their own metaphorical "survival" – for the cottage was far more than simply a place of leisure. Not being able to spend time at their cottage challenged these individuals' overall sense of well-being and their purposefulness in life, sentiments that I argue have links to those heroically memorialized as Canadian pioneers.

In the 1950s Wolfe (1977, 22) wrote,

> Part of the fascination of the [Canadian] Shield is reminiscence ... [Cottagers] can relive vicariously [the] moment of the strenuous era of their history simply by moving into the dark forests that stretch ... for hundreds of unbroken miles to the north. The great out-of-doors is, in Ontario, the out-of-doors against which the pioneers fought. Some of the activities that pioneers were, often with great hardship, forced into, are now indulged in for pleasure ... to be able to remember ... the pressing stuff of everyday life to the pioneers of a century ago adds exhilaration to the experiences and, to those who can feel it, the pleasure of helping to make history continuous. Thus in Ontario the cult of the wilderness is far from being exotic. It takes pleasure in experiences that were recently commonplace and difficult.[27] (See also C. Campbell 2005, 111; Hall and Müller 2004, 8; Luka 2006, 279, 291)

As Wolfe suggests, the remembrances of pioneer life are often romanticized and idealized, just as the early-nineteenth-century pioneer lives of Daniel and Elizabeth Stong were:

> 100 acres of land in the wilderness, clothed in majestic white pine, oak and elm trees, faced Daniel and Elizabeth as they started their life's farming work together [in Southern Ontario]. They knew it took hard work to build a productive farm ... Clearing the land, they built their first home, a small log house ... Their family grew [and] ... prospered.[28]

This short description hints little at the degree of hard work the Stongs would have exerted to "build a productive farm" from this densely forested land. Majestic pines may well have been seen as impediments to their efforts to claim arable land. More realistically, "John Carroll[,] a Methodist preacher[,] recalled, 'frugal fare and *work, work, work*'" (quoted in Baskerville 2002, 75, emphasis added). Nevertheless, as Ralph Bunce (1994, 36) has suggested, rather idealized narratives about "bygone lifestyles ... [are] fundamental ... [to Ontarian] values." They produce a fundamentally "utilitarian and functional" or, in McGregor's terms, "domesticated view of landscape" (ibid.; McGregor 1985, 39). Such sentiments resonate with trenchant Anglo-Protestant ideologies about the value of hard work and acquisition of private property – which could readily include a small Haliburton cottage – an ethos that continued to resonate strongly in post-war Ontario (Luka 2006, 291; Stevens 2008a; Warkentin 1966, 161).

To fully experience the beauty, healing, and inspirational properties of this unforgiving landscape that defeated many pioneers, middle-class Haliburton cottagers of the 1950s and 1960s engaged (as do their descendants today) the "utilitarian and functional" tropes of the settlers of earlier generations. Through their physical labours, these mid-twentieth-century middle-class "pioneers" reclaimed – or one could say "domesticated" – this landscape as an affirmation of their social, cultural, and economic position in the postwar world.[29] Through their "work, work, work" they claimed their identity as "real Canadians." As Merriman (quoted in Lowenthal 1989, 28) has pointed out, such nostalgic imaginings do not suggest that anyone wanted to actually return to the times of these pioneers. Rather they expressed a "desire to get out of modernity without leaving it altogether." Cottagers did not want to live as pioneers; they wanted a well-mediated experience of what is imagined as a simpler life. Many women advocated for the arrival of modern technology, such as washing machines, running water, and indoor plumbing at the cottage. Yet they expressed a desire to experience a purer, simpler, more "authentic" life, which the cottage was imagined to afford (Jaakson 1986; Luka 2006; Stevens 2008a; Williams and Kaltenborn 1999). Such sentiments, for many, captured imaginings of a previous time in history.

The acquisition of a cottage signalled that by the mid-twentieth century some of those who were descendants of earlier pioneering generations had the economic and social stability to invest in such capitalized leisure pursuits. But equally important, being a cottager allowed such firmly entrenched urban dwellers a chance to own, and in some cases reclaim, a piece of and a place in what had become an iconic Canadian landscape.

During our chat, Trevor quipped, "This place symbolizes that I am in Canada." I argue that cottagers use their cottage, at least in part, "to legitimize 'their nation,'" which Low and Lawrence-Zúñiga (2003, 23) have observed is not limited to the processes and actions of the state. Tropes of history and the mythic pioneer engage the challenge of carving out one's place in what is seen as a beautiful but unforgiving landscape, and instil value – economic, emotional, social, aesthetic, nationalistic – in the cottagers' "idea of Canada" (Luka 2006, 279; Wolfe 1977). The Haliburton cottage and the experience of it express what Valenius (2004, 14) calls a "less conscious" nationalism when compared to "official nationalism ... [that which is] expressed ... in the writings of politicians, historians, and other ideologues." It is "nationalism [that] suggests that nationhood is near the surface of contemporary life" (Billig 1995, 93). The physical, emotional, financial, and generational resources invested in this experience foster a "sentient or felt history" of the cottage (C. Palmer 2003, 427; see also Connor 1993, 384-85). Cottagers feel that they "belong" at the cottage, an experience far more powerful than any rational understanding of their citizenship within the Canadian nation-state (C. Palmer 2003, 427; see also J. Harrison 2010).

I discovered in my interviews that many cottagers know little of the specific history of the Haliburton area. Instead, they invoke a more generic Ontarian/Canadian pioneer. At play here are the spirit and iconic status of early settlers who prospered and thus achieved a particular social and economic positioning. In Kedourie's (1960) and Smith's (1991) terms, cottagers seek to connect with, and in some measure replicate, the "golden age" of nationalist development in Canada.

In contemporary theoretical terms, these "real" cottagers, in the manner of the earlier settlers, are seeking to protect what Giddens (1990, 92; see also 1991) has called "ontological security ... [those] feelings of security in the wide sense ... the confidence that ... human beings have in the continuity of their self-identity and the constancy of the surrounding social and material environments" (see also Williams and Van Patten 2006, 35-36ff). Williams and Van Patten (2006, 36) argue, in reference to a similar group of Wisconsin cottagers, again drawing on Giddens (1991), that cottagers seek "refuge from modernity's ... disorienting and fragmenting quality" (see also Merriman in Lowenthal 1989, 28). They do so by rooting themselves "in the local" (Pitkänen 2008). The Ontario zeitgeist continues to validate the cottage as such a refuge, fuelling, one could speculate, a consistently high demand for recreational cottages in recent years. Doreen Massey (1993, 63) suggested that such trends are driven by those seeking "a bit of peace and quiet ... stability and unproblematic identity" amid such flux in the postmodern urban sphere.

For the cottagers I interviewed, the "local" embedded notions of a nostalgic nationalism for a Canada they never really knew, but one that exists in mythic conceptions of those who laboured to build this nation. Borrowing from Benedict Anderson ([1983] 2006), such understandings require an examination of the assumptions of race, culture, gender, and class naturalized in the imaginings of the Canadian identity, none of which I found were scrutinized in cottage country.

The assumed centrality of the cottage experience to being Canadian was captured in an article in *Cottage Life* magazine, in which the author asserted, "Scratch a Canadian and you will find a cottage in his or her background" (Teitel 2009, 87). This statement suggests that the cottage is presumed to be an experience central to the history and the political and social realities of Canadians and the nation-state. Many cottagers would be happiest if any connection between them and the state, the nation and ideas of Canada at the cottage, were kept at the level of a metaphorical identity, a nostalgic nationalism. Many, then, were not pleased when the long arms of the state began to encroach more directly, some would say aggressively and worryingly, into life at the cottage. In fact, legal and policy intrusions of all sorts have inveigled their way into cottage country in recent decades, altering the experience both temporally and spatially. To some cottagers I came to know, the intrusions of such regimes of order were necessary to preserve life at the cottage; to others, they challenged its very essence, and warranted resistance. Contradiction, it seems, is the order of the day at the cottage, and at the heart of life at a Haliburton cottage.

4

Time and Order at the Cottage

Olive described arriving and settling in at the cottage as "getting the monkey off of your back." Once there, she considered herself released from the tyranny of all that ruled her life in the city. The steadfastness of all that constituted life at the cottage comforted her, while at the same time it was delightfully pliable, allowing for serendipity and creativity to flourish in all that she did there. But what Olive felt released from was steadily encroaching on the cottage, causing disquiet, if not outright anger, among some cottagers. Intrusive structures of order, regulation, and limitation were colliding with the perceived inherent and implicit freedoms of life at the cottage.

Yet, I argue that cottage life has ironically always functioned under well-defined, even if contradictory, regimes of time, order, and discipline. In this chapter, I describe how time was and is precisely marked and tracked at the cottage, and discuss structures that define and ideally capture the precious resource, "cottage time," which cottagers sought to spend wisely to maximize the indulgences of life there. I discuss other examples of regimes of order, many of which have only recently arrived, including new communication technologies such as cellphones and the internet, the 9-1-1 emergency system, and new tax systems that privilege the role of the market in the complex expression of the value of a cottage. Some claim that these intrusions seek to affirm and ensure the continuance of cottage life, but to many they constrain it, distilling it to a mere prescriptive representation. To some cottagers, lifestyle magazines such as *Cottage Life*, spinoffs like *Cottage Life TV*, or the semi-annual *Cottage Life* trade shows furthered the proliferation of a uniform, generic, and sterile representation of the cottage experience. Other, more formal documents such as succession agreements, lake plans, covenants, and even community petitions could also be seen as attempts to codify life at the cottage in the early twenty-first century.

Such prescriptive regimes were seen to be multiplying at the cottage despite an insistence that the joy of carefully measured "cottage time" would flow only if life there was experienced as something organic, idiosyncratic, and unfettered by external constraints.

Keeping Time at the Cottage

For the cottagers I came to know, simply being at the cottage, spending time there, no matter how abbreviated it might be, contributed to the easing of the tiresome load of life elsewhere. Time was transformed into something delightfully pleasurable at the cottage. It was not the iron-grid of obligation and duty that drives urban life ever faster in a cycle of deadlines and increasing responsibilities. Clocks, day timers, cellphones, and smartphones had no bearing on something so cherished. (I did observe, however, that this discarding of timekeepers varied generationally, as more sophisticated timekeeping technologies were often kept close by younger ones.) Urry (1995, 214-15) wrote: "[Clock time symbolizes that] time is money ... [it is understood by someone who] is aware and orientated to the passing of time that time is a resource which is to be organized, regulated and distributed."

Of course, time at the cottage was still marked, be it in the passing of generations, the annual pattern of the seasons, the anticipated rhythms of visitation, or the sensorial and almost intuitive responses to the experience. I came to understand that time was a multidimensional phenomenon at the cottage. It shaped the cottage experience. Many cottagers told me that they often lost track of what day of the week it was, or the date, if they spent more than a few days at the cottage. Yet time at its most basic was charted in a linear extension forward and back, despite cottagers' insistence that they "stepped out of time" at the cottage. Robert, along with many others, imagined time "stood still" at the cottage.

In reality, there is a shift from clock time to "social time" – which in Weber's terms was characterized by "sociability, idle talk, luxury, [and] even more sleep" (quoted in Lash and Urry 1994, 226, 229; see also

Macnaghten and Urry 1998, 134-71). Many cottagers suggested that at the cottage they escaped what Lash and Urry call "instantaneous time," time that is "so brief ... that it cannot be experienced or observed." What many imagined at the cottage was the opposite: time that is "imperceptibly changing, glacial" (Lash and Urry 1994, 242, 246-47).

Glacial time sees the relationship "between humans and nature [as] long-term and evolutionary," something that gives them "a special respons-ibility for its preservation [which] entails ... the taking of a very long-term perspective, certainly one extending ... beyond the lifetime of anyone presently living" (Lash and Urry, 1995, 247). As Trevor said, "It is cottagers who have been the long-term stewards of the lakes in Haliburton." His claim sounds like a very grand notion to describe what many saw as the mere by-product of the extended time they spent at the cottage. They observed small incremental changes in the natural and social environment around them, some of which just happened, others which they initiated, and still others that unfolded unwittingly around them. They valued the never-ending expanse of time as it unravelled at the cottage. Michael, who had inherited his cottage from his parents and was now retired, said, "The lake has never changed, it still seems the same to me." Delores reflected on how she understood the *longue durée* of the cottage, something that ex-tended well beyond her time there: "There's something about sitting on the beach where I grew up, where the sun has gone down in the same place for a thousand years ... it's zen."

In such a timeframe, one at the very least "strolls through" but prefer-ably "lives in" places as opposed to rushing through; this allows one to "feel the weight of history ... memories of that place, and to believe that [its] ... essence [will be there] in many generations' time" (Giddens quoted in Lash and Urry 1994, 243, 249-50). Such was the beauty of life at the cottage. It was a place that was imagined would endure in time and "persist as a distinctive entity even though the world around may change" (Relph 1976, 31). I would argue that particularly for those who spent their child-hood summers at the cottage when every day seemed to go on for a glorious eternity, these perceptions of time carry an unshakeable veracity, despite the fact that their adult and even adolescent lives challenged such notions. Such a weighty sense of history also helps to shape a rather nostalgic imagined past.

As mentioned earlier, time was indeed still measured: it was counted in decades, something unfailingly flagged by large maintenance projects – replacing roofs, septic systems, decks, foundation repairs – particularly if they were being tackled for the second or third time. Annually, time was counted in the rhythms and rituals of calendric and seasonal markers and qualities. But my conversations with cottagers regularly began with a discussion of the marking of time across a longer period – generations.

The cottage, as most told me, was "good for the kids" and grandkids. Many cottages in Haliburton were passing into the hands of the second generation, a few their third, and even a couple their fourth; in Muskoka, the Rideau region, and Georgian Bay, some cottages were now in the third, often fourth, fifth, or even sixth generations of familial ownership (see C. Campbell 2004).

It would seem that there has always been a preoccupation with the next generation in much of what goes on at the cottage.[1] There are books, workshops, seminars, and newspaper and magazine pieces that offer harrowing tales, strategies, advice, and guidance on how to actually go about passing the cottage on to the next generation.[2] When making contacts through various cottage associations in Haliburton, I was consistently directed to those who had been on the lake the longest, preferably the descendants of someone who was there before it was opened up for more expanded cottage development in the immediate postwar era. Being able to mark one's history on a lake in generations was something that fostered respect and admiration among those who considered themselves relative newcomers. For some, it also earned them bragging rights. One couple proudly told me they both had spent their summers as young children in the 1930s on the Haliburton lake. This common experience caused them to feel a great affinity for each other when they met years later in Toronto and eventually married. Now they owned a cottage together on the same lake.

In keeping with the deference showed to those who could mark such time, there was a strong desire among cottagers to instil in upcoming generations a love and commitment to the cottage. Becky's comments sum up such sentiments:

It's three decades now that our family has been enjoying this place. And from what I see, God willing, they are probably going to be here for

another four decades. Someday, this all will pass on to my son. And I
hope I will keep enjoying this place after it becomes his. And then his
children can enjoy it and keep it.

For those who remained seasonal cottagers, time was more immediately
marked in well-established patterns of annual rituals; a central one was
the opening and closing of the cottage each year. Even for those who kept
their properties open all year, in the fall their docks and diving rafts had
to be pulled in, boats, canoes, outdoor furniture, and PWCs put away, and
septic, water, and heating systems made ready for the onslaught of winter.
In the spring, much of this work had to be reversed.

Seasonal cottages were most consistently opened on the May long
weekend and closed up on Labour Day in September, or in some cases in
October at Thanksgiving. However, some cottagers tried to get up at least
once in late April or early May, and hoped to have their cottage fully functional for the summer season before the first long weekend. Charles said,

> We like to get up here early May as soon as the road is firm because the
> wildflowers are out and the loons are back and everything is so fresh.
> And you can see through the bush because the leaves aren't out.

Some seasonal cottagers came for sporadic weekends up until the end of
October or early November, depending on the weather in any particular
year. But for most, being at the cottage coincided with the months of June,
July, August, and, for those without school-age children, the early part
of September. Louise, a retired widow, did not like being at the cottage in
July, as it was "too busy," and thus opted to be there for the months of
August, September, and the early part of October. June was marked by some
as undesirable because "the bugs were just too bad."

Many who began cottaging as children talked of the regular pattern of
leaving for the cottage on the last day of school and returning to the city
on Labour Day Monday, ready to start school on Tuesday. More recently,
this pattern had changed, as some had winterized (or at least partially
winterized) their cottages, and in some cases replaced them with four-
season structures. Such redevelopment was the exception rather than the
rule among those with whom I spoke. Some of Michael's retired neighbours
spend April to early October at the cottage, and November to March in

Florida, the Caribbean, or southern Europe. Trevor noted of the cottages near him that many were winterized or permanent homes – the ritualized activities of opening and closing weekends had passed into history. That his and other cottages on the bay were easily accessible from a major provincial highway also made year-round access much more feasible. Those whose access was not so direct, particularly those on private roads and lanes maintained entirely by the cottagers and not plowed in the winter, more consistently marked life at the cottage with these annual calendric rituals. Some accessed their cottages outside of these months on snowmobiles, snowshoes, or skis, but for many these visits were sporadic and short in duration.

These cyclical markers were powerful mnemonics of childhood. Isabelle talked of the excitement she felt as a child each year when the first of May arrived. She knew she could then count the days before she would join her grandmother on the annual trip to open up the cottage. She remembered the smell of the cottage when she first walked into it each summer. Equally powerful were memories of closing up the cottage when September rolled around. Trevor remembered all the work that had to be done to close the cottage: "We had to put up the shutters on all the windows, put mouse traps all over the place, liberally place moth balls in things, and close up holes with tape and anything else to make sure that animals could not get in." In contrast to the excitement and anticipation of May, closing the cottage often prompted sadness and tears.[3]

Even a winterized cottage was rarely used twelve months of the year. Visits to the cottage were generally restricted to weekends, sometimes including an extended stay between Christmas and New Year's Day in winter. Only those who lived some distance away tended to come for a stretch as long as two weeks in the winter. Some months were seen as generally undesirable to be at the cottage. For many cottagers, the days were too short and the snow conditions unsuitable for winter sports in November and much of December. And while longer days and more light had returned by late March and April, melting snow, spring rains, dangerous ice conditions, and soft access roads dissuaded many from going to the cottage.

The months, weeks, weekends, or days cottagers spent at the cottage varied considerably, depending on such things as life stage, work commitments, family obligations, season, geographic location in relation to the cottage, and competing desires. Usage patterns generally tended to remain fairly consistent over several years, though they could vary over time as family dynamics and other commitments intervened. For example, because it was a fourteen-hour drive to the cottage, Richard and his family were limited to spending a two- or three-week summer vacation at the cottage when they lived in northern Ontario for eleven years, but when he was transferred south to within two hours of his family's cottage, he was pleased to adopt a pattern of taking his family there every weekend throughout the summer and making regular day or weekend visits in the winter. When Alice and Leonard retired, they marked their time at the cottage in terms of weeks rather than weekends. Michael often went back to the city on weekends to allow his daughter and her family to have the cottage to themselves. Disruptions to established patterns did happen: Howard and Emily were booked one summer with family weddings, which took up precious weekends. This pattern was one they hoped would not be repeated, as it distracted from the pleasure they derived from imagining the consistency with which they would spend time at the cottage over the next few decades. They had bought and sold several cottages, and at one point it took them a couple of years to find another one they wanted to buy. Emily admitted that that "two-year period was very hard," and she did not want to spend such a significant block of time without a cottage again.

Overall, the time spent at the cottage was marked out in a wide range of patterns. Cottagers variously told me, "We come every year for a month"; "we spend every weekend at the cottage all year"; "we come about three weekends a month in the summer and then spend our three- or four-week vacation here in the summer"; "I only get two weeks' holiday a year so I spend a week in June and another week in August here and I try to get up for a few weekends or two-day visits during the summer"; "our family comes for two weeks every year and the kids now come more frequently for a day or two when they can get here throughout the year"; "we are together as a family at the cottage every other weekend, and either my husband or I are at the cottage during the week with the kids"; "we always travel somewhere in the summer so there are two or three weeks when we do not come to the cottage on the weekends"; "we come for two weeks in the summer and two weeks in the late fall."[4] It did seem that weekends, particularly in the summer, were the most consistent block of time spent at the cottage, and in many cases it was the only time spent there. (No one opted to use their cottage only in the winter.) This pattern marks a shift from decades in the last half of the twentieth century when many more cottages were occupied almost full-time in the months of July and August by mothers and children, and the fathers arrived on weekends and for their annual two- or three week vacation.[5] This shift was the cause of some concern for Ava. She felt her grandsons could not possibly "dedicate their lives" to the cottage, as they would not have the experience of spending their entire summers there. They would have no capacity to sense the passage of time there at a visceral level and how it marked their own development and growth. For her, such things threatened the long-term viability of the family cottage.

Sensorial responses – visual, aural, haptic, kinetic – were another way time was marked at the cottage. For Becky, it was as simple and glorious as sensing the passage of time by the change in colours of the vegetation. She said,

> The seasons are beautiful here. In the fall the leaves change. In spring everything is bright green. You notice it, because it's lush. You are surrounded by it. Here all you see is light baby green everywhere. And in the summer it's dark green. And in the fall it's all different colors. Winter is just a white blanket.

Frances, who admitted that she did not like the cold, marked the passage of time at the cottage by the change of the colour of the lake. She always waited for "the blue to come back to the lake" and then she knew summer was soon to arrive. Don loved watching the first winter storms blow in and seeing the lake start to freeze. He also tried to get up early in the spring to watch and hear the ice start to crack up. The latter was a bit of a guessing game for him, as he was never quite sure when it might start to happen. Others indulged in the absolute quiet of winter – save perhaps a few snowmobiles roaring down the lake as a backdrop, but they were few in number and never constant. Dwayne said appreciatively, "[When they're gone,] it's very, very quiet." His wife concurred, "It is so peaceful here then." They talked of going for walks in the fall and how refreshing it was when the air was starting to turn cold. A few brave souls loved to be at the cottage when it was –30 degrees or so. The air crackled, the snow crunched, and the fire inside the cottage was intense and "toasty" at the end of an afternoon of skiing or skating. Neil admitted that his kids liked the cottage better in the winter, as they enjoyed the excitement of winter sports and the contrast between the cold frosty air and the warmth of the fire in the cottage.

Many took their cues from the weather as to when they either closed up the cottage or switched to coming up on weekends only. The timing of these shifts varied from year to year. If winter winds, snow, and ice disappeared early, then some cottagers who had good road access could get an early start to their cottaging season. Some simply felt it too uncomfortable to go to the cottage before the warmth of summer could reasonably be assured. Ida said that she rarely made such trips, as it was "just too cold" for her, even if her husband, Leon, enjoyed these times as much as any at the cottage. Several cottagers, noting that in recent years the snow seemed to be disappearing earlier, wanted to start going to the cottage earlier. Some had done a range of renovations to what were basically "summer only" cottages – the addition or improvement of insulation, the installation of some form of heating system – to make such visits more comfortable and enjoyable. Capturing a few extra days at the cottage, on no predictable schedule, was particularly sweet for those lucky enough to enjoy it.

Capturing "Cottage Time"

For cottagers, the most pleasurable dimension of time was its character. It is what made "cottage time." Time at the cottage was shaped by a range of distinctive structures. But it was also imagined to be without structure and hindrance. Time at the cottage could be captured, found, made, or even stolen – qualities that positioned it in contrast to time outside of the cottage, which was always something slipping away, that could not be accumulated and expanded. As such, cottage time was of course desirable, pleasurable, something in which one could indulge.

Jordan, Marnie and Norman, and Alice and Leonard all owned cottages that they only used in the summer. But that did not prevent them from transporting themselves in the middle of winter to the cottage, even if it was only in their minds. Marnie commented that she and Norman would spend much of the winter planning all that they wanted to do at the cottage in the summer; Leonard and Alice did the same thing. And while their imaginings were mainly about what work and improvements they wanted to make a priority, Jordan's children would talk about the places they wanted to revisit, or how they wanted to improve their water skiing or swimming abilities, or which of their friends they wanted to invite to the cottage next summer. He said of them, "There is no day that goes by in winter time [when they don't say,] 'We can't wait to go to the cottage!'" He mused that his children did seem to be wishing part of their lives away, but as they saw each summer as "an endless expanse of time when they remembered every moment," it seemed to be a fair trade-off.

Time, particularly social time, could be captured or made at the cottage. Vicky said she and her family "*made* time" at the cottage in various ways and, while there, they *found* time to take in the local arts fairs and cultural festivals, which they would not think of doing at home. Similarly, Becky noted that she *found* the time to write letters to her friends and family in Canada and Europe "the old-fashioned way, in handwriting." Drew's Aunt Peg *made* time to teach her daughters to sew. Deborah, as she sat on her dock, said that she would *take* the time "to sit, relax and talk" to her neighbours.

I learned that cottage time, a common phrase used by cottagers, was imagined as something found or made, extended, and ultimately expansive. As both an experience and a mindset, it was imagined to be part of the *longue durée,* whether it was actually only one day of a weekend, a short two-week vacation, or a full month of the summer. In telling the story of how it once took him three weeks at the cottage to start a project that he had initially imagined as urgent, Jacob asserted, "Once you get into cottage time, it simply becomes 'I'll get to it tomorrow,' and sometimes it just never gets done." The work that Howard had to do to finish his cottage was something that he could, as he said, "do on his own time." About painting his cottage, Roger said, "You set your timeframe; if you do not get it done, it will wait until next week, or the next."

Theresa described cottage time as "a stream of consciousness ... [like] a conversation that [happily] goes nowhere." Conrad said that time at the cottage stands in contrast to the rest of your life, "where you are just *doing* all the time." Cottage time is not a slave to the schedule of "work, get up, eat, go to work, get back," a cycle Aaron felt was only broken by the reward of finally "getting up here, just to be at the cottage, perfect." Henry commented, "You go to bed when you are tired, and you wake up when you are not. It's just whatever pace you feel." One of the joys of cottage time for

Robert was that "there is no such thing as a typical day at the cottage; every day is different." His friend Sean concurred: "One day you get up early, the next day you don't. One day you do some work on the cottage, the next day you wake up and decide to sit and read a book all day." Cottage time is understood and experienced as seamless.

In thinking about how cottagers spoke about cottage time, I came to reflect on the irony of the idiomatic link between the word/concept time and the verb "to spend." It speaks to the notion that time is a finite resource that can be either well or poorly spent. Time at the cottage – conceptualized as something that could not be commodified or limited in such a way – was ironically well spent. At the cottage, how one spent one's time was one's personal choice, or at the very most something structured by the desires of family and friends, who, it was presumed, would understand the need for, as well as the joys and texture of, cottage time.

Cottage time could also be frustratingly wasted or lost if demands were deemed unreasonable and contrary to what life at the cottage was intended to be. Delores remembered how she used to lose precious cottage time with her grandmother's imposed regimen of

> sit-down lunches at the cottage. So as a kid, you had to come and sit down on a hot day in the cottage and have lunch. Then you'd do the dishes. We lost an hour every day simply with lunch. We hated it. My parents bought their cottage as an escape.

Firmly grounded in a particular place, cottage time could not be found, made, or taken elsewhere. A treasured reserve, it was measured in glacial time over decades by families and friends. Cottages were, in Jordan's terms, "time capsules" that held the cherished essence and the legacy of how his family had experienced the cottage over the decades. Cottage time was also, however, something many saw as being undermined.

Spending Time Wisely

For Paul's mother, the purchase of a cottage in the early 1950s was a stabilizing investment for her son. It was a way for him to stop "wasting his time" with "his friends in the pub." This purchase thus had a moralizing element to it, as it was a distraction from what she deemed less desirable pursuits.

It was a way to get him "to spend his time more wisely," as he told me. In reality, for Paul a cottage was actually more affordable than a down payment and a mortgage on a house in the city.[6] To Paul's mother, who had come to Canada in the late 1940s as an immigrant from Poland, this purchase symbolized the increasing material success of her son. In fact, Paul's move to acquire a cottage paralleled those of other postwar cottagers. Like him, they were at least in part motivated by "a need to get out of the city and into the great outdoors," and to acquire something that was a "powerful status symbol ... [as] owning a vacation home signifies that one has enjoyed some social and material success" – even if in Paul's case it was as much his mother's desire as his (Stevens 2008a, 28-29). Such acquisitions also emulated the lifestyles of those deemed of higher social status. In keeping with what another middle-class tourist once emphasized to me, Paul and other early postwar cottagers I interviewed demonstrated that "you do not have to be rich" to do what the rich do (J. Harrison 2003, 11).

Paul bought his first cottage when he was only renting a room in a boarding house in Toronto. But his positioning slowly gained stability over the years, as he eventually owned three small cottages on the same lake, two of which were later transferred to his children. And as my conversations with Paul and his wife Sandra suggested, in the world of postwar reconstruction and prosperity, such purchases symbolized hope for their future and that of their family. They did not talk much of the rest, relaxation, peace, and quiet that this life was imagined to represent. There was much time to be spent working to do such essential labour as transforming the cottage from a mere wooden shell to a habitable structure, building roads and driveways, installing septic systems, and removing logging debris from the waterfront, as well as managing life with their small children with very limited resources and without basic things such as running water. When I talked to Paul and Sandra and members of their family about the centrality of life at the cottage to their familial identity, I saw that Paul had clearly done what his mother had desired: spent his time well.

Paul and Sandra would emphatically agree with the idea that time at the cottage was seen to accrue good things for one's family. Several cottagers mentioned it as a place that worked to secure the health and safety of their children. It provided an escape from "the dirt" or even "the evils" of life in the city, as Trevor said – the latter specifically important in relation to adolescents. Time spent at the cottage was seen to offer a morally sound experience, if not simply a healthier one. Garry told me the cottage was "a good place for young people to spend their time."

However, the cottage was also considered a protective place for those well past childhood/adolescence. Middle-aged or older cottagers saw the cottage as a place where they escaped many of the complexities and confusions that characterize life in the city in the twenty-first century. They saw themselves evading a world moving faster and ultimately, in some measure, out of their control. Their descriptors of their lives in the city suggested they felt a loss of control of their time: cottagers lamented "never having time," always "being in a hurry," struggling to "find enough time," always knowing that they "don't have time," fighting the "fast pace," or having only "one speed: go." They saw the city itself as "concrete from wall to wall" and "nothing but traffic," and complained that "everything was the same." Cottagers, I learned, see the cottage as the place where they can leave behind this whirlwind of time and its attendant banality, a place more secure and rich in desirable character.

When people set off for their cottages, they saw themselves exiting the whirlwind of what David Harvey (1989) calls the "time-space compression" of the postmodern world. Cottage time could, in fact, be seen as the antithesis of this phenomenon.[7] In such compression, time blurs spatial boundaries, accelerating the social life of those caught in it, willingly or not (Harvey 1989, 229-30, 240; see also Lash and Urry 1994, 244). A sense of place has the potential to suffer the erasure of its distinctive qualities, of being reduced to a more amorphous "generic space" (Lash and Urry 1994, 242). Evidence of this process are the cookie-cutter strip malls and big-box-store clusters, which line the "gasoline alleys" of many Ontario (and North American) towns and cities. Some cottagers I spoke with wondered what exactly they had escaped when two Tim Horton's coffee shops, including drive-thrus, opened in Haliburton. Their arrival prompted the closing of a long-standing, locally owned and run coffee stop down the road. Such intrusions were deeply offensive to some cottagers' ideas of what the cottage was, even if several acknowledged that the coffee was better at Tim Horton's. There were a few, at least initially, who had boycotted these new establishments for what they symbolized about changes in life at the cottage.

Some cottagers were apprehensive about the inevitability of the arrival of new technologies – exemplified by cellphone towers and high speed internet – that, Harvey argues, drive the frenetic pace of life in the twenty-first century. They wished the cottage to remain a place that was resolutely unlike other places, and being "unplugged" was one way to ensure that. Resisting such technologies was standing firm against any attempt to homogenize or genericize the cottage experience. Such obstructionist postures were not, however, new to everyone at the cottage. Cottagers told stories of earlier heated family arguments about, first, whether a telephone service should be installed at the cottage, and, then, whether television belonged there, even if it did keep kids entertained on rainy days. But such symbolic changes really began with the arrival of electricity at the cottage, allowing for electric lights and appliances, indoor plumbing and running water, things that everyone now took as essential amenities at the cottage. For many, the non-essential postmodern technologies, such as the internet and cellphones, had not yet gained the same level of acceptance. Many locals and some cottagers are pleased that such services have arrived in areas like Haliburton. Others see no role for them there and find the towers they require just another source of visual pollution. Such technologies seem to presume that doing things faster is unquestionably desirable, a basic tenet that challenges what many understand as cottage time. Moreover, several of those I interviewed saw such technological development as an attempt to homogenize and regulate all that encompassed the cottage experience, even if the argument could be made that they sought to enhance what many wanted the cottage to be: a safe and protective place. These criteria were what many of the external regimes of order being imposed at the cottage in the early twenty-first century were understood to achieve. The arrival of the 9-1-1 system in Haliburton exemplifies this tension.

"We Are Not in Florida"

Ava could not believe it when her newly arrived cottage neighbour registered the name of the small road that led to their cottages as Flamingo Lane. As she said, "We do not have flamingoes here, we are not in Florida." She wanted the access route called Centennial Lane to mark the fact that she and her husband had bought their cottage lot in 1967, Canada's Centennial, making it the first cottage property developed on that bay.

After much protest, she eventually succeeded in getting the designation and, ultimately, the sign changed to what she wanted. Her family's legacy on the lake was publicly acknowledged, but even more critically for Ava, the name change connected her "sense of place" to a celebratory moment in her country's and her own heritage.

Why was there any need to name the lane? Such ordering emerged in the late 1990s as a main preoccupation of those in Haliburton. A major telecommunications provider in Ontario had made a commitment to bringing the 9-1-1 emergency system – which relies on a well-organized system of road names and individual property numbering – to cottage country. With an ageing population, an increase in the number of permanent residents on some lakes, and an overall increase in the desire to engage in risk management practices that took hold in the late twentieth century (and multiplied exponentially following the events of September 11, 2001), it seemed from a public policy perspective like a good idea. Athough far from universally popular, the 9-1-1 move met with approval among many cottagers (Tillson 2000/2001). But not everyone was happy: for one cottager, it was part of a process of "transform[ing] ... a cottage, [his] sanctuary[,] into a subdivision" and he refused to put up his number or complete the necessary paperwork (Tillson 2000/2001, 29). In Luka's terms (2006, 12), this project indicated that the "the iconic or even 'sacred' spaces of cottage country are being transformed in unexpected ways, with growing anxiety over perceived changes from 'rustic' to '(sub)urban.'"

Haliburton was one of the last areas in Ontario's cottage country to be integrated into the 9-1-1 system. By the time the system was to be put into practice, it had become obvious that it was important to involve cottagers in its implementation. It was vital to let those who had properties on the maze of privately maintained tracks, lanes, and small roads determine the names for these routes. If cottagers boycotted or never got around to putting forward a name, one would be assigned. Previous efforts in other domains of cottage country had led many cottagers to conclude that the bureaucrats in offices in Toronto, who were trying to impose order on the pleasures of disorder, failed to understand the realities and delights of cottage life. And despite efforts towards a more inclusive process in Haliburton, many cottagers there felt the same way.

To facilitate the exact identification of a cottage location, there could not be any duplication of road names. But it turns out that cottagers had informally named many roads over the years. Sometimes these names were poetic and lyrical, other times they were entirely pragmatic; in any case, these were the names they wanted to keep. "West Bay Road," "South Shore Road," and "North Road," however, were common designations on several lakes. These all had to be changed in the 9-1-1 system, often to the frustration and anger of many cottagers who knew that their cottage was on "West Bay Road," even if there was no sign anywhere to identify it and even if there was another such road on a neighbouring lake. I was told, "Everybody knows where we are" – everybody, that is, except the emergency service dispatchers. When the 9-1-1 service providers suggested what they thought was a suitable alternative "cottagey" name, "Ripple River Road," to replace a duplicate "West Bay Road," it drew a mixture of hilarity and insult from those who lived on it – there was no "rippling river" in the area, and they would always call it "West Bay Road" anyway, no matter what the name was officially changed to.

I encountered one group of cottages on a particularly entangled series of lanes and driveways that had at least three different numbers posted on each property. It seems that a couple of informal numbering systems had been developed over the years, and they saw the 9-1-1 designation as just another system that was likely to fail, as their earlier attempts had done. Many continued to identify where their cottage was by descriptive annotations – "at the end of the lane, take the first driveway to the left, but watch for the dead-end that looks like a driveway" – rather than by any numbering system. Different people on the road chose their preferred number and used that when necessary, but more frequently they just assumed everyone knew where everyone else's cottage was – and if you did not, you did not really belong there.

Some rejected suggested names that did not capture what they saw as the essence of their life at the cottage, even if a neighbour had suggested them. To Norman and Marnie, their cottage embodied many positive things, but it was not to them a "cozy" place, and thus they did not want to have their road called "Cozy Lane." Deidre rejected the idea of "Rose Lane," a name suggested by her neighbour because the cottage reminded her of the rose gardens she knew as a child in England. But similar to Ava's response to Flamingo Lane, Deidre said, "This is not England!"

Other names, such as "Leisure Lane" or "Take-a-Break Trail," did capture what people understood the cottage to be. Many opted to defer to the wishes of those who had been using the lane the longest; it was assumed that they, who had been committed to the place the longest, would pick an appropriate name. Often, the names of these long-standing cottagers were selected – "Henderson Way," "Jackson Lane" – a demonstration of respect to a particular individual's or family's stature within the microcommunity of those whose cottages were on the same road. In recognition of an even earlier history, some wanted their roads named after the farmers who had originally sold land to them or their parents. If it had not been for their initiative, some observed, they would never have had the privilege of having a cottage.

Naming, rather than numbering, was a popular practice at the cottage for decades. "Snug Haven," "Happy Hollow," "Day's Rest," "End-of-the-Road," and "Peterson's Paradise" are just a small sample of the descriptors that individuals and families gave to their cottages. Such names were prominently posted on signs leading into a cottage, or sometimes mounted on the water. These monikers were understood to reflect what the cottage represented for its owners (see also Luka 2006). Such designations, while absolutely meaningless in the grid system of 9-1-1, were infinitely symbolic to their owners. They captured the familial legacies of many cottages and, critically, much of the emotional, sentimental, and nostalgic attachment that people invested in such places.

As a Lefebvrian "representation of space,"[8] 2747 Maple Road captures little of the same spirit – particularly, as was often the case, when there were no maples on the laneway into the cottage. It does allow for strangers to find a cottage more readily, something that is needed more often these days as many cottagers are now starting to rent their cottages. But it does not allow for the idiosyncratic character of individual properties, cottages, and cottagers to be immediately evident. Standard addresses shift each cottage closer to a "generic space." In its structure and what it symbolizes, the 9-1-1 system also robs cottagers of a sense of real escape – they like to be able to say, "nobody can find us here" or "if you know where to look, you will find us."

On a larger level, this system highlights even more boldly that cottage country is an ever-increasingly urban space. It also underscores that change is afoot: those who recently moved to cottages on access routes with such designations are unaware of past practice, and take the 9-1-1 designation as the accurate moniker of their new cottage. They may even take down the "Peterson's Paradise" sign, for example, as it has no historical or personal resonance with them. What matters most to them is that they have successfully acquired a commodity – a cottage – whose value and attributes, at least in the first instance, were established by the external forces of the open market. It will take time spent at the cottage, ideally over more than one generation, to shift away from this highly de-personalized assessment of what gives value to the cottage. But first one has to be sure that it stays in the family.

The Spectre of the Taxman

In 1998, the Ontario provincial government put in place an independent system of establishing a value for all properties in the province based on current market value.[9] Taxes based on rates determined by local municipalities were then set according to these assessments. This process prompted significant increases in the taxes levied on cottages. One Haliburton cottager saw his annual taxes increase from just under $1,000 to $3,000 in the space of two years.[10] In 2008, one study predicted that Haliburton cottage owners would see a 45 percent increase in their property assessment.[11] Cottagers protested vehemently against these increases, claiming it made their cottages unaffordable.[12] Many cottagers, particularly those who have owned their cottage for several decades and originally paid only a small fraction of their current assessed value, are offended by the imposition of current market values, because "[their] cottage is not an asset [they] have any interest in selling" (Langlois 2008, 41). Having frequently been the result of the productive labour of at least one generation of family members, a cottage was seen as something that could not in any meaningful way be alienated from that legacy; it could not become a commodity that could simply be sold on the open market. One cottager likened selling the cottage to "selling part of your soul." In A. Weiner's (1992) terms, cottages are understood to be "inalienable possessions." Thus, a cottage's market value was frequently incomparable with the value according to the cottager.

For the first few years of the twenty-first century, the market values of cottages grew at what seemed like an ever-increasing rate, but then so did the number of people who wanted to own a cottage.[13] In 2007, a Canadian

Mortgage and Housing Corporation report indicated that more than a million Canadian households owned a vacation property (Hayes 2009, 62).[14] In the summer of 2012, a waterfront land-access cottage in Haliburton cost anywhere from $250,000 to $1 million-plus. This amount is a long way from the $2,500 needed to buy a cottage on Haliburton Lake in 1953, or the $20,000 to $30,000 it might have cost in the mid-1970s (Teitel 2009, 88).[15] Such price increases heralded an increase in property taxes, at times to such a degree that the capacity to hang on to the family cottage was in question.[16] It was not an issue that many cottagers had expected to face in their retirement. Miller (1998, 138) says that such confidence "comes from the gradual expansion of a sense of what ordinary people may ordinarily expect as their standard of living combined with the growth in their incomes." This new instability was, therefore, fundamentally disquieting. The cottagers I spoke with did not want to dwell on what this potentially meant for their families and future generations; instead, they chose to remain optimistic that the family would be able to keep the cottage, despite an array of external regimes implicitly working to transform the cottage into something framed within more rational than affective structures.

Those cottagers who wanted to keep the cottage central in their lives were concerned about how the capital gains tax would be paid once the cottage was passed on to the next generation. A federal tax, capital gains tax was first imposed in 1972 with a list of exemptions, all of which were removed in 1995. This tax is paid on 50 percent of the appreciated value, based on the original purchase price. It is triggered when the cottage changes hands, either through transfer in an estate or direct sale to anyone, including a family member. Based on the steep rise in market value of many cottages, this tax can be in the tens or even hundreds of thousands of dollars. Naturally, cottagers worry that their children will not be able to pay the tax, and will thereby be forced to sell the cottage. There are various ways of deferring these taxes in the transfer of cottages between family members, but ultimately, at some point, the tax has to be paid.[17]

Codifying What Matters

As we can see, the future of the family cottage – despite all that people say they have invested in it and all that it symbolizes for them – is not necessarily secure. It has, however, prompted myriad agreements, rules, permits, laws, documents, instructions, information, and ultimately anxiety. What matters at the cottage now seems to require documenting and codifying, as the cottage has been progressively seen as a mere commodity in the eyes of governments and lawyers, with little attention paid to the sentimental and emotional value that cottagers attach to it. Legal agreements, "branding" by the popular media and trade shows, lake plans, and covenants are part of this codification process.

If a way is found to keep the cottage in the family, sorting out how a cottage is going to be used and maintained by all those who inherit it can – as many estate lawyers will attest – cause even more tension. Even siblings who grew up at the same cottage may, as they pass into adulthood, have very different understandings of what good times at the cottage actually are. Popular seminars at *Cottage Life* shows are those given by an estate lawyer on how to minimize family feuding over the cottage once it passes into the hands of the next generations (Lillico 2009). Central to this lawyer's recommendations is the preparation of a legally binding agreement that all parties – usually siblings or other relatives – sign before the cottage is turned over, or before the death of the original owner(s). These agreements should range from details as specific as to whether food can be left in the fridge at the end of the visit of one sibling and his/her family, to how the ongoing maintenance costs will be covered, to what happens to the share of the cottage left to the family of a sibling that dies/divorces/remarries. Key to the success of these agreements is their clarity and the dispute resolution processes they endorse, which could range from majority rule to bringing in professional mediators or arbitrators. Failing such specifics, disputes can often end up in court (Cheney 2002).

In the late twentieth and early twenty-first centuries, other agencies besides legal firms played a role in what some would see as the transformation of the cottage into a marker or signpost of a particular status and lifestyle (Urry 1995). As the editor of *Cottage Life* acknowledged, the cottage, while being "a state of mind," is also "a marketable brand" (Caldwell 2007, 13). *Cottage Life*, *Cottage Life TV*, and *Cottage Life* shows,[18] all classic examples of Lefebvre's ([1974] 1993) "spaces of representation," are Canadian (largely Ontarian) media that have contributed considerably to the popular image of that brand, and cultivated people's desire to have the cottage experience. These media fuel the idea that the cottage is a place "to be gazed upon," that fosters "anticipation, especially through day-dreaming and fantasy, of intense pleasures ... so that what is then seen is interpreted in terms of these pre-given categories" (Urry 1995, 132). Such representations have helped construct the cottage as fundamentally desirable.

Many cottagers I met subscribed to *Cottage Life* magazine; a smaller number had watched episodes of *Cottage Life TV*. Some had visited the bi-annual *Cottage Life* shows in Toronto. A review of the editors' columns, letters to the editor, and various regular columns of the magazine since its inception in the late 1980s suggests that it is, in fact, aimed at the "do-it-yourselfer," the cottager with a desire to preserve a particular tradition of cottaging, who is more of a traditionalist than a socialite and is definitely not a transient, who tries to be as "green" as possible, and who is concerned about retaining all of what is seen as desirable and rewarding about the cottage experience.

Some regular magazine subscribers or sporadic visitors to the trade shows found the content interesting even if they felt some frustration with how cottages and cottage life were represented. With specific reference to the magazine, several cottagers said it featured structures and representations that lacked a "cottage feeling," as they were "too fancy," or "too new," or simply "too perfect." Some acknowledged, on the other hand, that they found the magazine's how-to columns and the handyman tips dispensed by various vendors at the bi-annual *Cottage Life* shows helpful. Others said that such media did not capture what cottaging was to them, and they dismissed them as completely irrelevant to their cottage experience. One cottager wondered why anyone would want to read about an experience that he felt could only be understood by spending time at a cottage. What was missing from these shows, the magazines, or any TV program, he and several others felt, were the most vital elements of the cottage – those affective, if intangible, qualities that made life there all that it was. How to capture this essence was the dilemma faced by those cottage associations I learned about that were developing lake plans.

Provincial legislation played an important role in shaping various aspects of cottage life by imposing such things as mandatory septic system inspection, limiting the square footage and placement of cottages, restricting the degree of deforestation that can be done on any cottage property, and regulating the use of non-biodegradable household products in a cottage environment. Most cottagers saw such protocols, even if annoying, as positive for the future of cottage life, as they sought to protect shorelines and water quality. Such formal rules, however, operated at a macro level. Many cottagers recognized it was important to understand, and ultimately manage and monitor, their behaviour at a more micro level to ensure the *longue durée* of their cottage on the lake. In the twenty-first century, such grassroots monitoring began with the aforementioned lake plan.

Lake plans synthesized volumes of data – physical, biological, geological, geographical, ecological, climatological, historical, and, some would say, social and cultural – about a particular lake. They integrated qualitative and quantitative information collected and digested at community meetings and consultations, in surveys, focus groups, interviews, and through archival research – all of which cottagers considered as important as any scientific data on water quality, local habitat, or shoreline degradation. In doing so, the plans were intended to capture what really matters to those who own cottages on the lake and were intended by many to be used as proof that no further development should be allowed on "their" lake. But the capacity of a lake, from a water quality point of view, may in fact be quite different from what cottagers think the more qualitative social and cultural capacity of life on a lake should be.[19] As one employee of the Ministry of the Environment told me, "Every cottager thinks anyone who wants to build a new cottage is a developer; but every cottager who already owns a cottage is an environmentalist; cottagers intuitively want to keep things just the way they are."[20] Leon, one lake steward I met, seemed to suggest this bureaucrat was right. He mused about the interest of some of those on his cottage association executive in doing a lake plan:

I'm on the committee to investigate whether we should do [a lake plan]. But people who are pushing it are concerned that we can monitor the development of time-shares or condos based on this study. They do not want any more boats. They do not want any more development. They think that if they get a formal planning study done that we'll be able to sort of leave this lake frozen in time. I think that if we have a study done it might just say that this lake is under-developed. There are 262 cottages on this lake. I know that the water quality is fine so we are not going to be able to build a case that says, "Hey, you've got real problems here." So if you do a study, it might backfire on you. If you take this to the municipality they might just say, "Let's hand out the permits."

As of the spring of 2009, there were approximately eighteen Haliburton lake plans being developed. An example of a completed plan from a Haliburton lake is one sponsored by the Kennisis Lake Cottagers' Association, titled "Kennisis Watershed and Lakes Management Plan" (2007).[21] The document stated very specifically that it was intended to rise above "the special interests" of those who own cottages on the lake and consider the broader issues of human behaviour that impact "the natural environment and the overall health of the local ecosystem" (ibid., 6). It identified twelve priority issues: water quality (and what threatens it); over-development; public-use land (and its disappearance); natural shorelines (and their destruction); water levels (and their fluctuation); power boating (the disruption, destruction, and problems it causes); wildlife (habitats and their fragility); tranquility (and its increasing absence); night skies (and light pollution); traditional rights-of-way (and their masking); sustainable forest management (and what this means); and history (and the need to know the story of the lake to "learn from the past") (ibid., 113-22).

The implementation of these recommendations would require changes to, or at least adjustment in, the behaviours of some cottagers, particularly those newly arrived or youthful in age. In conjunction with a community-based research organization and a local university, those who worked on the plan developed a "social marketing" plan for what could be seen as the code of expected conduct to realize the priorities established in the report.[22] As part of its lake plan development process, another cottage association wrote "a cottagers' code" (see also MacLean 2006). Its stated purpose "is not to dictate how people must behave, but rather to suggest an approach to certain fundamental issues surrounding cottage life that ... will preserve the lake's serenity and beauty for the enjoyment of all."[23] The code was intended to ensure the safety of swimmers; a healthy and natural shoreline; abundant wildlife; deter the usage of fertilizers, soaps, and shampoos; discourage noisy parties and music; and limit PWC noise and excessive speeds.

Such codes were only one example I encountered of documents aimed at managing the behaviour of cottagers on a lake. Other cottagers I interviewed had been required to sign "covenants" when they bought their cottage. These documents restricted such things as the size of boat motors, the colours one could paint one's cottage, shoreline treatment, and the duration and decibel limits on noise and boisterous behaviour. One purchaser told me that his lawyer felt such a document "would never stand up in court"; regardless, it was all about social sanction, and its enforcement was handled through pronouncements of expected behaviours at meetings and in newsletters. Petitions were presented both directly to those acting in what were seen to be inappropriate ways and, in an effort to achieve their goal through public humiliation, at property association meetings. Other cottagers practised more passive resistance strategies, from lining up their boats across the lake to prevent the repeated landing of a new cottager's plane as he took his friends for joy rides every weekend, to stealthily removing water skiing slalom course markers in the dark of night, ensuring that the offending buoys could be collected by their owners as long as they moved their course to another part of the lake.

The limits to the exuberance of social life on many lakes have likely always been informally sanctioned to varying degrees, but because the essence of what many value at the cottage is considered under threat, or at least misunderstood, these limits are now being explicitly expressed through the development of lake plans or owners' covenants. Those who orchestrate such formalization, including those who adopted more subtle and unspoken sanctions of behaviour, understand themselves to be the "real cottagers." Set in the context of the noblest of goals – protecting all that constitutes the natural environment – how could anyone argue with a code of behaviour? But such a code is also aimed at fostering certain social behaviours that have come to be accepted as part of cottaging on Haliburton lakes. What these documents suggest is that the "real" cottage experience is not something accessible merely by the act of purchasing a cottage. To consume it "properly" required, rather as Gullestad (1993, 158) would argue, "a very complex interplay of [learned] ideas and practices."

Consuming the Cottage

John Urry has argued (1995, 130) that "a considerable amount of work is involved ... [to] transform what is purchased ... into an object of consumption." For example, Vicky and Dwayne's purchase of their cottage in 2000 was the first step in their consumption of the cottage experience. Neither of them came from families who had owned cottages. Frustrated with the vagaries of car-camping and even travelling in an RV, they saw their cottage as providing them with something more. Vicky said, "There's some family things that just don't evolve out of camping." When seen to nurture social relations among friends and family, the cottage is transformed from merely a purchase to a much more complex phenomenon. If Vicky and Dwayne had failed to return regularly to the cottage once they had bought it, or had not invested the labour and resources to attend to the repairs and upgrades necessary to keep it structurally sound and comfortable, or had neglected to establish their own familial set of cottage practices and rituals there, this shift would never have happened.

Places, Urry elaborates, can be consumed in a variety of ways (1995, 28, 129). One way is through lifestyle, or place-specific experiences such as those found at the cottage. What people do at the cottage is different in very large measure from what they do elsewhere. Even replicated domestic chores – food preparation, cleaning, child care – are seen to have a different character at the cottage. The cottage becomes a place people own on many levels, just as Vicky and Dwayne came to own their cottage and, by extension, claim the lake adjacent to it as "their lake." In the process of consumption, cottagers laid claim to Haliburton as part of the landscape of cottage country, masking its realities as a county with limited possibilities for economic development and subsequently some of the highest poverty rates in the province for the local population.

Images of Haliburton as cottage country are used to sell products and services consumed by cottagers and "wannabe" cottagers. Examples of these "spaces of representation" include cottage real estate advertisements, an endless number of cottage rental websites, a wide array of media – newspapers, brochures, websites – that detail what vacation services are to be found there. At a broader level, *Cottage Life* magazine and trade shows suggest that the experience of the cottage as a readily consumable product. Such representations, some argue, reduce the experience to merely a commodity, "fetishiz[ing] or ... diminish[ing] ... [the powerful] personal and social values" attributed to it (Marx quoted in Miller 1998, 152). Regardless, it is true that there are long lists of treasured commodities purchased while at the cottage. These include locally produced maple syrup, homemade pies made with locally picked wild raspberries or blueberries, or certain brands of ice cream only sold in cottage country. Such things could be understood as simply commodities, devoid of "personal and social value[s]." At the same time, indulgence in such consumption is greatly relished at the cottage and, over time, becomes layered with densely symbolic and ritualized meanings through specific associations with life there.

Goods, services, places, and the social and cultural life that links them all together are thus all part of the consumption of the Haliburton cottage (Urry 1995, 130). But these processes do not diminish the potency of such a place and the value of times spent there to those engaged in such practices. In the minds of most cottagers I interviewed, life at the cottage was not trivialized and rendered superficial by these processes any more than it can be effectively regulated by particular regimes of time, structures of bureaucracy, demands of the taxman and strategies of lawyers, pressures of market forces, and the results of structured self-study or covenants. It was a far too complicated and contradictory experience to be diminished in any meaningful way by such things. What was deeply valued about life at the cottage was rooted in a complex web of personal experiences, feelings, and histories; class, race, and gender assumptions; and cultural practices and social relations. I turn my attention in the next chapter to that which grounds the experience at a most fundamental level and thus encourages intense resistance to any such reduction – the disciplining, measuring, marking, and undeniable pleasures of the *body* at the cottage.

5
The Cottage Body

What had prompted the tears? I found myself pondering this question when, in the middle of some of my initial interviews with cottagers I had only just met, several of them began to quietly weep. Usually this was followed by a nervous apology and a little embarrassment, particularly if those shedding the tears were men. Drew explained,

> You just do this [that is, getting people to talk about life at the cottage] on purpose ... just to get people misty-eyed ... you go around giving people the opportunity of recovering their whole life again.

Why did Drew see his "whole life" embedded in his stories about the cottages he knew as a child and, as I learned in the course of my conversations, in the hopes he had for the future of his own family at the cottage he was building on a small Haliburton lake? What was it about life at the cottage that prompted such bodily responses from him and others? I came to learn that bodies performed, learned, absorbed, endured, and expressed a response to, and often love of, the cottage – at times unwittingly and spontaneously. I also came to understand that the "cottage body" was a disciplined body, and thus a good body. It was a body that expressed Raymond Williams's somewhat ambiguous "structure of feeling," which Nigel Thrift reworked as "what we live through." The latter captures the "movement of bone, of body, of breath, of imagination, of muscle," a culturally shaped bodily comportment that expresses "emotion, bodily practices, the physical character of places" (quoted in Knowles 2008, 168; see Thrift 1994, 193-94). Or as Marcel Mauss earlier suggested, such bodies manifest particular "techniques of the body ... [the] ways in which ... men [and women] know how to use their bodies ... [which] vary ... between societies, educations, proprieties and fashions, and prestiges" (Mauss [1935] 1973, 70, 73). Cottage bodies were, as I came to understand them, comported or "lived through" in very particular ways.[1]

Making Good Bodies

My analysis here intersects with many of the themes raised by David Crouch and Luke Desforges (2003), who argue that the tourist's – in this case, a domestic tourist's – body is one in motion; it is a sensuous body, whose subjectivity is responsive to such things as the technologies, the performance, and all that is encompassed by being in the world, what I (and many others) gloss as Heidegger's notion of "dwelling" (see also J. Harrison 2003, 92-138; Obrador Pons 2003; Chapter 2 in this book). Such a body is always deeply meaningful and never neutral; it is at once a social and a political entity, and with its capacity to act in certain ways, it can be a "good body."

What I am calling here the "cottage body" is richly sensorial and, despite all that is said about being free at the cottage, it is, I would argue, highly disciplined. Gendered bodies are highly disciplined at the cottage, with particular reference to work and labour, a theme I return to Chapter 7. Here I discuss less obvious forms of bodily discipline at the cottage.

There are two things I take as givens in reference to the cottage body. When referring to a physical cottage body, I first assume the "embodied nature of the mind" (Csordas 1994, 8); or, using Lyon and Barbalet's (1994, 63) wording, I see this body as "a biological being and a conscious, experiencing, acting, interpreting entity." Second, the cottage body has flesh; it is a real physical body that does real things; it makes choices and often challenges, or frequently only partially accepts, any disciplinary practice. It is not a "passive representationalist body" (T. Turner 1994, 13), which Turner sees as "begotten [entirely] out of discourse by power" (ibid., 36).[2] Regimes of power do play a role in shaping the cottage body, but these regimes are "far from being automatic and unidirectional" (Dyck 2008, 14; see also Obrador Pons 2003). Noel Dyck (2008, 1) argues the value of exploring the "stylized and innovative ways in which regimes of self-discipline are ... cultivated within voluntary realms of leisure and self-development." To him, examinations of discipline need to extend beyond the "technological features and mechanisms, the 'it' of discipline," turning to the "relationships and dealings with those who would apply discipline and those to whom it would be applied" (ibid., 3).[3] Discipline, Dyck argues, is not "implacable, seamless ... [an] inscrutable force *sui generis*" (ibid., 4). He also highlights the limitations of Bourdieu's notion of *habitus,* arguing that "disciplinary schema" cannot be seen to "encompass inexorable aspects of a social and political structure or inscrutable manifestations of an un-conscious habitus." Such schema are rather "generated, maintained, resisted and manipulated in everyday life" (ibid., 13). Attention needs to be paid, Dyck suggests,

> to actual performances of discipline, not to mention reports by subjects of sensual experiences and memories of disciplinary practice. *What is smelled, felt, tasted, and experientially linked to given disciplinary settings becomes socially ... instructive ... [as do] symbolic and communicative processes.* (ibid., emphasis added)

Discipline offers "practical and reliable means for constituting and incul-cating suitable selves for oneself and others." In the process, it offers opportunity for "reflexive selves capable of exercising agency ... intentional choice" (Dyck 2008, 14). The emotionally fraught debates and arguments among cottagers as to the place of the new, noisy, high-powered PWCs on cottage lakes is just one example of resistance by some to what is presumed to be the "proper" behaviour of the cottager, particularly in their playful practice. To be effective, discipline must revolve "around belief, for its symbolic and expressive dimensions possess deep emotive and practical significance" (ibid., 15). It is, as Collins (2008, 181) suggests, all about "doing the 'right-thing' ... [something that] is a never-ending process of negoti-ation informed by an apparent and contested, though always and already available, moral-aesthetic code." This was, to my mind, unquestionably the case for the disciplined cottage body. There was much that seemed to challenge what was the "right thing" and thus the implicit "moral-aesthetic code" at the cottage.

In reference to organized children's sports in Canada, Dyck (2007, 114) suggests that they "can be seen to furnish an attractive and pliable medium for mounting projects of social and political engineering under the rubric of play." I would make a similar argument for much of the play that goes on at the cottage. Dyck observes that at "the heart of athletic performance rests the attempt to exercise control over stylized uses of the body so as to accomplish desired movements ... [such] sculpting of malleable bodies may be ... extended to guide the disciplining of other aspects of ... deportment and behaviour." Such processes begin with learning the "desired movements," which is central to the playful, competent body of the cottager. This frame of thinking fits in with what others have said about the experience of tourists in general. Vacationing requires skills; "it takes a great deal of effort to enjoy a vacation" (Löfgren 1999, 5; see also J. Harrison 2003; Schroeder 2002, 75).

It became clear to me, as a non-cottager, that the cottage body had much to learn, even if only to have fun. The pleasures of the cottage body were moulded in part by texture and detail – these bodies needed to learn early in their lives such things as how to swim, or how to drive a boat (even if it was only a small one with an equally small motor); how to play games and sports; or how to simply hang out at the cottage. Formal and symbolic structures further shaped cottage bodies, which signalled accepted assumptions about gendered identity and roles, desired physical and technical competencies and capabilities, class position and values, and national and racial identity. Such bodies have particularly complex relations with notions of what makes life at the cottage satisfying and pleasurable. The cottage body is also, it is worth noting, implicitly assumed to be an able body.

I turn my attention now to exploring the cottage body at its most pleasing: as playful, competent, sensual, well-fed, relaxed and healthy, durable and destined for transition, and, with only a touch of irony in light of my comments above, liberated. In short, a happy body. However, as I discuss at the end of this chapter, it is also a fearful and, ultimately, racialized body.

The Playful Cottage Body

It might seem odd based on what I have suggested so far that anything at the cottage could be seen as boring. But, as Lorne admitted, "you can run out of things to do ... it can get boring." Thirteen-year-old Abigail confessed at the end of one summer, after reciting a long list of all that she had done at the cottage, "I read about sixteen or eighteen other books because I was bored." Several cottagers suggested that the games they played, the sports they participated in, the time they spent socializing with friends and family, or anything that they did that could be labelled as a leisure or recreational activity or simply fun – what people did, or what their parents organized at the cottage – were intended, at their root, to keep boredom at bay. Several cottagers admitted that they found being at the cottage alone an unpleasant experience; Sean said there was "nobody to do things with."

The playful things people did at the cottage in large measure required a physically active body and a willing mind to, as one might say, "go along with the game." Ideally, such activities were done outdoors. For many cottagers, the water was the central focus of their play. Cottages were often bought based on their accessibility to the lake. The lake as "playground" was an important trope in such decisions. Several cottagers said they could not imagine a cottage that was not on the water, even if they admitted that they went in the water only rarely – they still wanted to be close to it. Some cottagers looked for gently sloping sandy beaches to make the water a safe and accessible place for young children to play. Others wanted a protected swimming area so they could swim a good distance without worrying about boat or other water vehicle traffic. Others wanted the water immediately adjacent to their property to be deep enough to allow for safe diving and the playing of games such as water polo or "water football," as one family called it.

Games, many of them played in teams – horseshoes, bocce, beach volleyball, croquet, and badminton – were played regularly at the cottage, some on the beach, others in specially constructed areas. Many of these activities did require what Mike Michael (2000, 107-8) labelled "minimal technologies" – mallets, nets, birdies, balls, racquets, horseshoes – items that in some cases had been passed down through the family, and so were far from new. The surfaces that they could be played on varied, and needed little, if any, development. Some pastimes at the cottage required only "mundane" or even "invisible technologies," the latter exemplified by such things as "walking boots" (Michael 2000).

Alice remembered when things got boring at the cottage for her children:

[I recall] packing them a lunch and telling them they could go [for a hike]. The neighbouring empty lot ... was high and rocky and so it made a nice hike up, with a beautiful view way up above the lake. The kids called it

Pine Mountain. So whenever there was a boring period, that's where they went. It was a big adventure for them.

For Delores, a cottager in her mid-forties, childhood summer afternoons spent catching tadpoles in an old sealer jar were some of her happiest times. For her, good times at the cottage were all about "making your own fun," obviously with minimal technological assistance. She remembered times with her friends at the cottage: "We used to be gone for hours, playing in the woods and building forts and chasing frogs and doing whatever." Several cottagers observed that inclement weather did not keep them inside – their mothers sent them out to play in the rain. But if it persisted, board games, card games, jigsaw puzzles, or comic books kept children amused – all of which continue to be common rainy day pastimes for all ages at the cottage. And due either to the constraints of the size of a cottage, or the desire to simply not be alone, many cottagers talked of sitting and reading – newspapers, magazines, or a novel – in the company of others.

In the winter, skates, toboggans, skis, and snowshoes allowed the cottager body to be playful despite snow and cold temperatures, as did snowmobiles, which were more readily accepted by some cottagers than PWCs.[4] There has been a general trend towards recreational activities involving somewhat more elaborate technologies in the last couple of decades, and in some cases requiring a much more elaborate infrastructure. In Haliburton, these things included golf courses, whitewater kayaking routes, and planned and mapped hiking trails.[5]

Jordan remembered that when he was a child, he and his mother rarely left the cottage property during the summer. There was simply little opportunity to do so, as his mother did not have a car during the week. This hardly mattered to him: he was happily entertained by what there was to do in his immediate surroundings. For him, and for others, a trip to the town of Haliburton, Minden, or especially the somewhat more distant Huntsville had been a major expedition that was undertaken only two or three times a summer. But that seems to have changed. He noted of his own family,

My wife and my kids now are in and out of the town several times a week. They are getting involved in activities like golfing, and taking in a movie, or going to dinner. So, there is a lot more doing things off the lake. But I think it adds to the lifestyle to a certain degree, although it makes it probably a little more hectic. But they seem to enjoy it.

Television – which some claimed was only used to watch a movie on a rainy day, and for others was "just to keep on top of the news" – computers, video games, and, more recently, high speed internet are recreational technologies that have arrived at the cottage. But for some I spoke to, these developments presented a challenge to what they understood to be the playful cottage body, contested all that the cottage experience symbolized, and in particular what a cottage body was supposed to be: both physically and mentally active. What one did at the cottage in the name of fun should be something that stimulated or tested one's physical body, creativity, energy, curiosity, imagination, and independence, all of which they felt needed little technological support – even if it fell into the realm of what Urry (1995, 197) calls "quiet recreation," like reading or simply observing nature from the dock.

Some cottagers countered resistance to new technologies at the cottage by pointing out that they were only supplementary to what remained the key site of play at the cottage – the water. On many cottage beaches and waterfronts today, a wide array of "cottage toys" can be found tied up to an elaborate system of docks and walkways. Such toys generally fall into two categories: those that require an engine or motor, often of significant power, and those powered by human energy (canoes, kayaks, paddleboats) or natural elements (sailboats). (It is important to note that canoes have been a standard feature at many cottages since the earliest years, as have been small, usually aluminum, boats – with at most a 10hp motor, "just enough to putt you around the lake to fish," as one cottager said.) Diving rafts, water slides, and inflatable trampolines are other non-motorized technologies that enhance fun at the cottage. Such things keep many a cottage body playful on a twenty-first-century summer weekend.

Personal watercraft, power boats – preferably with high-powered motors to pull water skiers, wakeboarders, and water tubers – and pontoon boats were all popular technologies of play – at "too many cottages," as some of those I interviewed bemoaned. Brigita lamented her adolescent son's recent complaint that they "don't have any toys" at their cottage; she told him that if he wanted a power boat for water skiing, "he was going to have to purchase it himself," as she was happy with their small aluminum "tub" that she and her husband took out fishing. Megan, a cottager in her mid-fifties, found her playful body "too old" for a PWC; she had to nurse her aching knees following a ride on one. Thus, such enhanced play demanded certain bodily competencies and capacities. But then, whether it is learning how to swim or knowing where and how to catch tadpoles, figuring out the basics of paddling a canoe, or, more recently, knowing how to ride a wakeboard, a competent body has always been valued at the cottage. It is understood that the cottage body has the capacity to be more playful if in fact it is a competently skilled body.

The Competent Cottage Body

Roger described for me in meticulous detail what is involved in the art of water skiing, from the fears of the beginner to the competencies and thrills of someone more experienced:

> The real challenge is, first of all to get on the top of the water and then to stay there. And, I know it sounds unusual, but if you've never tried it, it's a tremendous feeling. When my son [who knows how to ski] is behind the boat, he is probably on one ski, not two skis. To get up on two skis is hard, to get up on one ski is harder. Because it's harder, it's more desirable. If my son is behind the boat and his cousins are driving the boat, then it becomes the challenge between the driver and the skier to see if he will stay up or be made to fall ... If my son goes left behind the boat, the boat driver will then turn quickly to the right. What it [probably] does is ... [double] the speed that the skier is going when he's going around the boat, around in a circle. Now, at that point, you are going very fast ... then what the driver will do in order to try to knock him off the ski, he will then turn to the left. When he does that, the rope goes slack. And at that point the skier goes in the water. It's a game they play.

In the course of this interview, Roger went on to explain what is involved in first getting up on water skis and how it would be unfair to play such games with a novice, who would still need to learn the basics and "gain their confidence."

The details of what it took to get someone up on water skis were well known to Laura and her children Jacob and Theresa, who made it a project, as Jacob said, to ensure that "anyone who would come to visit us couldn't go home from the weekend if they didn't get up on water skis."

Theresa: Everybody who came up had to go water skiing ...
Jacob: If you'd never skied before, that's even worse, because that means a lot more effort.
Theresa: Dad would get you to water ski whether you wanted to or not.
Laura: We'd bring out the video camera and the tape at the end of the weekend and they'd all be proud because we'd put them through some pain and glory and some challenges.

Learning these skills, even against your will, was something this family assumed would inculcate into their visitors the pleasures – and the thrills – of the cottage experience. With an almost missionary zeal, they talked about wanting everyone to appreciate life at the cottage. Getting up on water skis was symbolic to them of larger life lessons. It represented the confidence and perseverance needed to overcome the challenges of actually getting up on water skis and, once there, to enjoy the experience. It was also something that demonstrated the joys of collective experience, as it was often a true group effort that finally got someone up. Neil said of his godson Adam,

[He] was up here last week and ... I said, "Come on, Adam, we'll teach you how to ski" ... He replied, "Oh, I don't know." We urged him on. I said, "Come on, Adam, we'll teach you." On Saturday we had a couple of attempts that didn't work out. But on Sunday when he got up and started going around the bay, skiing and hootin' and hollerin' ... oh it was great.

Whatever the skills needed to competently water ski and to outwit those who tried to make you fall, at least one person in the group had to know how to skilfully drive a boat. It was a skill that allowed for others to have fun water skiing or, more recently, wakeboarding, or tubing. Many who had grown up spending summers at the cottage proudly boasted that they had known how to drive a boat long before they knew how to drive a car.

Some kids were driving small boats at the cottage when they were just ten or eleven years old. These small boats had equally small motors, but many soon moved on to much larger boats with much more powerful motors. Delores remembered,

> When the car pulled out with Dad on Sunday night [as he went back to work in the city], we, the kids would become the runners. We'd head to the store in the little boat to get milk, the eggs, the bread, or whatever during the week.

Japanese anthropologist Shiho Satsuka (1997), who did research as a young woman, and whose writings inspired this section of the chapter, quickly learned that her inability to drive a boat denied her access to cottages in Georgian Bay, where she planned to undertake fieldwork. She was assured that this was not a skill she could quickly learn, for not only did she lack the physical knowledge of what was involved in driving a boat, but she also lacked the knowledge of the waterways and rocky shoals that abounded in the area. Her difficulties in accessing island cottages were quickly alleviated when she hired an adolescent boy to chauffeur her around in his parents' boat. Having grown up cottaging on the islands, he possessed the necessary skills and knowledge.

Knowing the basics of guiding a canoe on the lake,[6] of putting bait and a hook on a fishing rod, accessing and diving safely off the cliffs – these are examples of desired competencies of playful cottage bodies. Unquestionably, however, the most critical and ubiquitous skill for a competent cottage body would be knowing how to swim. Isabelle recounted her times spent at her grandmother's cottage:

> You learned to swim there, so you didn't have any fear of the water. My Nana made sure all of us swam, [she felt] we should learn to swim and that's part of being at the cottage.

Or as Harry told me,

> I said to my daughter when she had her boys, I said, "One thing if you're [going to be] at the cottage, I want my grandsons to swim."

Learning how to swim was a practical safety strategy, but it was also seen to exponentially increase one's ability to have fun at the cottage. Some children learned to swim at the lake if lessons were offered under the auspices of the local cottagers' association, or they took lessons in the city in the winter, or learned at summer camp; others were simply taught informally by family and friends. Children had plenty of time to practice. They often spent hours in the water swimming and playing games over the course of a summer. Many told me that they lived in their bathing suits all summer long.

But not all cottagers knew how to swim. Some cottagers admitted that they had never learned, and that they continued to have a fear of the water even after spending many years going back and forth to a water-access-only cottage. These feelings made them even more adamant that their children know how to swim, to increase both safety at the cottage and their enjoyment of the experience. If one could swim, then one's potential fear of the water was significantly reduced. It also provided a sense of security when children went out for a boat ride, drove small boats, or even went for a ride on a PWC or larger power boat. Personal flotation devices (PFDs), or life jackets as they are more commonly labelled, further enhanced the sense of security cottagers had in and around the water, both for themselves and for subsequent generations.[7] The combination of wearing a PFD and knowing how to swim increased one's chances of survival should the boat capsize. Yet statistics continue to show that not everyone chooses to wear one.[8]

Basic competencies for many cottage bodies included knowing how to swim and dive at a level that one felt comfortable in the water, paddle a canoe (no matter how awkwardly), drive a power boat or a PWC, water ski (sometimes on one ski), or, more recently, ride a wakeboard. Richard proudly said of his daughters, whose bodies – he hoped whose minds and hearts as well – had been well disciplined at the cottage,

> They're both good water skiers, they're both excellent swimmers. They learned to swim in the lake, not at swimming pools and swimming lessons. And they know how to drive the boat. They know how to paddle canoes. They respect the water. I hope that they both have it in their blood and will always want to come back.

Other less technologically engaged cottagers emphasized things like possessing the capacity to swim a set distance each morning, or complete a lengthy walk each day.

There was a moral imperative in such pleasures and proficiencies. In a manner somewhat parallel to other regimes of physical activity, there was a "moral duty to actualize [the] potential" of the body to play competently (Harré 1989, 193). Certain skills focused on facilitating fun and enjoyment at the cottage were to be ingrained in subsequent generations. They represented values – self-reliance, tenacity, and determined accomplishment – held dearly by the Haliburton cottagers I met.

Such shared experiences fostered a *communitas* among cottagers. Many hoped the resulting sense of belonging would endure "on a more or less permanent basis" to help ensure future generations would know the joys of the experience (V. Turner 1982, 49). But this sense of belonging was established not only through the nurturing of active and specifically skilled bodies. As Dyck explains, "What is smelled, felt, tasted, and experientially linked to given disciplinary settings become[s] socially ... instructive," and, I would argue, hones a particular aesthetic sense. The cottage body is also very much a sensuous body whose sensorial responses are specifically conditioned to enjoy life at the cottage.

The Sensuous Cottage Body

When asked what it was she thought people like about the cottage, Frances replied, "The whole package. You can sit on your front porch and *listen* to the loons and *feel* the breeze, *read* a book, *enjoy* the view of the lake, everything." To her, there was no doubt that much of what was pleasing about the cottage was its potential to stimulate the senses.

It is taken as a given that of the five bodily senses, the visual is most privileged in Western cultures (Howes 1991, 1; see also Urry 1990, 1995). And clearly what cottagers saw, what they gazed upon, was central to what many found beautiful and awe-inspiring about life at the cottage. This kind of gaze has resonances of the "romantic tourist gaze," which, in Urry's (1990, 45; 1995, 198) terms, emphasizes "a personal, semi-spiritual relationship with the object of the gaze."

The visual beauty on display at the cottage could capture the attention of even those who have not grown up there. Kevin and Delores told the story of a friend's son who had spent a couple of summers in Haliburton with them in his late teens. Delores said, "He was so busy being cool he could hardly put two words together." He found work at a local restaurant. One night, when he got home two hours later than usual, Kevin asked if he had been busy at the restaurant. "No," their friend's son replied, "it was really misty and the lake was really nice and the stars were great. I turned off the motor and lay in the boat and looked at the stars." Delores noted, "For him to actually put those words into a sentence, that was a big thing." He had started to appreciate the beauty of the cottage. In their assessment several years later, he had not forgotten what he had learned to appreciate there, and if given the chance he would move to Haliburton "in a heartbeat." He remained, in their minds, a "wannabe" cottager.

The magnificent sunsets across the lake, the stars, comets, meteors, and northern lights in the night sky, the shades of pink of the Canadian Shield granite, the waves caressing the shore, the magnificent trees – all were visual elements that formed what many cottagers took to be a quintessential Canadian landscape. But it was also the more intimate sights – "sun-dappled leaves on a forest path," "the hummingbird who visits the wild flowers," "the tadpoles, the minnows, the lily pads in the water," "the fireflies hovering in the black of night," "the moonlight filtering through the hemlocks on a bedroom wall" – that added to the visual beauty of life at the cottage.

Of course, the cottage body had other sensorial receptors, which many felt "went into overdrive" at the cottage. For some, their hearing and smell were particularly heightened. As Aaron said, "You get the feeling of the lake, when you are up here for a few days – the smell, the sounds, the waves ... at night you are sleeping and it's windy, you hear the water crashing." Marnie said, "You're very aware of weather when you're at a cottage, as you can hear it." Trudy recalled distinctly, "Whenever we would come up, when I got out of the car on a Friday night, it was like, everything fell away as I could *smell* the pine and the earth and the lake."

Cottagers frequently contrasted the sounds and smells at the cottage to those of an urban environment: the disruptive aural and olfactory assault of sirens, traffic, garbage, and polluted air. Whether these senses were actually any more attuned at the cottage is difficult to assess, but cottagers had been socialized to perceive the cottage soundscape and the scentscape as more pleasing. Still, such "scapes" were painted in broad brush strokes by cottagers, as few had specific knowledge of what these sounds and smells actually were. Beyond one or two common bird calls, for example, many could not distinguish one bird from another, but that did not really seem to matter.

When walking at the cottage in winter, Neil found all his senses to be heightened by "the frigid temperatures ... because it's a very crisp cold ... you can walk at night ... the sky is just so bright with stars and the reflection from the snow ... and sometimes you can see and hear the northern lights." Leonard told me how, when lying quietly on the dock on hot summer afternoons, he felt his conscious awareness lessen and his sensorial receptors heighten. He said,

> You hear the little fishies dart around ... the little chipmunk running around through the leaves, it just sounds so huge ... and you can hear the lapping of a boat [when] the wake comes and hits the shore ... it's a delight.

Others expanded his list of sensorial experiences at the cottage: "feeling the water in the lake when you are swimming"; "the smell of the cottage, the air"; "the waves lapping on the shore and the winds in the trees"; "the birds singing"; "the crunch of the leaves underfoot on a fall day in the woods"; "the feel of the air on your arms"; "the smell and the sound of the wind moving through the hemlocks and the pines"; "the force of the wind on your face as it moves up the lake during a storm"; "the scolding of a chipmunk"; " the sound of the fish com[ing] up to eat at night"; "the drone of the cicadas"; "the bull frogs in the early spring"; and what some considered the quintessential Canadian sound, the "call of the loon." All of these sensorial memories were mnemonics of pleasurable moments at the cottage.

The intensity of the sun at the cottage was less oppressive than that of the city, as it was usually tempered by a breeze off the lake. Marilyn admitted to enjoying this more temperate heat while relaxing on the dock "catching a few rays" to enhance her tan. She had long associated such sensorial experiences with the cottage. This kind of luxuriating is now more tenuous due to the increased level of ultraviolet (UV) rays, the potential for serious burns, and the more pervasive fear of skin cancer. Despite the moderating effects of the water, increased UV rays are leading to higher summer temperatures at the cottage. This incremental change has increased the use of air conditioning, or in some cases forced cottagers to return early to their air-conditioned homes in the city. Generally, cottagers wanted to indulge in the sensual pleasures of the cottage only when the conditions were deemed to be at their most optimal.

In the same vein, the sensuous cottage body also reveled in absences. A good summer at the cottage was one in which "the bugs were great" – that is, there were fewer of them. Cottagers were also happier if they were not being bombarded by "non-cottage" sounds. Vicky said, "The quieter it is, the better it is for us. If there is no movement on the lake, that's the best." Many emphasized that the absence of loud noises, particularly those not considered natural sounds, was one of the things that they preferred about being at the cottage midweek, when many of the weekend cottagers had gone home. It was then that the noise of PWCs and high-powered boats was at its most minimal. Their sounds generated annoyance, if not outright anger, among some cottagers, as they were reminiscent of the "rattlin'" roar of the city (Altmeyer 1976, 23).[9]

Such absences had elements of what Csikszentmihalyi (1975, 36, 38) would call "flow," "the holistic sensation that people have when they act with total involvement ... [when they merge] action and awareness" – a state Victor Turner (1982, 58) said was "to be as happy as a human can be."[10] Flow is a condition of heightened awareness, a sense of being in the moment. It can have elements of thrill and challenge, as in Roger's description of what it was like to be on water skis:

> Have you ever ridden [in], say, a convertible? You know, where you are getting an air flow around you? It's something like that when you water ski. Except it gives you a tremendous thrill to be behind the boat.[11]

Flow is a state that one can move in and out of over a period of time (Csikszentmihalyi 1975, 38). Roger was hardly the only cottager who could see himself in this fluid state of flow while at the cottage. As Conrad reflected,

> I read a lot of Proust when I was studying [at university]. I had a really vivid recaptured memory here one evening. It was partly the elevated porch that did it. We had a front porch in north Toronto where I grew up and I can remember as a little boy, I would pretend that porch was the Toronto Island ferry and I was its skipper. Well one night, it just came

back to me and just like Proust describes, it comes back with such force that you relive it but it's actually a stronger experience. I can't sit on the screened porch without thinking about it now. How many chances do you get to just cerebrally let go and just see what happens?

Anna reminisced about one summer night:

One year we went out to sit on the dock at midnight. We were with my sister, my two young sons and a friend from France. We all went out in the dark and we talked from midnight till two o'clock in the morning. We watched the moon change and rise over the lake. We saw all the stars. You could see and hear everything. We were in awe.

Sam afforded his mother-in-law an experience that allowed her to transcend her fears and have a "peak experience," a moment of flow. Joan told me how her husband

took [her] mother [who had lived her life in Philadelphia] out in the canoe one night. She was terrified of the water, but she was dying of cancer. He took her out at eleven o'clock to show her the stars. I remember it being a real bonding experience for them. It was this huge moment of trust because she would never have done it had it not been for the fact that she was dying. But it was certainly probably one of the most moving and important moments in her life to see all the stars as you can only see them on a clear night at the cottage.

And as Delores remembered of her childhood,

There used to be a store down the road, down the highway from our cottage to a little general store. I used to go there with my friend, whose parents and grandparents were two doors down from our cottage. We would walk to the store on hot days, barefoot. There were cattle in the fields, there were fat farm ladies in white aprons hanging clothes on the line. We would go with our fifty cents to buy candy. It had this old floor, when you pushed the little carts, they went da-da-da-da-da-da over the floor. They had a red Coke cooler with the stainless steel lids. It [also] had Orange Crush and 7-Up. And you'd plunge your hand into this icy cold water, b-r-r-r, and then open your little bottles of pop, psssht! right on the front of the Coke cooler. You'd get a little brown paper bag of candy you'd picked up from the old man behind the counter.

As Urry (1995, 27) concludes, it is imperative to "'remember' that memories are embodied." Connerton (1989) argues that bodily actions and remembered sensorial responses "sediment memories" in the human psyche. What is striking about the cottage moments I describe here is their ordinariness. Save one, they do not describe once-in-a-lifetime experiences. Most may well have been repeated several times. And even as Sam took his mother-in-law – a non-cottager – out to see the stars, it was clear from talking to him that she *had* to have this experience at least once in her life, as for him it was something that was completely unparalleled. Such experiences became transcendent of their particularities and firmly imprinted the cottage as a place of treasured corporeal memories.

One sensorial remembrance highlighted by many cottagers was the taste, and to some extent the smell, of certain foods. Being at the cottage sanctioned the decadent consumption of particular foods and sometimes drinks (the latter often included alcoholic beverages). They were always consumed in the presence of others, and thus prompted fondly remembered occasions of sociality. All such pleasures contributed to the well-fed and nurtured cottage body.

The Well-Fed Cottage Body

The candies and the ice-cold drinks that Delores and her friend bought likely tasted better due to the effort exerted in getting to the store on a hot summer afternoon, and all the sensorial indulgences stimulated in the process. And while candy and soft drinks may not be the most nutritious foods, they undoubtedly satiated their young cottage bodies in other, maybe more important ways. Many cottagers told me about stops at their favourite store to purchase locally produced ice cream, often a ritualized part of the journey home from the cottage. In the same manner, a dessert of raspberries and ice cream tasted its absolute best at the cottage. As Fred reminisced,

I can remember sitting having dinner and my father saying "Well, we've got raspberries, I'll get the ice cream" ... So he'd jump in, we had a kayak, it was the fastest boat on the lake and he'd take the double paddle and go across to the store [at the end of the lake]. They'd wrap the ice cream up in newspaper and he'd have it back before it melted.

Cottage bodies, whether those of family or friends who gather at the cottage, are well-fed – and I do not mean only in terms of their nutritional needs being met. As Isabelle said, "We eat and drink, it's just fun." What is eaten, how it is prepared, and how, where, and with whom it is consumed have powerful symbolic dimensions at the cottage. I observed that roasting marshmallows by a Saturday evening bonfire with friends and family gathered around is probably the best example of all that food can symbolize at the cottage. Sticky, gooey, sweet, and delectably toasted over a roaring fire, it was particularly exciting for young children. Such things would rarely be eaten anywhere but at the cottage. They were very simple to prepare and they were eaten outside the context of any scheduled meal. They were generally eaten in the company of those with whom one had meaningful relationships and they were yet another family tradition at the cottage. Grandparents and parents enjoyed them as much as younger generations. These indulgences captured the specialness of food at the cottage.

If one were to look at issues of *Cottage Life* over the years, one might assume that all cottagers have finely honed palates, and that many are striving to be gourmet chefs. Most of the cottagers I spoke with did not seem to imagine themselves as having such talents. These skills were not part of the world of the cottage as they knew it in Haliburton, but were instead, they felt, more likely to be found in Muskoka. Nevertheless, I did in fact encounter a few cottagers like Conrad, who admitted, "I've certainly used *Cottage Life* recipes," but without any real pretence that he considered himself anything more than an adequate cook. He noted that one of his favourite recipes from the magazine is "good-naturedly referred to as the 'official appetizer'" of all his company's potluck functions.

The food I was served by cottagers, and the food people told me they ate at the cottage, was generally much more standard and simple fare. Many of the meals I was offered could be classed as plain fare – tuna melts, grilled cheese sandwiches, devilled eggs, and cold cuts: things that one finds recipes for in standard cookbooks from the 1950s, '60s, and '70s. Following a supper of corned beef hash made with Alice's mother's recipe, Alice admitted:

The cottage is not about preparing fancy meals, although we certainly admit to doing a lot more entertaining at the cottage than we do at home. It's just a lot more casual, somehow a lot easier and something that you have time for at the cottage.

Even Conrad admitted that his more regular cottage fare included

something that I know is just gonna be heat-and-serve later, or often just cold barbecued chicken, some medley of raw vegetables and dip, and some nice bread or something like that.

But he did say that there was an element of indulgence in the foods that he had at the cottage: "This fridge is better stocked than my fridge at home ever is, except maybe at Christmas time ... [but] it's just ... fun stuff." And a key priority for him was that "often I will make something that I can prep, because once I hit cocktail hour, I just want to have as few duties as possible."

But food and its consumption also took on another quality at the cottage. As Roger reflected,

Breakfast is more leisurely [at the cottage], we can go a little longer without breakfast. And we have a chance to talk and enjoy a second cup of coffee.

Many emphasized that meal times at the cottage were typified by flexibility, in keeping with the rejection of rigid scheduling commonly enacted at the cottage. For Lorne, a satisfying element of cottage meal times was the sense of indulgence that allowed everyone simply to "eat when [they were] hungry." Meanwhile, Garry remembered how as a child, he sought out lunch not only when he wanted it but where he wanted it (or where he was able to find someone to give it to him). When he and his friends were out for the day "fishing, swimming, hunting frogs or walking in the swamp, [they] would find somebody's house to have lunch at, or head home if [they] absolutely had to."

For Sean, eating at the cottage was as much about getting together with his friends as it was about what was consumed. He remembered particularly when he was younger and fewer of his neighbours had established families:

Everybody would get together and cook dinner at one spot or another. We would bounce around the lake doing this. We would arrive and ask, "What are we eating tonight?" Or we might decide, "Let's go to so-and-so, see what he's got for dinner." When we got there, he would ask, "What do you guys want?" And he would go to the fridge and see what he had.

Food and its consumption at the cottage was, for many, about the ease of preparation, which led many to often use barbecues, in both the summer and winter, to prepare simple but tasty meals at the cottage. And even when "serving anywhere from ten to twenty people" on any given weekend, as Laura regularly did, the preparation, presentation, and consumption of a simple meal was presumed to satiate everyone's nutritional needs, and, more critically, to foster a socially and emotionally well-fed collective cottage body. In addition to being nurtured in this way, cottage bodies were understood to be – I would say disciplined to be – able to let go of stress, worry, and tension while at the cottage. Doing so resulted in what many said they desired and ultimately produced at the cottage: a relaxed, restored, yet invigorated, and therefore healthy body.

The Relaxed and Healthy Cottage Body

A true cottage body knows how to relax at the cottage. It knows how to "stay quiet ... [to] not do anything useful" (Gullestad 1990, 44). I heard various stories of visitors – that is, non-cottagers: those who had not been disciplined as to how 'to be' at the cottage – who left early from a weekend visit as they did not know what to do with themselves at the cottage. Several cottagers relayed tales about someone who was given the use of a cottage, or had even rented one for a week, but left halfway through as they could not find anything to do. Then there were those like Conrad's friend below, who lacked the self-reflexivity to know how much he needed "cottage time." Conrad told me that his friend came to the cottage,

for a couple of days and drove me crazy because he wouldn't stop looking at his cell phone. I felt like saying "Why don't you put that bloody thing away!" [The evening he got here] he was asleep on the couch by 9:00 p.m. He said, "I'm so sorry I conked out" and I said, "You've been conking out on me for a long time and I don't take it personally. It didn't matter. I just went to bed a little earlier than normal." But the second day we didn't have dinner until 9 and we were still up at 11. [Now] this is a guy who never sleeps in but I had to tap on the door at about 9, the next morning. He was just beside himself [apologizing]. But I said, "you really needed some *cottage time*, you definitely do."

Relaxation at the cottage could follow from the exhaustion and excitement of play and work, or from the heightened stimulation of the senses, including the indulgences of satisfying food and shared meals. Conrad and others might well have also agreed that it came from the indulgences – in moderation – of the cocktail hour. For others, there was just something comforting and restful about simply being near the water that dissipated tension. John put it most simply: "being by the water is just relaxing." For others, it was just not being at home in the city; as Emily said of her husband, "he'd never relax there."

The sensual stimulation at the cottage was so rich and intense, and at the same time so calming and rejuvenating, that many cottagers did not want to miss a moment of it. Sally – whose Canadian grandfather had first brought her father to spend his summers on a lake in Haliburton, something that he subsequently did for his family – now worked for the Philadelphia Emergency Services Department. In the years and months since taking her paramedic position, she had regularly made the trip to her parents' cottage, often leaving mid-week following her night shift for the ten-hour drive. As she said,

I find this place very restorative. When you're [working in life and death situations], then you come up to this place, you just sort of get grounded again. But I don't want to ever sleep when I am here. I want to just absorb as much of it as I absolutely can to carry me through until I come back again.

For Sarah, the cottage was a place of creative and intellectual stimulation for her mind and body. As she said,

I am creative at the cottage. I did a master's degree several years ago. I remember I was struggling trying to get [a paper] written. And I went to the cottage and wrote [it] on a weekend. I just set myself at the table and inspiration arrived. The cottage for me is my relaxation place. So, as soon as you can relax you can get rid of all other stuff that impedes creativity.

The social stimulation and emotional support of the company of good friends and family also greatly contributed to the sense of calm, peace and general 'letting-go' that many cottagers talked about. As Becky said of her cottage, "This is the place I feel the most relaxed and at peace." For others, it was simply a place where life was more casual. Even the necessary labours and responsibilities of cottage ownership, she stated, "feel effortless here, I don't know why that is. Even cleaning is [easy], whereas at home it can feel as a chore." At times I really wondered if anyone actually saw her or himself to be working at the cottage, or whether they had been disciplined to think otherwise.

A relaxed cottage body was a healthy, restored body, one imagined to "be whole" (Gullestad 1990, 44). Being able to be at the cottage, which I would parallel with what Urry (1995, 130) describes as being "able to be on holiday ... is presumed to be a characteristic of modern citizenship which has become embodied into people's thinking about health and well being." In keeping with this, Deidre and Roger called their cottage "a restful place, therapeutic place for us, where we can rejuvenate our energy or creative spirit."

Aaron's cottage was his "therapy place," where his body and mind could become whole again. Vicky summed it up, saying, "Peaceful down-time [at the cottage] gives you back your sanity after going at a hectic five days." At her cottage, Hannah commented, she could regularly exercise her body by swimming or walking, which left her with a feeling of well-being and rejuvenation. Several cottagers told stories of how their time spent at the cottage helped heal them following accidents or illness. The cottage was where Becky's father went to recover from his stroke. Alice broke her leg at the cottage one summer by slipping on acorns and pine needles. Her doctor told her that she should return to the lake and go swimming every day. In doing so, she could avoid having physiotherapy. She took pleasure in being under doctor's orders to both return to her favourite place and resume doing something she dearly loved to do – swim regularly in the lake. Ben, who suffered terribly from ragweed allergies as a child, recounted,

In [the Toronto suburb] where we lived, on the outskirts of what had just been developed, there was a lot of ragweed ... part of coming here was an escape from that. It was so much better for me.

Several cottagers remembered very clearly that they remained at the cottage well into the fall rather than going back to Toronto during the polio epidemic in 1952. Being at the cottage, it seemed, kept one's body healthy.

The founder of the charitable organization *Cottage Dreams* was initially motivated by her conviction that the cottage was a healing and restorative place. This is the way the cottage had been seen from the earliest days of its development: a place free from the pollution, disease, and unsanitariness of the city. As the website for *Cottage Dreams* says, "For over a century, Canadian families have been finding peace, tranquility and inspiration in cottage country." *Cottage Dreams* matches cottages with cancer survivors and their friends and families, allowing them to spend a donated week at a cottage to, as the website says, "reconnect and rejuvenate with family and friends after successfully completing treatment."[12] It is implicit in these statements that the bodies, if not the souls, minds, and hearts – of family, friends, and cancer survivors themselves – will be healed and restored, aided in their individual and collective recovery by spending time at a cottage. Such premises are grounded in the notion that a cottage body is a durable body, one that can rebound and be healed. Cottage bodies unquestionably need to do this as they age and move through life stages, at each transition encountering, if not necessarily happily accepting (and at times disregarding), new regimes of discipline. The cottage body, I learned, was a durable and resilient body, but one always in transition.

The Durable Cottage Body

An Ageing Body/A Failing Body

Jack and Lily spoke with great admiration about two of their neighbours who lived at the cottage year round. They exemplified what they, and several others, hoped would be their fate at the cottage, even if they remained only seasonal cottagers.

> *Lily:* There are two widows who live alone [down the road].
> *Jack:* How old is she? Eighty? The other is eighty.

Lily: Eighty-five. She looks wonderful. Then we have the other [one] who in the winter can't even get her car down to the cottage. She has to drive up a hill so she bought special shoes with cleats in the bottom. She does remarkably well.

Jack: Oh, she's quite a lady.

Unfortunately, many of those I interviewed who were middle-aged or older expressed anxiety and concern about how long they would be able to continue to visit the cottage on a regular basis. Charles and Sophia, whose cottage did not have indoor plumbing, used what Charles called the "'arms-strong' water delivery system, which is a pail on the end of each arm!" They worried about how much longer they would be able to manage on their own to get water to the cottage, as they were both over seventy-five. Charles lamented,

We want to keep coming as long as we can but my legs are not in good shape ... I can't cut the firewood and split it the way I once could. And I'm nervous about a chainsaw now because of sheer physical strength ... And we don't come in the winter anymore just because of age, but we used to. The two of us would snowshoe in and you never heard anything so quiet in your life. I mean it was wonderful.

Many had given up a wide range of physical activities such as snow-mobiling, water skiing, hiking, and much of the heavy physical work of cottage maintenance and upkeep. Some lamented their need to rely on the younger, stronger bodies of their children to do much of this work. Several visited the cottage less as they found it difficult to face the fact that they simply could not attend to its ongoing maintenance. For Norman and Marnie, who had built their original cottage (and the addition put on to accommodate their yet-to-arrive grandchildren) themselves, so much of their fun at the cottage had been about "doing everything ourselves." But Norman now had a series of health issues and, as Marnie said, "he is just not strong enough" to keep up that pace.

It was clear that those who lost these capacities through accident or illness would have a difficult time at the cottage. While I did learn of a couple of cottages that had been outfitted with ramps to accommodate the needs of a family member who was confined to a wheelchair, such possibilities of access were rare. The cottage body was undoubtedly under-stood as an able body. Isabelle noted that they had built a bedroom on the ground floor of their cottage because they "knew that they would not always be able to climb stairs." Others noted that they feared that if their bodies failed them while at the cottage – if, for instance, they had a stroke or heart attack while there – they were a long way from medical services. These fears curtailed several people's desire to move to the cottage permanently. Some had observed neighbours who had done this and had lived relatively contentedly there year round until they hit their seventies or early eighties. Then they found themselves needing to move to be nearer to medical fa-cilities, and simply to escape the isolation of living on the lake throughout the winter.[13] For Richard's mother, fears of her failing body actually brought new technologies to the cottage. At the insistence of her children, telephone service was installed, just in case anything happened to her when she was there, particularly if she was there alone. She acquiesced, but wanted it put at the opposite end of the cottage from her bedroom, and resolutely refused to answer it when it rang.

Becky noted that the physical activities that she enjoyed at the cottage had changed over the years as her body had aged:

I think you learn to enjoy different things at different stages of your life. I still like going out in the boat. But it doesn't do the same things for me as it used to. I like going out in the kayak. Last week when we were here, it was 8:30, it was a really nice sunset. So, we went out in the kayak, the water was like glass. And we watched. We didn't have the urge to go get out in the power boat ... My brother used to come up here and we would water ski. We were mad about it for about fifteen years. But one day recently we were sitting here and he said, "Remember when we were younger?" And I said, "Yeah, we would be out there cutting up the lake." And now I just want to have my coffee and read my Globe and Mail. So, I think things change with age.

An Adult Body/A Working Body

In reviewing the materials and interview transcripts gathered for this project, it became obvious that there were four stages of the human life-cycle that cottagers highlighted: childhood (most frequently), adoles-cence, adulthood/middle age, and late middle age and beyond. Adulthood

– roughly encompassing, for my purposes here, ages thirty to sixty years – was a period that seemed initially to yield little reflection. But then I realized that it was not overlooked; rather, it was just the time during which cottagers were very busily engaged in what constituted work at the cottage. Deborah, a cottager in her mid-forties, summed it up succinctly. Their cottage, which they had recently completed building, had been "just so much work."

Many of those who were middle-aged now had de facto responsibility for a cottage that still belonged to their parents, and which needed seemingly endless repairs and maintenance. Parents came to rely on their adult/middle-aged children – those with stronger, younger bodies – to do much of the physical labour at the cottage. Other adult cottagers had bought their own lots and had a cottage built (or built one themselves), undertakings that always required more time and energy, not to mention resources, than anticipated. Leon, in his mid-forties, estimated that it would take ten years to get the cottage built and other improvements on his property completed to the point that they would not require his full-time attention every weekend.

Competing with these demands was the fact that people wanted to spend their cottage weekends simply resting from the pressures of their work week. Neil found that his body's need for down time often conflicted with his children's desires "to do things"; he admitted guiltily, "I just want to sit and read." Consequently, it seems that whether living through this period or simply remembering it, many cottagers preferred to highlight what the cottage meant for their young or adolescent children – even if the latter rarely demonstrated what it might mean to them.

An Adolescent Body/A Recalcitrant Body
Ben laughed when he asked me, "How eager do you think a fifteen-year-old kid is to come to the cottage for the weekend and spend all of his time helping with chores?" Adolescent bodies at the cottage were by and large understood to be recalcitrant, somewhat lazy, at times trying, generally resistant, and certainly operating on their own biological clock. As Darcy said,

> They live in a different world than us at the cottage. We go to bed about 11 o'clock which is when they [his adolescent and young adult children]

start to party. They go until about 4 a.m. And then we do not see them until early afternoon of the next day. They miss the best part of the day at the cottage but they do not seem to mind.

Many saw the adolescent body as something that "simply disappeared" from the cottage. The resistance to coming to the cottage, many asserted, began about the age of fifteen and lasted until about twenty-five years of age. Friends, rather than family, became the priority social group during this time. Emily said that to try to counter this, they had "always done the friend thing" to keep their children's interest in the cottage. They had even built two sets of bunk beds in one of the bedrooms at the cottage to facilitate additional visitors on a regular basis. Being able to find a friend to bring to the cottage was not necessarily an easy task for an adolescent. It seemed that not everyone saw it as a desirable place to spend a weekend. Some had no experience of this resistance, as their children had continued to be keen to come to the cottage through their adolescent years. These parents realized that their experience was the exception – something for which they were grateful.

Some parents felt that adolescent children could be won over by regimes of discipline unique to the cottage. Indoctrinating one's children into the wholesome fun and simple pleasures of the cottage, according to Sam, was particularly intended to keep them "out of trouble" once they got to be teenagers. He wanted the love of the cottage so ingrained that his children would never waver in their enthusiasm for the experience. And he had been quite successful: his two daughters, now young adults, insisted that it had remained their absolute favourite place to be.

The teenage body at the cottage could also be disciplined through the securing of paid labour at a local marina, lodge, restaurant, store, or other nearby business. It would then have to maintain schedules and work habits at the behest of someone other than parents, even while at the cottage. It was not, however, as easy to find work as it had been ten or twenty years ago, because many of the small marinas and local businesses had since closed (K. Barker 2010). Furthermore, many of those looking for work simply did not want to be anywhere near the cottage. They wanted to put as much distance as they could between them and their parents, and thus obstinately sought work in the city. In spite of such adolescent contrariness, there was an overwhelming consensus among cottagers that they just had to wait a few years and their progeny would be "magnetized back," as one said, when they realized that life without the cottage is "not very much fun." Alice and Leonard had contemplated selling their cottage, as their adolescent children had not shown any real interest in it for several years. Once this idea was made known to their children, the children protested strongly, insisting that "*their* cottage could not be sold." Their parents bargained that they would not sell it only if their son and daughter contributed their labour to its upkeep and maintenance, and spent more time there.

Some cottagers, meanwhile, did not necessarily want such unmanageable bodies at the cottage, and were happy to have them stay away. They came to the cottage only "to party, drink, and drive like madmen on the lake," one cottager said. There was a consensus among some cottagers that their experience was ruined by so and so who recklessly drove high-powered boats up the lake, threatening swimmers and causing shoreline erosion, or, even more annoyingly for many, by the youth that, as more than one cottager observed, "drove round and round in circles at high speed endlessly on a PWC, 'wake-jumping,' making noise and waves, often doing this in groups of five or six for hours."[14]

Tracy, a woman in her mid-forties who was much younger than many of her neighbours, was approached by one neighbour to sign a petition in an attempt to stop these kinds of youthful activities on their small lake. The majority of those on the lake had already signed, but she refused to do so. She said that those driving the PWCs were there only a couple of days a week, and felt that everyone should "cut them some slack as they were young." It seemed to her that her neighbours had forgotten what it was like to want to do these things, and to have the kind of energy and physical resilience needed to enjoy the speed and thrill of them. Tracy was also angry that those marshalling the petition had not talked with those who were targeted by it. She retorted, "But these are your neighbours, they are people too." Her stance on the petition had resulted in her being shunned by some of her neighbours on the lake, something she was happy to endure.

Several cottagers I talked to highlighted that their first paid jobs had been at a local establishment near their family cottage. Such things were in fact part of a long list of rites of passage that occurred when many cottagers were adolescents: the first stirrings of sexual desires, a first love, first kiss, the loss of one's virginity, a first heartbreak, a first hangover, the first sign that their parents saw them as at least somewhat responsible and let them come to the cottage at some point without them. The intensity of some of these memories was what generated some of the tears I mentioned at the beginning of this chapter. They seemed to carry an emotional wallop quite unlike experiences that happened at home in the city.

Structured recreational activity was another way that a potentially problematic adolescent body could be managed. Various cottagers talked of cajoling their children into taking tennis, golf, or advanced swimming lessons as teens. For others, summer classes at a local fine arts school provided a perfect outlet for creative and expressive energies.

Harry, a cottager now in his eighties, had one particular experience that resulted in what many parents and grandparents wished for as they negotiated the often turbulent years of their children's adolescence. In the 1960s and '70s, "Boshkung was a water skiing mecca, eventually spawning national water ski champions" (M. Perkins 2005, n.p.), some of whom emerged from the semi-professional water ski team, based on the lake, for which Harry had driven the boat. But beyond the many accomplishments of the water ski team, he treasured the values that the kids who participated had gained. They became "extremely strong," and learned to both endure pain and have confidence in their abilities. They learned that the success of the group was larger than their individual discomforts. These experiences forged lifelong friendships among many of the skiers; as Harry said, the experience "drew these kids together ... and now, in the next generation, their children are also very close." Lifelong bonds among the people one met at the cottage were frequently brought to my attention, and these friendships often stretched back to what many saw as their most formative and treasured moments at the cottage, the times they spent there as children.

A Child's Body/A Blissful Body

"I came up July 14th, 1951. I was five weeks old." While unique in its specificity, the precision with which Kevin was able to pinpoint his arrival at the cottage was not so in what it signalled. Several cottagers proudly announced that they had been coming to the cottage long before they were consciously able to remember the experience. Several were sure that they had been conceived there. When they did eventually become cognizant of their world, being at the cottage was already well established as a normal part of their life. It was what you did in the summer. Delores said, "My brothers and I all trundled up on a Friday night as babes in arms and that's the life, that's what we always did." Or as Tim summed it up, "I have been here forever." And it was the desire of several of them to replicate for their own offspring the cottage experience as they had known it in their childhood. Bill said, "It's my roots. I want to make sure that my children and my wife come all summer so that they have what I had when I was a kid." In her divorce settlement, Tracy was adamant about keeping the cottage she and her husband had purchased, so her kids would have the experience that she had had at her parents' Muskoka cottage as a child. Theresa said, "I wish that everyone could have as much fun and as much happiness as a kid that I had coming up here." Such sentiments had prompted several of the people I interviewed to purchase a cottage if the family cottage had not been passed on to them.

As Leslie Paris (2008, 2) posited for children's summer camps, and as I argue in a parallel manner for cottages, they "helped to consolidate the notion of childhood as a time apart, at once protected and playful." Kevin summed it up: "I never had to do any [work] ... sometimes I'd mow the lawn but that would be about it ... I used to romp around a lot, outdoors in a canoe even when I was quite small ... it was nothing to go down the lake to my cousin's by myself."

Time spent at the cottage as a child was an experience many treasured greatly. As Harry suggested, from a child's point of view "you're not in school, you don't have all the rules and all of that kind of stuff that, as kids, you don't particularly love." Cottage time imprinted an understanding of what childhood was assumed to embody: happiness, freedom, adventure, and wonderment at the world. All this was achieved in what was perceived as a secure, manageable, and controlled milieu that tempered fears of the darker elements of nature and at the same time offered protection from the evils of the urban world. A very consistent theme among all those I interviewed was that the cottage was, and still is, a "good place for kids."

The playful cottage body was very often grounded in childhood play at the cottage. I often sensed that, as bodies aged into adolescence and adulthood, many were nostalgic for the innocent and never-ending fun of their earliest days at the cottage. Roberta recalled that her early years at the cottage had been:

barefoot and fancy free ... it was a great, great experience for us ... I have a lot of memories of the cottage ... it was so fun growing up here. And I know some people grow out of the cottage, but I've never grown out of it.

Frances felt that the times spent at the cottage as a child – with a bit of adolescent foolishness thrown in – were what predisposed you to "love the lake." For Emily, life at the cottage was one way to recapture the joys of being a child. She said, "It brings out the child in you and as you get older, you want to keep that child in you and enjoy."

Many cottagers remembered and observed of their own children that at the cottage play groups were not necessarily made up of kids of similar age. Jordan said,

In the city when kids go to school, they focus on their age group and you don't see very much variation in ages of kids that play, chum around together, do activities together. They are usually about the same age, give or take a year. But at the cottage age seems to disappear. And these kids [pointing to those playing in the water in front of his and his neighbour's cottage] are all the way from 9 to 19 years old. I mean they do pair up for certain things. But if it's boating or skiing or water activities or bonfires at night, there is really no age distinction. And there are a lot of kids that chum around together and there can be a five year age difference. It doesn't seem to matter.

Physical age and ability were something that transcended the collective experience of doing playful things together, sowing the seeds of community at the cottage.

Play at the cottage also taught childhood bodies many things. Marnie valued not only the skills her son learned in sailing his raft but also the independence he gained, and the freedom he had to express it at the cottage. She said,

Norman built him a small raft-type boat, just a sheet of plywood on the bottom ... so it was very, very safe. And that boat for him was every-thing. He took a piece of old duck cloth, the stuff that was used to cover mattresses, and turned it into a sail. He sailed between the points here, always in view of us. Then he got a little seven horsepower motor to put on it and oh, were we in business then. And he and his buddies used to meet with their boats out in the middle of the lake and they'd all go in nose-to-nose and chat out there, away from us, as he got a bit older.

From the perspective of someone who had gathered with his friends on the lake as a child, a slightly different realm of learning also went on, which had much to do with the stirrings of sexual desire. Trevor remembered,

> When I was young, every child over about eight had to have his [or her] own boat of some sort. You paddled, rowed or motored to see your friends and often rafted up a bunch of boats in the middle of the bay and talked, sunbathed (we had never heard of skin cancer or ozone), swam and played. The older kids flirted and set up dates and did a lot of splashing and dunking and a little groping.

Despite, or maybe eventually because of, such awakenings, the youthful body as a site of freedom and pleasure was a recurrent theme among cottagers. At the same time, it was also, as I suggested earlier, subject to an array of what Dyck (2008) would call "regimes of discipline." There were many things to learn "to accomplish desired movements ... to guide the disciplining of ... deportment and behaviour" of a cottage body, to ensure that it could have fun at the cottage (Dyck 2007, 114). Regardless, the cottage body as a free body remains a most durable ideological assumption. For many, the cottage body well past childhood years was still seen as free, even if such liberation took on different forms as the lifecycle progressed.

The Liberated Cottage Body

At the cottage, a liberated body was one that had escaped the constraints of the everyday urban world, which implied for many the restrictions of their working and professional lives. The cottage offered respite from the sensory overload and physical congestion of the city. "Freedom," "being free," "carefree," and "escape" were some of the words that were repeatedly used to describe what cottagers felt was central to the joy and pleasure of the cottage. As Richard said, "Life's burden seems to rest in the city. And to me, when you get to the cottage, you can leave it alone."

Liberation took various forms at the cottage, but how one clothed or adorned (or not) one's body seemed for many to be symbolic of numerous other freedoms at the cottage. Henry talked about the "un-disciplining" of his attire at the cottage:

> What we wear around the cottage we would not likely wear to the local store. And even at home [in the city], I don't think we'd dress that way and have our neighbours over. Everything is very casual [–] bathing suits, shorts, sandals. You don't have to worry so much about what's in your closet. And every time we come [for an extended time] we bring additional items of clothing, just in case we go out and do things. But they usually don't get worn. The first day back after our holidays [here], it's always hard to put your shoes back on and go into the office. [Here] you don't have to worry about what you wear on a daily basis. Nobody is judging you by what you wear. It's not important.

In a similar fashion, Lisa took pleasure in that she "could go around without makeup on, even if my neighbours come over to visit." And Becky rejoiced, "You can walk around with your shoes on [in the cottage], doesn't matter if they have sand on them, you can sit on the couch with your bathing suit on ... you can be comfortable." Jack's ageing body also indulged in such un-disciplining at the cottage: "You can sit here half-naked and have no pretensions about who or what you are." And of course, one can be free of clothes altogether if one has sufficient privacy on the lot, or gets up early enough for the morning swim, or indulges in a late evening skinny dip under a full moon – a popular and much-enjoyed practice for some. If one could wear somewhat more informal clothing at the cottage – or, as Fred acknowledged, expose more of one's body – the bikini and, more recently, the minimalist male speedo bathing suit tested the limits of what could be classed as "clothed" at the cottage. The scantiness of these swimsuits varied with certain fashion trends and understandings of what was morally appropriate or aesthetically desirable, but their basic form never failed to titillate and undoubtedly stimulate much adolescent – and, for that matter, adult – sexual desire on hot summer nights or even sultry afternoons.[15] The cottage body was thereby further defined as one of heightened sensual stimulus and response.

Susan rejoiced in letting her body set her schedule: "In the middle of the afternoon, if your body feels like it needs a nap, you can take one." Elaine's emancipation was about "not having to be busy if you don't want to be." Becky claimed that simply being at the cottage "cleared [her] mind." As Emily observed of her family's life at the cottage, "It's just very easy-come, easy-go, there are few rules ... we get up and go off for a walk, they [her son and daughter-in-law] sleep in." Sally, an emergency medical officer, said, "When I come to the cottage, I just can be there and be quiet. I enjoy the complete shutdown."

Deidre saw herself as a different person even if she inhabited the same physical body at the cottage:

> Here you forget your name and who you are and what you do for a living and who you work for, because none of these are important when you are there. You can put behind you those things that tie you down or trouble you during the week ... When you are here you can just escape.

In liberation was transformation. A tired, stressed, distracted, ever-older body could even fleetingly be seen again as something beautiful, sensual, and whole, something accepting of limitations yet indulgent in its very being. An adolescent body was forever changed as it passed through critical rites of passage, and was slowly reclaimed from its recalcitrance. It was a body that gained freedom as it gained competencies, continually learning how to be a cottage body (see Satsuka 1997, 123-26). A childhood body is strategically disciplined to enjoy the adventures, wonderment, thrills, and excitement of the life and world of the cottage – and it remains for cottagers a key symbol of all that the cottage is imagined to be. Even if, as Darlene sanguinely reflected, one has to adapt to the inevitable transitions, and eventually the failings, of the cottage body: "You have to learn to enjoy different things at different stages of your life." Bill summed it up: "It's life. You have to expect change."

Regardless, the ordinary, the habitual, and the progressive disciplining of the cottage body are far from being just "fun, banal and depthless" touristic pursuits (Obrador Pons 2003, 63). Rather, they symbolize the past, the present, and hopes for the future of one's lived bodily experiences, and the cottage is a place where these can be carefully curated.

As I suggested above, losing the capacity to go to the cottage and experience the physical and sensual rejuvenation and bodily pleasures attributed to it, is a cause of considerable anxiety for the ageing body. But there were other anxieties expressed during the interviews, too, and they were not limited to the ageing cottage body. The fearful body counterbalances the liberated and pleasure-laden cottage body. Several things at the cottage clearly challenged prevailing notions of its unflagging good times, but some fearful experiences can stimulate intense sensorial responses, making it difficult to skirt the fine line between pleasure and pain. As Terry Eagleton (1990, 28) suggests, aesthetics can be both emancipatory (pleasurable and freeing) and repressive (painful and confining). While the cottage body indulged in the pleasures of all that was considered beautiful at the cottage, in some cases, it also found itself constrained and anxious in this world of pleasure. To acknowledge the cottage body as something that was at times fearful suggests a somewhat darker side of cottage life.

A Fearful Cottage Body / A Prescient Body

The theme of fear and fearfulness at the cottage percolated through many discussions I had. For some, overcoming fearfulness, or even revisiting its source, generated much intense pleasure for a cottage body, and could help it achieve a state of "flow" (Csikszentmihalyi 1990). Physical activities such as water skiing, wakeboarding, wake-jumping on a PWC, and in the winter, snowmobiling on- or off-trail, over (or on the edge of) open water, had the capacity to induce intense thrills and excitement. Less-technologized activities, such as a distance swim across the lake or bay that challenged the swimmer's strength and endurance, could have a parallel effect.

I wondered whether the fearful cottage body was a prescient one, symbolic of the seemingly ever-expanding realm of concerns about the future at the cottage. Those with ageing cottage bodies who expressed their worries to me could be seen as metaphors for what lay at the heart of much anxiety about life at the cottage. One cannot stop the ageing process; the body will get older and progressively less able. And no matter how much one had initially wanted to continue coming to the cottage, at some point it just might no longer be physically possible. Was a sense of losing control over all that made the cottage a beautiful place at the heart of fearfulness at the cottage?

Many of the disciplining strategies of childhood and adolescent bodies were aimed at alleviating fears of the water, and teaching how to play safely at the cottage. Learning how to swim, wearing a PFD, and knowing how to safely operate a boat or PWC were all part of managing the cottage body in or near the water. As Ken noted after his detailed description of what was involved in the skill and thrill of water skiing, it was important that such activities be "done in a safe manner." In recent years boat safety Transport Canada regulations have been formalized and updated. Now to operate a motorized boat, one must be of legal age and have passed the necessary test to obtain a Pleasure Craft Operators Card (PCOC).[16] The cottage body is now very formally disciplined in this regard. Such strategies are, among other things, intended to heighten awareness of the illegal and often deadly mixture of boats and alcohol (Lifesaving Society, 2003, 2008; Stevens 2008b).[17]

As I have suggested, cottagers have a very ambiguous and even conflicted relationship with nature. While nature was what many people said encapsulated so much of the cottage's beauty, it also caused a great deal of trepidation. Several cottagers said that they no longer went for walks around their cottage because there were too many bears around since the provincial spring bear hunt had been cancelled in 1999.[18] Fear of wild animals in general has prompted some cottagers to install powerful exterior lighting, which others consider nothing more than a form of pollution. At a purely aesthetic level, such intrusive light blocks the beauty of the night sky, thought by many cottagers to be one of the most pleasing aspects of life at the cottage.

The arrival of the West Nile virus in Ontario also caused concern, particularly among those with small children. Alice noted that her daughter was constantly worrying about how to protect her children against the possibility of being bitten by mosquitoes that carried the virus. Hanta virus had arrived with deer mice and their droppings, which news reports acknowledged was difficult for cottagers to avoid.[19] Deer ticks brought Lyme disease, which is expected to appear more frequently in cottage country as global warming continues (Bauer 2006). Additionally, several cottagers noted that they were preoccupied by the increase in the level of ultraviolet rays and the consequent higher potential for rapid and severe sunburn and risk of skin cancer. All of these things were potentially life-threatening, and heightened anxiety about the vulnerability of the cottage body. Many cottagers had been disciplined over time to change their bodily practices to adjust to these new threats and anxieties.

Fear curtailed the physical activity and freedom of many children at the cottage. Delores, Marnie, Ava, and Garry were just some of those who expressed a real sense of loss that children at the cottage today could not experience the absolute freedom of movement that they had known as youngsters, or had allowed their offspring when they were growing up. As Delores observed of her days as a child,

> We'd be gone for hours, playing in the woods ... but now there is the danger of the highway, of abduction, of any kind of real or perceived threat in a changed community. Now if a kid is not seen for ten minutes, it's 'Where's so and so?' Parents are ever vigilant. They weren't like that when I was a kid. Sure we got nails in our feet, but we survived.

Marnie lamented that kids used to have "so much freedom here. I look at the youngsters now and feel so sorry for them because they really do not enjoy the lake as our youngsters did." Children now need to be disciplined to not stray far from the cottage and to be wary of what has become an increasingly unfamiliar environment.

Some felt the reduction in the amount of time that children spent at the cottage contributed to that alienation. Fewer children had the opportunity to spend from the last day of June until Labour Day in September at the cottage, as had been standard practice for many cottagers a couple of decades ago. Several cottagers felt that this prevented children from becoming comfortable and relaxed at the cottage and in its environs. Many mothers now have professional careers or are working full-time in a wide range of jobs and employment situations, and as a result do not have the opportunity to spend the summer at the cottage with their children. The endless days of a childhood summer at the cottage were something many saw as relegated to history. As Trevor lamented, now even children's time at the cottage is tightly scheduled, "with lessons here and lessons there requiring even children to have a Day-timer." It would seem as if the child's body is becoming subject to ever more discipline at the cottage, while at the same time participating in what some would see as a process of moving away from the cottage – by pursuing structured off-site activities that in many cases could just as easily be undertaken in the city.

Some might well suggest that both parents and their children have a certain· fear of copious amounts of free time at the cottage.

Dyck (2000) makes the point that enrolling children in organized activities is perceived by Canadian middle-class parents as giving their children the necessary social and educational capital to be competent, successful, strong, and independent adults. At the same time, this suggests that they are "good" parents, and good parents know that "basic" Canadian values are grounded in the legacies of those who founded the nation. But those ancestries also presumed certain racialized identities. As Jiménez (2006) has suggested, cottage country could be called "the Great White North," a place where one could expect to find specifically raced bodies.

"The Great White North": The Racialized Body

Trevor commented to me, "Once you get north of Highway 9, it's a very uniform cultural mix ... I am not trying to be racist but it's just true. In the whole [of Haliburton] county, I don't think that there are fifteen Korean families; there's a couple of black families, and that is it. Everyone else is WASP." More than one cottager commented to me that what they observed – and for some what they liked – about life at the lake was that they were surrounded there by others like them. Such statements could be taken in many ways, but it is obvious that cottage country – with specific reference to Haliburton here, though in significant measure this applies to all areas of cottage country in Ontario – is overwhelmingly populated by those who, in racial terms, would be labelled white.

Marina Jiménez, a senior writer for Canada's largest national newspaper, wrote an article in 2006 titled, "Why They Call Cottage Country the Great White North." She began her piece with the story of her own mixed-ancestry family's ambivalence (especially that of her non-Caucasian father) about the idea of venturing into Ontario's cottage country. It was deemed too isolated, lacking the pleasures and crowds of an urban environment. The woods were threatening and scary, the lakes dark and uninviting, the wildlife menacing, and the cultural practices of swimming, boating, cottage maintenance, or simply hanging around one's dock seemed entirely unappealing (F1; see also Kaltenborn and Bjerke 2002). She went on to discuss the racial distinctiveness – that is, largely white – that characterizes cottage country in Ontario.

The influx of new Canadians over the last thirty years from places such as China, India, Pakistan, Korea, the Philippines, the Caribbean, and Latin America have not in large measure made their way to cottage country. There are exceptions, but they are relatively few in number.[20] When a group that arranged recreational camps for Muslim youth purchased a small resort shortly after the events of September 11, 2001, on one of the Haliburton lakes, their behaviours were viewed by some as rather curious, and by others with some suspicion. As they did not appear to swim or canoe, some saw them as not knowing how to "use" the lake and wondered why they had chosen such a location; others saw them as perfect new owners precisely because they did not use the lake and thus left it for those who did; and still others eyed them with misgiving in the climate of wide-ranging paranoia about anyone who claimed to be Muslim post-9/11. In essence, they were viewed as not really belonging in Haliburton cottage country.

In my own observations over four years of fieldwork, I noted little racial diversity among those I encountered in public spaces in Haliburton. On the rare occasions that I did see someone who was obviously of non-white ancestry, often they appeared to have married into a family of white cottagers. Toronto-based, Trinidadian-born black Canadian poet Dionne Brand (1997, 73-77) wrote about her experiences driving out of the city and being targeted as or assumed to be someone who did not belong there. She and her travelling companions were, it seemed, out of place in a non-urbanized space of "whiteness."[21]

What does it mean to call Haliburton cottage country a place of whiteness? An ever-expanding body of academic literature would suggest that whiteness is not an uncomplicated notion. John Hartigan (2005, 1) suggests that white people see themselves as "'normal' and racially 'unmarked,'" and so in their eyes their racial identification is invisible. Dyer (1997, 1) observed of those who are white, "Other people are raced, we are just human." Hartigan further argued that whites are obviously "racially interested and motivated," a view that solidifies the implicit assumptions of "whiteness as a *system* of privilege" (Garner 2007, 5, emphasis in original), affirming its "structural position ... [of] power" (Frankenberg quoted in Hartigan 1997, 496; see also Kendall 2006; Levine-Rasky 2002). Blindness to the racial character of being "white" is implicit in the way Canada describes itself and its various categories of citizens. Himani Bannerji (1993, 183) points out that the term "visible minority" is used to identify those "racialized others" (Levine-Rasky 2002, 3) whose skin colour (and, by extension, cultural practices) makes them stand out against the "invisible white, that is non-coloured normative, majority" in the Canadian population. She argues that the intention is that such noticeable individuals "get lost," disappear, just fade away.

However, as with other racial categorizations, white racialness should not categorically be presumed to define "a unifying ideology or a [singular] shared sense of identity" (Hartigan 1997, 500). Hartigan (see also 2005) argues that "the heterogeneous aspects of white racialness" must be acknowledged (see also Bonnett 2000; Levine-Rasky 2002). At the very least, racial identities are, as Faye Harrison insists (1995, 63), "always lived in class- and gender-specific ways." So, some would add, are sexuality, age, (dis)abilities, politics, and religion (Dyer 1997, 3; Levine-Rasky 2002, 4). Caroline Knowles (2008, 168; emphasis added) states that whiteness, as with other racial identities, must be seen as something "produced ... made into (human and spatial) matter in the quotidian scenes and interaction of *daily existence*" in practices that are embedded in the *places* where such activities unfold. She affirms that place must be seen as "an active constituent" of what it means to be white, of producing whiteness. For Knowles, whiteness "is not an intrinsic human property ... [but] it is dynamic, acquired and performed" (2008, 169; 2005). It is, she argues, "like other versions of race ... made in where people go ... and how they comport themselves once they are there" (2005, 103).

Steve Garner (2007, 2) adds an important layer to this link between place and racial identification, specifically with reference to whiteness. To him, "'white' is a marked racialized identity whose precise meanings derive from *national* racial regimes" (emphasis added). This connection between racial identification, place, and national specificities is of direct relevance to my discussion here. The whiteness of the Haliburton cottagers was shaped by their understandings of and attachments to their cottage. Haliburton cottagers exhibited a certain slippage into the presumption of their right to own – and retain – a cottage for future generations of their Canadian family. Their family presumes the opportunity to continue to access the power and thus the resources needed to do so. Such assumptions are implicitly embedded in understandings of what it means to be a real

Canadian, which historically has implied a certain, if rarely articulated, racial ancestry.

I suggest that the sense of a racialized identity among Haliburton cottagers was something that had shifted over time, having been greatly influenced by the urban realities and experiences of cottagers. As noted previously, Luka argues (2006) that Ontario cottage country must be seen as an extension of metropolitan urban space. Knowles (2008, 171) further highlights that no rural/non-urban space can be seen as isolated from the urban reality. Any such spaces are "not a separate sphere from the urban, and it is important to stress rural connectivity, local, national and global, to other (urban) places, people and social contexts ... [r]ural contexts are as networked as urban ones."

When many of the parents or grandparents of cottagers first acquired their cottages, their city homes were in largely homogeneous white, and thus "invisibly raced," spaces – new GTA suburbs or small Ontario towns or cities. Those employed outside of the home mostly worked in similarly "non-racialized" spaces of professional, business, or corporate or public sectors. But with the changes in immigration policies in Canada over the past forty years, many such spaces are now much more racially and culturally heterogeneous. Such diversity has not in any significant respect made its way to the Haliburton cottage. The cottagers I interviewed identified the space of the cottage as a place of whiteness, a space of racial coherence, something that differed from what they observed of the spaces they moved through and occupied in the GTA. As such, despite the academic claims of the embeddedness of the cottage in the realities of the city, this was to Haliburton cottagers yet another quality that distinguished the cottage from the city.

Cottagers I interviewed observed openly that everyone looked like them at the cottage. It was, as one of them said, "a very white place." And to many, this reality gave significant comfort. As one said, "Everyone likes you up here." One cottager who was deeply involved in "diversity issues" in his professional life was observed by his partner to be "the most at home in a very, very white space, the cottage." This tension was something he himself ruminated over.[22] The cottage did, in fact, begin to presume a certain ideological and cultural coherence to some cottagers – white values derivative of a taken-for-granted reasonableness, rationality, self-reliance, and dependability, qualities that reinforced and incrementally enhanced a sense of "deservedness" to be able to enjoy life at the cottage on their terms.[23] For Trevor, these values were reflected in common understandings of space, distance, and "appropriate" interaction:

> The vast majority of cottagers hail from cultures that have a relatively larger interpersonal distance and a cool, formal, almost taciturn cultural background. Many feel uncomfortable in cities because of the crowds and, especially in the GTA, the larger immigrant population that feels too close and too noisy.

His comments flag racial, cultural, and ancestral characteristics of many in the GTA as being different from those he expected to find at the cottage in Haliburton.

Local Haliburton realtors claim that it will take until the second or third generations of these more recently arrived "new Canadians" to "fall in love with cottage country" (Jiménez 2006, F1). But this move is not necessarily so predictably assured. Some would claim that the desire to own a cottage has to transcend generations, that it must extend from an ancestral, almost mythical tradition that lauds the virtues of recreational pursuits in the realms beyond the city. Engaging in these pursuits can be seen to affirm an enhanced class and upwardly mobile social position. In keeping with these imaginings, valorizing these activities would have to be assumed to be part of the racial and cultural stock of the United Kingdom, Ireland, and Western Europe, as over 88 percent of those I interviewed identified these places as their ancestral homes.[24] But these were truly distant links: over 80 percent of those I interviewed were from families who had been in Canada for over three generations, 30 percent for five generations or more. In keeping with the consistency of racial types found at the cottage in Haliburton, the ethno-national ancestry of the cottagers I met was similarly uniform. These were the ancestries whose trademark "cool, formal, almost taciturn" mode of interaction gave Trevor comfort. He knew what to expect in such engagements. He valued the tenaciousness and assurance of such traits, and he was not alone. Ultimately, he saw these characteristics as "fundamentally Canadian," like the Ontario cottage experience.

Diego Muro (2005, 575) has suggested, "Nostalgia will come to the surface during epochs of intense social change." Canada in 2008 was not the Canada of the 1950s and '60s. Canada's immigration policies began to change dramatically in the 1960s. In 1962, the essentially racist "all-white" immigration policy was abandoned, and a point system to encourage the flow of skilled immigrants was created. In the 1950s, 84.6 percent of immigrants were European by birth, but by the mid-1980s, only 15.6 percent of immigrants were born in Europe or the United Kingdom. By 2011, over 70 percent of Canada's immigrants came from Asia, Africa, the Pacific, or the Middle East. Only 14 percent of immigrants came that year from Europe and the United Kingdom.[25] The Citizenship and Immigration Canada website also notes the following:

> Over the period of 1986 to 2001, the number of immigrants living in Toronto increased by almost 800,000 or 65%. In comparison, Toronto's Canadian-born population increased by almost 400,000 or 18%. Immigrants accounted for two-thirds of Toronto's total population growth between 1986 and 2001.[26]

The Canadian population, and specifically that of the GTA, is now much more racially and culturally diverse than it has ever been before. It has moved a long way from the Canada First movement's notions of Canada being solely "a ... country inhabited by the descendants of Northern races" (Haliburton quoted in Berger 1970, 53). The country's population is also much more urban, as 80 percent of Canadians now live in cities; the percentage is even higher for the province of Ontario. This "new" population may challenge the classic, if clichéd, assumption that the opportunity to watch the sun set over the rocky shores of tree-lined lakes with one's immediate family or circle of close friends is somehow a primordial Canadian desire. The assumed link between rusticity and pleasure is not something to be taken for granted. These "new Canadians" do not necessarily have any connection to the mythic narratives of settler experience and all that was endured in laying the foundations of the Canadian nation. And urban technologies, entertainments, and luxury might just be deemed central to any leisured experience; such sentiments are not necessarily restricted to this group. Leaving one's home to live with more modest amenities just may not be appealing: as one representative of this "new" population told me, she had left her original homeland to get away from such basic conditions. Returning to them for the purposes of leisure was not something that she was interested in doing. The cottage demanded of her an uncomfortable, if not altogether unknown, bodily comportment.

In contrast, those I came to know were well conditioned in cottage behaviour by those they knew to be family, a process that in the end assured them that they belonged at the cottage.

6

Family at the Cottage

During my conversation with Caroline, my Australian friend whom I introduced in the first pages of this book, she commented on the intense sense of familial connection among her in-laws. She attributed this connection to their having grown up spending summers living in close quarters at the cottage. She felt that this closeness, a circumstance allowing for little physical distance between family members for several months each year, translated into strong emotional bonds among those who shared this space. She had flagged for me something that the cottagers I would later interview steadfastly affirmed.

When I asked cottagers what they liked most about being at the cottage, a common response was, simply, "family." Or as Sean put it, "It is family up here." Susan summed up what her cottage meant to her: "You come here and you've got your family." Aaron devoted significant time, energy, and resources to the maintenance and upkeep of a cottage for which he did not claim ownership; instead, he insisted it was "the family cottage." For Emily, many things at the cottage were "about family." Isabelle concluded our conversation with an especially powerful statement: "I would not have a family if we did not have a cottage." These references to the role of family at the cottage resonate with what others who have studied the second-home phenomena historically and in other national contexts have found. As Pitkänen (2008, 182) observed of the Finnish experience, "Only the nearest and the dearest [are] accepted as part of it."

Isabelle's statement, however, hints at something less positive that pervades popular, political, and academic discourse about the family: it is a fragile phenomenon. It could disappear. It is not a given. In the discussion that follows, I will use family to refer to the social unit that in broad terms is responsible for the biological survival and social development of its off-spring, or those to whom the state grants such responsibility; and 'family' to denote what the cottagers indicated was something additional, albeit complementary, and which sometimes fully overlapped with the former family.[1]

In 2003, sociologist John Conway's book, *The Canadian Family in Crisis*, came out in its fifth edition. His preface to that edition began, "The crisis of the family in Canada is one of monumental proportions, and it touches [us] all" (xiii).[2] Social historian John Gillis (1996a, 4) observed that "scholars as well as the families they study prefer to think that things have always been better in the past" for families. Meanwhile, Judith Stacey's book, *In the Name of the Family: Rethinking Family Values in the Postmodern Age* (1996), forcefully argues against any lament for the loss of the traditional heterosexual two-parent nuclear family. In her view, society – in her case, American society – needs to embrace and support new forms of family and family life that gained a place in the public consciousness and social fabric, not always willingly, in the late twentieth century. These scholars' critiques, which amount to only the tiniest representative fraction of all that has been written on the contemporary dynamics of families in the Western world, revolve around three dominant themes in the discussion and analyses of this social institution: it is generally imagined to have been a more robust and stable social institution in the past; it is in a present state of crisis, or at the very least transformation; and its future should be seen as more than a little tentative, a reality that could lead to large-scale social disintegration. 'Family,' cottagers would argue, should be understood somewhat differently.

As I mentioned at the beginning of this book, 'family' is a more expansive collective than what is assumed to be the hetero-normative nuclear Canadian family. It can include more than just those with shared biology – as I discovered during my interviews, not all family was necessarily "family." As I have already discussed repeatedly, despite the fact that the cottage is a resolutely modern institution, it was frequently imagined as something that stood outside, or at least in resistance to, all that constituted modernity. In Bruno Latour's (1993) language, many 'family' members would like to imagine themselves as "never having been modern." In my research, 'family' is an example of the anti-modernist imaginings that grounded understandings of the cottage. It had its conceptual and emotional locus and legacy at the cottage and was kept vibrant in large measure by regular return there. The social relations of 'family', which I would argue were embodied in the very cottage itself, were kept alive by all that 'family' shared there. 'Family' was a group narrated into being by the stories and memories of previous generations and experiences at the cottage, life at the cottage in the present, and the hopes for the future of life at the cottage. It was a group understood to be "kin" by the very fact that they shared memories of milestones, repeated annual cycles, and expanses of ordinary life together (Carsten 2000b). It was also understood to be a hetero-normative family; as Bruce Erickson (2010) has argued, "queering" all that constitutes the discourse of the wilderness, nature, nation, and ultimately cottage country is still a goal waiting to be achieved.[3] As such, 'family' was meaningful and treasured and embodied passionately held "habits of the heart" (Tocqueville quoted in Bellah et al. 1985, viii), or, in more prosaic terms, particular 'family' values. Grounded in these values, 'family' believed it had what was needed to resist all that for Conway, Gillis, and Stacey characterized family life in the early decades of the twenty-first century.

But no family is without its secrets. I came to understand that some kin were more welcome 'family' members than others, while others willingly chose to exclude themselves from this collective. In what follows, I discuss 'family' as it extends through time and space, and how familial social relations are embodied and materialized at the Haliburton cottage. I conclude with a discussion of what counterbalanced the "habits of the heart" of 'family' – the glue of 'family' secrets.

There's Family, and Then There's 'Family'

Social historian John Gillis identifies a tension between the two different families that many in the West experience; a family to "live with" and a family to "live by." The former is associated with the public sphere, "often fragmented and impermanent ... [something] much less reliable than the imagined family to live by." The latter, according to Gillis, is "constituted by myth, ritual, and image [and is] forever nurturing and protective (1996b, xv). 'Family' was taken to be the latter, even if it was not unambiguously experienced by cottagers.

In anthropologist Janet Carsten's terms, 'family' is a kin network that is "made," not simply "given" (2004, 9; see also Carsten 2000b), which makes it an example of Bourdieu's practical – as opposed to official – kinship. The former exists

> only through and for the particular functions in pursuance of which they have been *effectively mobilized;* and they continue to exist only because they have been kept in working order by their very use and by maintenance work ... and because they rest on a community of dispositions (habitus) and interests. (1977, 35, emphasis in original)

In Micaela Di Leonardo's (1987, 443-44) terms, "kin work" – something she says is largely done by women – is the locus of activities that lubricate the kinship networks; that turn relationships within the nuclear and extended family into something more than structural links; and allow others who did not necessarily share biology to become part of it if they showed true appreciation of all that such networks symbolize. It was important for 'family' to keep various nodes on this network alive, for as Carsten (2007, 22) observed, "familial history is always partially fragmented between different bearers and paths of transmission, as well as the chance occurrence of family life."

'Family' shared a sense of connection grounded in an understanding that life at the cottage was something to be deeply treasured. The habitus of the 'family' cottage was deeply rooted in what Bellah et al. (1985, 154) call a "community of memory," kinship bonds, shared experiences, and a "sustaining hope for the future."

Anthropologists, sociologists, and historians have repeatedly demonstrated that the family is a social institution that cannot be easily defined. In the 1940s, anthropologist Bronisław Malinowski argued for the notion of the universal family, based on his research in the first decades of the twentieth century. He argued that the social institution of the family could be taken as a universal, because humans everywhere had clear understandings of who could have sexual intercourse with whom and, subsequently, who would be responsible for any offspring of such couplings. These "related" individuals recognized themselves as a distinct grouping, occupied some form of shared space, and shared emotional bonds. Malinowski positioned both fathers and mothers as key players in the endurance of this social unit (Collier, Rosaldo, and Yanagisako [1992] 2001, 12-13).

Understandings of the family have clearly moved a long way from Malinowski's ideas. The cultural specificity of his conclusions has long been obvious, even if the role of women and mothers as key nurturing figures in the lives of their children is one element that remains. Critics of these early reflections on the family challenged any purely functionalist interpretation – that is, the universal family as a predetermined institution, grounded in the biological and socialization needs of the human species (see ibid.). From the comparative perspective of anthropology, it is clear that such a collective is not the only structure that can meet human survival and socialization needs. Even in Western societies there are other institutions that accomplish these tasks. One has only to think of children raised in orphanages and boarding schools, or of the role of long-term care facilities in maintaining the lives of the elderly.

Feminist thinking in the late twentieth century argued that a more helpful framework to understand family is one that recognizes it for what it is: an "ideological unit" that carries "a moral statement" (ibid., 20). The assumed normativity in the Western world of the nuclear family unit of a father (breadwinner), a mother (homemaker), and the biological offspring exemplifies their point. Furthermore, as extended kin became increasingly attenuated throughout the twentieth century, it was expected that any such nuclear family would operate by and large as a social isolate, as Michael Gauvreau argues (2004, 184-85, 187). This winnowing down of family coheres well with the increasing focus throughout the twentieth century on individualism. With its roots in the Enlightenment, modern individualism, some would claim, has turned into a twenty-first-century hyperindividualism fuelled by social media, online communities, and the ever-emerging new technological interfaces seemingly designed to eliminate direct social contact. Those who study the family have questioned whether, with the independence of the individual having continually expanded through the twentieth and now twenty-first century, the family itself will soon become nothing more than a "marginal, residual category in modern society," an institution that will begin to fail most notably as an institution of "cultural transmission" (ibid., 389). 'Family' would appear to be a social unit that is embedded in values intended to counter this prediction.[4]

As the closing decades of the twentieth century unfolded, there was, particularly in North America, a long-overdue recognition that the nuclear heterosexual family was not as much a norm as public discourse and policy had suggested. In fact, single parents, most frequently mothers, head a significant percentage of today's families. An increase in the number of blended families with the easing of divorce laws, gay and lesbian marriage/ parents, surrogate mothers, a wide array of new reproductive technologies facilitating conception outside of the human body, and a surge in the search by adoptees for their birth parents due to changes in legislation and policy further challenge any simplistic notions of what constitutes a family in the Western world (see for example Carsten 2000a; Conway 2003, 20-22; Edwards 2000; Stacey 1996).

These realities have prompted demands from conservative, often religious, groups for public policy and legislative changes to champion a return to family values.[5] Critics of this conservative rhetoric begin with the fundamental question, "Whose family values?" Why should it be assumed that there exists a ubiquitous and commonly validated set of moral and social values, and that the necessary crucible of their promulgation is the modern nuclear family? Mid-twentieth-century popular television featured families – the Cleavers (on *Leave it to Beaver*), the Reeds (on *The Donna Reed Show*), the Andersons (on *Father Knows Best*), or the Cunninghams (on *Happy Days*) – that embodied certain biological, social, and moral absolutes. These idealized values presumably formed the glue that held these social units together.

At their most basic, such ideas are grounded in particular cultural, ideological, class, and gender assumptions (see Popenoe 1988, 73-79). This is not to deny that there were many Canadian families in the postwar period that, at a biological and broad social level, fit the model of the nuclear family – in fact, many of the cottagers I spoke with came from them. At the same time, this fact does not necessarily presume that any defined set of values or socialization processes were rigidly adhered to by such collectives. For example, there could be no expectation that members of these families would agree on "normal" gendered behaviours or desired familial responsibilities and expectations, or even that a cottage was a "good" place to take one's family in the summer.

Even when considering the pluralities of its configuration, the Western family remains embedded in the capitalist system, and is broadly understood to stand in opposition to the world of business and commerce (see Collier, Rosaldo, and Yanagisako [1992] 2001; Gillis 1996b). As a social institution, with the rise of the urbanized, industrial, market-driven world, the family steadily lost its role as a site of the production of economic capital. The family in this dualism came to be understood as characterized by "affection and love," "cooperation rather than competition," to be "enduring rather than temporary," not "contingent upon performance," and "governed by feeling and morality rather than law and contract" (Collier, Rosaldo, and Yanagisako [1992] 2001, 17-18). Family evolved into the institution of nurturance, whose role was to ensure the biological survival and social development of its members.[6] Gillis (1996b, xvi) states that in the late twentieth century, this role took "on a greater cultural significance in mediating tensions and contradictions built into a political and economic system based on the values of competition [and] instant gratification" – a role, he claims, that families found "difficult, if not impossible to sustain on a daily basis." In contrast to Gillis's families, 'family' would not find it quite so burdensome. 'Family' is something special, greatly aided by the belief that there is no such thing as pejorative daily life at the cottage (1996b, xvi-xvii).

'Family' incorporates elements of what Jeanette Edwards concluded about the residents of the Lancashire town Bacup and their ideas of kinship. In Bacup, kinship emerges from "an interplay between the biological and the social rather than an elaboration of natural facts" of shared biology. Cottage 'families,' as with Bacupian kinship, presume the former but accentuate the latter (Edwards 2000, 28; see also Edwards and Strathern 2000, 162; Schneider 1968; Stone 2004; Strathern 1981). Paralleling what Edwards and Strathern see as the effect of kinship in an English village, 'family' sets limits "on how far ... connections" can be claimed and under what circumstances they can be claimed (2000, 159). In Carsten's terms, 'family' at the cottage was about relatedness, "a term that allows [movement] away from ... ideas concerning kinship in terms of biological connection" (quoted in Stone 2004, 251; see also Carsten 2000a, 1-36). To be 'family,' one's biological connection is often a starting point, but primarily one must be committed to all that makes cottage life meaningful and thus is understood to be fundamentally good.

In reality, biological kin may not in the end be any more passionate than those who arrive at the cottage lacking biological connections to 'family,' but it was assumed they had the potential to be. In my research it was evident that blood relatives were rather like "a cup half-full," in part because of what was expected to be their "natural" response to the cottage, but also because their socialization often began at a very early age. Blood ties could be seen to generate forms of social, cultural, and, ultimately, emotional capital for potential 'family' members. They situated individuals in networks that fostered reciprocal ties and expectations about what being a cottager was all about, and they exposed individuals from their earliest moments to what was required to successfully navigate the cottager's habitus, where the cottage functioned as a centric force for 'familial' social relations.

Cynthia Comacchio's (2000, 218) description of family as a "multi-dimensional symbol system" resonated with what I was hearing from cottagers about 'family.' Within such a system, I wondered what the symbolic referents of 'family' were, and if the 'family' functioned in Gillis's (1996a) terms as a site of "cultural production," a crucible capable of nurturing desired moral and aesthetic values, and social relations deemed healthy and tenacious. Those 'family' members I came to know would resoundingly answer: yes.

"It's a Good Thing": An Extended 'Family'
In his critical review of the research of social scientists and historians on the family in Western society generally and in postwar Canada more specifically, social historian Michael Gauvreau (2004, 385) noted that the "most significant aspect of postwar discussion of the family by Canadian social scientists was the conviction that the isolated nuclear family shorn of ... kin, and intergenerational connections ... was synonymous with modernity itself." In postwar modern Canada, living with an intimate knowledge of one's extended kin was thought to be the exception. Life at the cottage, however, could for many be seen as an exception to that exception. As I and others (see Luka 2006; Stevens 2008a, 2008b) acknowledge that the cottage is a modern experience, no matter how rustic or anti-modern its imaginings, I also have to assume that none of these researchers who claimed this separation hung out at a cottage, where for many "kin and intergenerational connections" were central to the experience. These very links are what made 'family.'

Many of those I interviewed began what I called the "origin narratives" of how they came to be cottagers by situating their story at a particular cottage, or on a specific lake, or in a 'familial' legacy of Ontario cottaging. Extended kin, reaching back at least one generation, were central to many of these narratives. For example, for Laura's family, life at the cottage had always been about extended family, reaching back three generations. It was at the cottage that Laura's grandmother had gotten to know her great-aunts and -uncles, when they all established cottages on the same lake. And these relatives were later made real to Laura through the stories her grandmother told about them. She noted that even when her grandmother was a young woman, it was otherwise hard to get to know these relations, as none of them lived near each other in the city, particularly during the interwar years. Several of these origin narratives began somewhere other than Haliburton. Isabelle had spent her childhood summers at her grand-parents' Muskoka cottage, which had links to her great-grandfather. He started the 'family' tradition of the cottage. She said,

> My great grandfather started cottaging up in the 1800s ... He bought a whole lot of land [up there]. He had nine children so he gave them each a section of land for their cottages ... I used to stay with my Nana and Pop ... I fit right in. I loved it because my cousins, [actually] my grandfather's sister, my great-aunt, owned the island across [from my grandparent's cottage].

Isabelle went on to explain that her grandparents' property had, however, not been passed on through her family, as it had been sold following her mother's untimely death and her father's resultant disinterest in returning there. In time, her own cottage became the centre of her attention, and those whom she understood as 'family' shifted to her husband's family.

Leonard's grandfather had owned recreational property in eastern Ontario and his great uncle had a cottage in Muskoka. As a child, he was invited to spend summers in both places. And Drew's earliest and dearest memories of 'family' were based on the times his parents rented a cottage on Pigeon Lake in the Kawarthas when he was a child:

> The times there [were] when we had the most fun. We got to know our relatives because we lived some distance from [Lakefield] and most of our relatives are from around there. So it meant that we knew my grand-mother, my uncles, my aunts, my cousins ... It was just a very special time.

These links to extended kin worked to situate the cottage/cottaging experience in Lash and Urry's (1994) "glacial time." And they were therefore relished for their "weight of history," the memories they embodied, and the desire that they would endure "for many generations' time" (ibid., 250). 'Family' affirmed the cottage as a place rich in "social time" – its bonds were grounded in "sociability, idle talk, [the] luxury [of time spent together]" (Weber quoted in ibid., 226, 229).

In the early days of their courtship, Isabelle was thrilled to learn that several of her future husband's extended family owned cottages on one lake in Haliburton. Eventually she and her husband jumped at the chance to buy property there, and they eventually built their cottage. She was keen to replicate her childhood cottage experiences among an extended multi-generational family. Peppered throughout my visit with her were references to the relationships her children had with her husband's parents, uncles, aunts, nephews, and nieces, many of whom currently owned cottages on the same lake. This 'family' legacy had begun forty-five years ago, when her husband's uncle had first bought a cottage there.

Enamoured with the idea of spending time at the cottage, based on his childhood experience, Leonard bought a piece of property on a Haliburton lake in 1955. He was nineteen years old, and as he was too young to legally sign the papers, he needed his father to do so.

Drew and his family lived outside of Canada for thirty years, but they never failed to return for a few weeks in the summer to a friend's cottage in Haliburton. These experiences kept alive Drew's memories of his early childhood at his relatives' cottage. As he approached retirement, he sought out property in Haliburton, the region that he and his family had come to love, on which to build a cottage. When interviewed, he was in the final stages of seeing this dream become a reality.

Kevin's Haliburton origin narrative began with his grandparents:

My grandparents had bought 900 feet of frontage on [a Haliburton lake]. My father built a cottage on part of it. He started building a cottage before he was married so that would have been '48 or '49. Then he married and I came along so he modified the cottage, changed it and made it bigger and we went there for summers. No electricity, no running water, no heat. Later I spent from the age of ten on complete summers [there] because my grandmother taught at University of Toronto, so she had summers off and my grandfather was retired, so I just came with my grandparents.

At the cottage, 'family' took the time to look inward, and implicitly back-ward, rather than constantly being distracted by the outside world and its forward orientation. It was an experience that Delores imagined as paral-leling early pioneering ancestral lives on the farm. She imagined her youth at her 'family' cottage to be like

> going back to the old farm days and it was all family and very close. You had all ... the "rellies" over and that was your social circle ... the aunts and uncles, you would see a lot more. If my family had been at home [in the city], my grandparents would not have been with us. They would be at their house. I would be in my room reading a book; my brother ... would be in his room making a little model; and Bruce, the eldest, would be downstairs watching TV. We wouldn't be unified. We would be a family living in a home engaging in separate activities.

Not all cottagers I interviewed had multi-generational histories at a cottage. 'Family' thus did not always reach very far back, though it could extend laterally. Roberta told me how her parents had come to acquire the property on which they later erected their cottage:

> On a piece of land that my uncle Herbert ... farmed ... we built the cot-tage in 1936. There was this little piece, fifty feet or so, I can't remember what it measured, but he suggested it was a good place for a cottage. He used to bring the cows up here to the stream for them to drink and there was always a breeze on this hill. So anyhow, we bought it [from him].

If aunts and uncles could be considered 'family,' so could cousins. Some cottagers considered their cousins whom they knew only at the cottage their best friends, and thought of them only incidentally as biological relations. The relationship that Roberta had had over fifty years with her cousin Grace was "like that of a sister." When Grace died, Roberta thought of selling the cottage where she and her cousin had shared so many memorable times together. Then Grace's brother, who still lived adjacent to the cottage, reminded her, "Well, I'm still here." She decided not to sell.

Strong bonds between cousins were not limited to those who had had close relationships over many decades. Isabelle's children were very close to their cousins. More recently, her daughter's children were developing bonds with her cousin's children, expanding the familial network to the third generation. Marianne described the endless tears her young son shed at the end of every summer when he had to say goodbye to his cousins. He countered suggestions that he would see them again at Thanksgiving and Christmas in the city with the point that those visits would be for only "two or three days." He longed for the extended periods when they could be together again, which happened only at the cottage.

Several first-generation cottagers had the potential to turn family into 'family.' Those who did not yet know all that the cottage could foster needed to be inculcated with its virtues. Beyond parents and children, siblings were another group ripe for conversion. In the world of the modern nuclear family, relationships with siblings can wither over time as brothers and sisters go about establishing their adult lives centred on their own nuclear families, often some distance from their natal home. But the cottage was repeatedly identified as a place to keep those bonds alive and vibrant, or even reinvigorate them. Hannah noted,

> I am from a large family. But we have had a lot of occasions where we've had the entire family [at the cottage] for a weekend or a couple of days to celebrate a special birthday or anniversary ... Those times were nice, because it's very seldom that everyone has a chance to get together.

Anna and her siblings shared ownership of their Haliburton cottage. They could not afford to each buy one individually, but as a collective they were able to do so. When asked if such an arrangement caused any problems, she and her ten-year-old son Cameron replied,

> *Anna:* No, we love it.
> *Cameron:* We love sharing with other people.
> *Anna:* The kids are all cousins, so it's really fun for them, because that provides them a lot more time together than they might get, certainly in

the city. Normally we can get together briefly on birthdays, but up here we get to stay together overnight and have weekends together. It's fun.
Cameron: All of us live so far away from each other. [At the cottage] it is pretty much the only time we see them.
Anna: It's actually a big thing about our cottage. The fact that we do own it together is a big thing for us. It's a good thing.

Roberta had inherited her parents' cottage, where she and her two brothers had spent their childhood summers with their mother. Her brother, who as she said had "more or less married the Maritimes" because his wife was from there, had visited the cottage only sporadically for many years when his own children were growing up. But once retired and a widower, he went to the cottage for a three-week visit one summer and didn't leave until it was time to close up in early September. He returned again the following spring, announcing that he was staying for the summer. When Roberta's city friends asked, "Is your brother still with you at the cottage?" she replied, "Well, what do you do with a fellow who thinks it's utopia, it's ecstasy?" She felt that he had rediscovered what he had known as a child as he relived their shared memories. And she remarked later to me, "every cottage needs a man." He always remembered her birthday in the summer, and was happy attending to repairs on the property. His daughter was now bringing her family to the cottage in the summer – as Roberta said, "moving the experience along through the generations."

Several grandparents I interviewed made similar comments. They took great pleasure in watching their grandchildren discover the joys of the cottage. Of particular note were grandchildren who wanted to come and stay at the cottage, independent of their parents, affirming bonds across multiple generations and, ideally, the future of the cottage as an important place in the 'family.' The cottage was often the place where grandparents got to see their grandchildren for extended periods. Richard's family cottage had been expanded so it could comfortably accommodate three generations: Richard's mother (the original owner following his parent's divorce); Richard, his wife, and his sister; and his two adolescent daughters. Richard noted that it was the only time that he and his family got to spend time with his mother, other than seeing her at infrequent family weddings or funerals.

Parents took equal pleasure in watching the love of the cottage catch fire in their children, often clearly articulating a sense that they were playing an important role in passing along the legacy across multiple generations. As Deidre said of her now-deceased father-in-law's dream:

> I'm just glad that my father-in-law bought this place sixty years ago. When you think about [the] sacrifices he made to do that ... back then he wasn't making a lot of money. He always had two jobs. He raised a family with four kids. It was a tremendous sacrifice for him to do this. And now his family is continuing the institution ... and it will be sent out to the next generation.

As the cottage could knit together relations across generations and into the realm of extended family, it could also foster closer ties among members of a nuclear family. Jacob remembered that as he was falling asleep in the car on the Friday night drive to the cottage, his parents "would always talk the whole way up." His mother noted that it was a time when she and her husband could catch up after a busy week, uninterrupted as the kids slept in the back seat.

Roger summed up the role that the cottage had played in nurturing his 'family' into being as that of a

> focal point ... It is a place of one hundred thousand memories. It is the place where I brought my girlfriend who became my fiancée, who became my wife, who had my children. It's just a huge part of my life. It's a core of so many things.

From the point of view of children, the cottage was the place where they could get close to their parents. Richard and Sam, both long-term Haliburton cottagers, told of parallel experiences with their fathers at the cottage. Their fathers were both theologians, both with demanding professional lives. These pressures allowed Richard and Sam little space in their fathers' lives for most of the year. But when the family came to the cottage for several weeks each summer, that all changed. They went fishing, canoeing, played games together, did repairs and maintenance as a team, and just generally spent time together. In Carsten's (2004) terms, these men were the fathers Richard and Sam were "given," but at the cottage they became fathers that were "made." At the cottage, each of their fathers turned from reverend to dad, whom they could get close to. Such was the stuff of deeply treasured memories of 'family' for these two men.

The next generation of potential 'family' members literally can be produced at the cottage. Several cottagers I spoke with regaled me with stories of how they had calculated that they were conceived at the cottage (see Illouz 1997, 141). Other new additions were often officially welcomed into the 'family' there. Cottage weddings were popular among 'family,' and provided an opportunity to introduce to a betrothed all that the experience meant to his or her in-laws-to-be. Garry and Lana built their cottage after their children were well into adolescence. So they were thrilled when their son, who had returned to the cottage infrequently – having chosen to live on the West Coast for most of his early adulthood – told them that he wanted to be married at their cottage. His fiancée from the West Coast knew little of the experience but had agreed to this idea. Lana and Garry responded as if they were welcoming home a prodigal son. They thought the symbolic role that the cottage would gain in the young couple's lives, as the place where they exchanged their wedding vows, boded well for the full incorporation of both of them into the 'family' as their marriage matured. As Garry concluded, even though his son had not spent much time there, this decision signalled that it was "a really significant part" of who he was.

There was no question in Trevor's mind as to whether or not his partner Brenda was 'family.' Trevor and Brenda had grown up at neighbouring cottages on the same lake, enjoying summers in their childhood and youth together. They drifted apart as they entered adulthood, married others, then both divorced. But they had never lost touch with each other, as they returned regularly to their parents' cottages over the years and Brenda eventually came to live there permanently after having inherited it following her parents' deaths. As romance bloomed, Trevor soon became a regular weekend visitor at his neighbour's cottage. Their shared passion for the cottage was a firm base on which to establish a long-lasting relationship. He intended to retire to live at the cottage with Brenda year round.

Those who married into 'family' and made clear their love of the cottage were truly celebrated. Isabelle said of her son-in-law,

He's Serbian, he's first-generation Canadian. His Mom and Dad think he's crazy. They've got a trailer forty-five minutes from London, it's on a man-made lake and they say, "This is nice. Why do you travel four hours, that's stupid, you're crazy!" He says, "Ah, but once you're up there," he says, "it's not crazy. It's beautiful." He just loves it. So it makes us feel good to see him so excited about being here.

Sam's daughters took pride in the fact that their respective husbands, despite having no cottaging experience in their family or cultural backgrounds, had come to truly appreciate it. Sally's husband, Patrick, originally from India via the United Kingdom, didn't like the water and was not familiar with the notion of a vacation, but he had learned that spending time there was a good thing to do. One could sit and talk, read, and unwind in the company of 'family.' He particularly liked the fact that it was a time when 'family' gathered in one place.

Frances took great pleasure in hearing her brother-in-law, originally from Australia and whom she said had travelled the world, say to her one day as he lay in the hammock at the front of her cottage, "This is one of the two most beautiful places on earth." And when she asked him where the other one was, he said, "I don't know, I'll tell you when I find it."

Other non-biological kin, what anthropologists would at one time have called fictive kin, were viewed somewhat skeptically until they declared and demonstrated their love of the cottage. Neil told of how his godson Adam was steadily socialized by Neil and his children to get rid of his fear of the water and his complaining about bugs, and the absence of TV and internet. Adam was eventually transformed into someone who was always asking when he could next go to the cottage. Love of life at the cottage opened the door to strong emotional and social attachment to his 'god-family.'

'Family' was materialized, embodied, and materially embodied at the cottage, giving substance to Comacchio's (2000, 218) statement that family can be seen as a "material, embodied set of social relations." The social relations of 'family' were materialized in such things as the culture of everyday life and leisure, the furnishings, and even the cottage itself. The things 'families' physically did together at the cottage, including the rituals they enacted, made their social relations real. 'Family' was materialized in the collective interaction of bodies at the cottage, and it was embodied in material things there.

Embodying 'Family'

'Families' *do* things together at the cottage. For anthropologist Joëlle Bahloul (1996, 136, emphasis in original) "repeated interactions" of 'family' articulate the "*practice*' [of the cottage]" where practice, following Bourdieu (1977), is taken to mean "its social making by its agents, who actively inhabit ... rather than [simply occupy] fixed and preestablished structures" (Bahloul 1996, 144). Paralleling the remembrances Bahloul collected about an Algerian house forcibly abandoned by a Jewish family in the mid-twentieth century, the cottage is remembered by 'family' as the "symbolic locus for the *embodiment* of social practices experienced [there]; it constitutes a system of 'bodily practices'" (ibid., 136, emphasis in original; see also Connerton 1989; Lakoff 1987). In John and Jean Comaroff's (1985) terms, what goes on at the cottage are "tangible practices of identity."

The vast majority of things that cottagers talked about doing were both collective and physical. The individual body was rarely alone and inactive at the cottage. Such "bodily practices" of kinship produced social relations of 'family' (Carsten 2004, 37). These shared activities cultivate affective bonds, mutual amiability, friendship, and a sense of a shared collectivity, all of which fed a sense of responsibility and obligation to one another.[7] In Urry's (1995, 131) terms, they constitute the necessary sociality of the touristic experience: what people want to consume in these experiences is "a particular social composition of other consumers," in this case 'family,' which can also include friends and neighbours.

In my research, I discovered that over time, some of the things 'family' did together became layered with meanings beyond any obvious purpose or objective that they may at one time have had. These repeated doings became ritualized. They are what Bellah et al. (1985, 154) would call "practices of commitment," as they "define the patterns of loyalty and obligation" that affirm that life at the cottage is meaningful. In Relph's (1976, 32) terms, "any form of repetitive tradition reestablishes place and expresses its stability and continuity." Those I interviewed clearly acknowledged that the cottage was something far more than just a structure to provide shelter. How could it not be? It was a second home. Its ritualized role therefore outweighed its practical purpose.

'Family' rituals became things that *had* to be done with regularity and consistency at the cottage. Gillis (1996a, 15) said, "Rituals provide not only those moments when families are actually with one another but, more important, when they imagine themselves as family" – or, in my usage here, as 'family'. They played a key role in defining the particularities of each 'family' experience, because they constituted a form of "insider" knowledge – only 'family' knew what had to be done and why. They constituted important parts of 'familial' legacy; they symbolized a certain constancy, a certain continuance of what 'family' valued, or what Bellah et al. called "habits of the heart." Such habits must be understood in their contexts.

So what were some of these rituals? Many were very simple acts: saying certain phrases when the final turn into the cottage driveway was made; making only Grandma's dressing to stuff the turkey when the 'family' gathered at the cottage for Thanksgiving; having Christmas, Thanksgiving, and Canada Day with 'family' at the cottage; ending the summer with a 'family' visit to the Kinmount Fall Fair; having an annual 'family' picnic in late August; preparing one's marshmallow stick in a particular way and ensuring that the bonfire was laid out in a certain way; going for a swim immediately upon arriving at the cottage; ensuring that you have a drink in your hand and are sitting on the dock by 5:30 each night to celebrate the day at the cottage; saying goodbye to the lake and the diving rock before leaving on Sunday. Other rituals involved the annual opening and closing of the cottage in the spring and fall, respectively.

Rituals have social effects on both those who enact them and those who observe them. But ritual behaviours are also in some way supposed to accomplish things. They send a "message of pattern and predictability" (Myerhoff 1984, 350). Saying goodbye to the lake each week, for example, could be seen as a proclamation of thanks for all the fun that had been had there, but also as an expression of desire for the opportunity to have those positive experiences repeated on the next visit. When queried, cottagers suggested that rituals denoted a connection across generations; a promise of a return to the cottage; an omen that each visit would be a good one. They cited the richness and meaningfulness of the cottage experience and a desire for its continuance; rituals were something that might just aid and abet any divine or supernatural powers in working towards these goals.

There were some repeated behaviours that might be seen at first as rituals of penance. But ultimately they too were about assuring good times at the cottage. These rituals were largely lacking in any notion of magic or spiritual powers. They involved much basic physical labour. As Deborah reported:

> I've always had high expectations of my daughters kicking in and doing things. I'd always do lists and just say, "Okay, you know, today's going-home day – bathrooms need to be cleaned, the floors need to be vacuumed or swept and washed." On Sunday morning the list just came out. [The cottage] is cleaner than the house [in town] because it got a good cleaning every Sunday ... We'd come back a few days later and it'd be so nice and clean. I want them to appreciate what they have and respect it, and have ownership [of it] ... not to be pampered. I guess it is a horrible ritual, but it works.

Other cottagers spoke of being met at the door upon arrival at the 'family' cottage with a list of things that needed doing that weekend. Everyone agreed that there was always something that needed repairing, painting, replacing, or installing at the cottage. Particularly for the men in the 'family,' physical labour and its predictability became a ritualized part of cottage life. Such labours were the prelude necessary to ensuring good times at the cottage. If the septic pump was broken or if squirrels or mice had invaded the cottage and wreaked havoc, a visit there could be far from enjoyable. Such tasks could additionally serve as a bonding experience between 'family,' as the labour was shared and the final product a joint accomplishment. Sophia noted that working with her husband at the cottage was "teamwork, it was very reinforcing [of our] partnership that we were doing all this together." To Deborah, such teamwork was "like a Mennonite barn-raising," where the collective action exceeded the sum of any individual labour.

'Families' do many things together at the cottage, but not all of them take on the character of ritual. Some were singular events that constituted vital moments in 'family' relations. Ben and his father built a boat together, the one used for many years to ferry the family and their belongings to their cottage, which did not have road access. Ben said, "The best time I spent with Dad was building the boat, and it all came about because of the cottage." His comments echo those of Richard and Sam about their theologian fathers.

Many put great emphasis on the physical sports and recreational activities in which 'family' participated. Swimming, tobogganing, water skiing, skating, tubing, wakeboarding, canoeing, boating, golfing, snowmobiling, hiking, fishing, badminton, volleyball, and horseshoes were just some of the activities and games that brought 'family' together. Others talked of board games, card games, or of doing jigsaw puzzles. Neil noted,

> Stephanie and I will walk, sometimes one of the kids will join us for a walk in the winter, but typically we walk by ourselves ... [then] we'll get into a big Rummoli or Scrabble game. I think our kids are a little exceptional inasmuch as they've kind of grown up with us kind of pushing the family games and the board games. They say to each other, "Oh, they want us to play." And then they do and they enjoy it.

Neil's description of 'family' time at the cottage highlights a couple of aspects of why, as some cottagers would argue, these shared, often physical activities were what made 'family' time at the cottage so much more treasured than any other family gatherings held throughout the year. At the cottage, individuals were allowed opportunities to go off and do things separate from others. The frequency with which 'family' gathered at the cottage brought with it a familiarity with what the 'familial' expectations were, allowing for some flexibility with their compliance. Stephanie noted that sometimes her son did not want to play board games with them, and they just let him do "his own thing." 'Family' had the potential – albeit one not always met – to be far less of a pressure cooker for any gender, generational, in-law, sibling, or extended kin tensions that might simmer beneath the surface (see Gillis 1996a).

Some activities that bonded 'family' together simply addressed basic human needs. The preparation, at times the gathering, and always the sharing of food was one frequently cited example of something 'family' did together. Such activities are fundamental actions of nurturance and socialization. As Anna said of her extended family, "We eat together lots" at the cottage. The food that was shared could be quotidian or it could be special feasts and treats. It could be the butter tarts made by Delores's mother, the hot dogs roasted at Laura's family's weekly bonfire, the potlucks organized by Isabelle for her husband's summer birthday, or the August long-weekend barbecue hosted by Jack and Lily. Marnie set the direction of her grandson's future career when she taught him how to make pastry one rainy afternoon at the cottage. He paid his way through university working in restaurant kitchens, then went on to become a professional chef, building on the countless summer afternoons when he and his grandmother had baked pies, made jam, and prepared meals together at the cottage. Isabelle told stories of the blueberry picking excursions her grandmother regularly organized with her grandchildren. She would then proceed to make real blueberry pies, while the grandchildren mimicked her actions with the mud pies they made outside. And while her handiwork would be enjoyed by the whole 'family', the children's was appreciated and judged as to the quality of their decoration when 'family' gathered to eat the real pie. Another food foraging experience that was fondly remembered was fishing with one's grandfather, father, or favourite uncle. Several cottagers remembered that these fish tasted like no other, a sensuous experience that could never be recaptured as they grew older.

Preparing and eating 'family' meals together may not have seemed worthy of note among an older generation of cottagers. But as Deborah, a cottager in her mid-forties, observed of her husband and their teenage daughters,

> We will actually eat a meal together here, instead of [each eating a meal alone] at home. And I can have help here [with the cooking] ... the kids are great. They are not always available at home; they're very involved with so many things. So when we are here, I have great help. Ed [my husband] loves to cook. He's a phenomenal cook. It's more of a together time.

Susan, also a middle-aged cottager, agreed:

> I always tell people that when we eat here as a family nobody gets up from the table for an hour and a half. We'll eat dinner and we'll be talking for a couple of hours after it is over. The conversation is still going.

It may just have been that shared meals at the cottage had become so meaningful to family *because* they had at one time been the assumed norm, and so these activities took on a symbolic role with a younger generation. Sharing a meal was presumed to bond 'family' together. When engaged in any of these activities – sports, games, cooking, fishing, eating, cleaning, repairs, and construction, even joining in rituals – as Adrian said, "you talk, you communicate with each other."

Smell was a sense that cottagers indicated as a powerful mnemonic of 'family', particularly cooking smells: the smell of toast cooking on Grandma's woodstove or of raspberry pies – made with berries everyone helped pick – baking in the woodstove Mom had used for years; the smell (and sound) of freshly caught fish – a "shore lunch"[8] – prepared by Grandpa, or of freshly roasted corn pulled from the bonfire, which Dad prepared every Saturday during the late summer; and, of course, fresh coffee brewing in the morning.

The conversations that emerged when 'family' did things together obviously covered a wide range of topics, including commentaries on the state of the world. Marnie said, "The problems of the world have been solved sitting in front of our fireplace at the cottage." They also covered topics of a much less weighty nature: the events of the day, the ubiquitous Canadian fascination with the weather, the logistics of meals, arrival of guests, the various comings and goings of 'family' at the cottage over the weekend or over the summer, or the beauty of the sunset last night – the list is endless. Furthermore – and this was something that many greatly valued and specifically noted – 'families' shared stories about the cottage. Of her memories of such storytelling times, Marnie remarked, "There are lots of funny stories. It is absolute hilarity when we get going on them. Someone should write them down." Tales about past times at the cottage: the first time a 'family' member caught a fish – and then had to fillet it; or got up on water skis or swam across the bay; or how everyone endured Grandpa's snoring; or how embarrassingly loud Mom cheered as her children won three-legged or sack races at the annual picnics – this was the stuff of good 'family' stories. Several cottagers seemed to have a practical joker in the 'family' whose antics and pranks provided good fodder for storytelling sessions. Short-sheeting beds,[9] hiding the clothes of those skinny-dipping, stealing the paddles for the canoe left behind by the young lovers who thought that they were alone on the island, or listening to the swearing at the fizzing sound, prompted by the Alka Seltzer tablets that somehow had found their way into Grandma's "thunder mug", as she relieved herself in the middle of the night – these constituted good 'family' stories. This list of anecdotes highlights what many of these stories centre on: bodily functions and actions. In contrast, those who were non-familial visitors to the cottage were often afraid of doing bodily things such as swimming in the lake. They feared for their physical safety as they thought deer would eat them, or they worried that there would be a bear waiting to attack from behind every tree, or, desiring to satisfy their gustatory cravings, they wondered where the nearest cappuccino might be.

The telling and retelling of these stories helps narrate 'family' into being. Through my interviews, I discovered that all the physical activities that 'family' engaged in at the cottage worked to produce social relations seen to have a distinctive character. In Knowles's (1996, 189) terms, 'family' "is generated in the minutiae of [its] daily performance [at the cottage] in the lives of its members; actions and interactions are [its] (unwritten) narratives." 'Family' was imagined, according to Gillis (1996b, xv), to be "forever nurturing and protective," demonstrating "cooperation, lasting loyalty, and moral consideration." The shared activity of individual bodies produced the metaphorical collective body of the 'family', which embodied a certain degree of ambivalence about the possession, or not, of shared biology. This collective body was made material in other ways at the cottage. Possibly, Miller's (1998, 150) description more aptly captures 'family' bonds: they can be described as not romantic love but "love as the ideological foundation for the complex relations that exist between household members ... which may be [those] that [are] derive[d] from the given and negotiated relationships of kinship as [much from] the sought [after] relationships of partners and friends ... [they are those that are] just-about-good-enough-if-you-make-allowances."

Materializing 'Family'

Sophie Chevalier (1999, 83, 92-93, emphasis added) suggests that French family country residences are the "materialization of family identity [as they] contain [the familial] lineage ... *anchoring* it to a particular locality."[10] I argue that the cottagers I interviewed considered their 'family' cottage as just such a material anchor. It grounded them on a particular Haliburton lake. The cottage was the place where they felt they belonged; it was "home" for many of them.[11] And as one of McCracken's (1989, 176) interviewees aptly observed, "You just can't have a family without a home." 'Families' who had owned their cottage for more than one generation asserted this emphatically, for as Chevalier (1999, 92) noted, "time plays a fundamental role" in constructing this sense of belonging. For her, the "process of 'anchoring' is necessarily long."

How are such lineages materialized at the cottage? Carsten (2004, 35, emphasis in original) suggests "that [through] the very qualitative density of experiences in the houses we inhabit ... kinship is *made* ... within domestic space." In the minds of the cottagers with whom I spoke, the domestic space where such processes are intensified and potent was the cottage. Roger captured this idea in his assertion, "Our cottage is just an extension of our family." Before his wife Deidre married him, she made it clear that it was "marry me, marry my cottage"; she saw it as an extension of herself. Roger quipped that he knew it was a toss-up between her cottage and him before he agreed that he would make it a central part of his life as well. For Deidre and many others, then, the cottage was clearly more than a physical structure – to borrow from Carsten (2004, 37), cottages "are the social relations of those who inhabit them." The physical structure of the cottage and the objects it contained materialized the social relations of 'family' (see also Bourdieu 2003 [1971], 270-83; Marcoux 2001, 83).

Stories of 'family' were made and embedded into the very structure of the cottage. A frequent element of my initial research visit was a tour of the interior of the cottage, followed by a walk around its exterior that usually covered the entire property. We visited docks, decks, retaining walls, beaches, gazebos, paths, boathouses, arbours, bunkies, outhouses – either abandoned or in use – and even septic beds; I was told when they were added, last used, or rebuilt, and by whom.

Each cottage, I learned, had its own biography, which the 'family' proudly knew (Kopytoff 1986). In cottages that had passed through more than one generation, detailed descriptions were often offered about what had been the original cottage, with emphasis on what had been changed and by whom. The accompanying narrative of these tours drew attention to the specific labours of grandparents, fathers, uncles, sometimes mothers, siblings, or other family members in the construction, modification, or reconstruction. As Isabelle noted of her cottage, "Everyone in the family, every member of the family, both sides, have all had their hand at something here." It was often difficult to visualize the original cottage because it had been almost entirely swallowed up by subsequent remodelling and additions, but this did not thwart an elaborated discussion of its initial form. I was struck by the importance placed on highlighting the physical structure from which the familial legacy of the cottage had begun.

Even if the cottage had not been built by the owners I met, they shared as much history about its original construction as they knew. Two cottagers were in the process of constructing new cottages when interviewed. In these cases, tours of the construction sites, details of what had been on the site previously, and plans for the future of the property – and, most importantly, how these spaces would be used by 'family' – were carefully delineated. Drew told of the tussle with his daughter over who was going to get the loft bedroom in the new cottage, which had begun when he pointed out where his grandchildren – even though his daughter was resolutely single – would sleep. Ida and Leon emphasized how they had planned for large family gatherings – Ida had seven siblings – in their new cottage. For those who over time had owned more than one cottage, photos of the earlier cottages were often proffered up for inspection, accompanied by a narrative of what changes had been made to them, or why they had been deemed inadequate to meet 'family' needs and thus sold. These stories emphasized the integration of the social relations of 'family' into the physical structure of the cottage itself.

'Family' was also mapped onto the lake. Often a boat tour around the lake concluded my initial research visit. Many cottagers had 'family' members for neighbours. These 'family' enclaves had often evolved from the splitting of the original piece of property purchased by grandparents or parents into two or more lots on which offspring had then built cottages. Other cottages had been specifically acquired because they were next door to a brother, cousin, or some other relative. Lorne told me that his neighbours at the cottage were all his former in-laws. When he and his wife divorced, he took the cottage even though it had originally been her parents' and she got their house in the city. Such arrangements facilitated a stable transition for their children. And they both agreed he was better able to maintain the cottage than she was. They both also assumed that the cottage would ideally stay in her family, as her children would one day inherit it. Being surrounded by former in-laws did not bother him; in fact, he liked it. As he said, they still treated him as 'family', since he had clearly demonstrated his love of their cottage. Often, while touring the lake, the identification of cottages and properties formerly owned by those considered 'family' prompted a lament for the loss these represented.

Popular stories abound of the value and memories layered on objects large or small, expensive or monetarily worthless, new or old, at the cottage.[12] Following Miller's (1987, 107) claim at the broader societal level, I argue that 'family' has "an extraordinary capacity to ... consider objects as having attributes which may not appear as evident to outsiders." For example, the furnishings at Alice and Leonard's cottage exemplified what had been a traditional pattern at many Ontario cottages, particularly in the 1950s and '60s. A dresser, which now functioned as a sideboard in the dining room, had come from Leonard's maternal grandparents' guest bedroom; the old radio had belonged to Alice's father – and was the first thing that he bought for himself when he came back from World War II with his discharge money; her mother had passed along her coffee percolator and a sewing machine; a chair had come from her aunt's home and the couch from an uncle. These objects materialized 'family' at the cottage; they concentrated the family legacy in one place.[13] Both Alice and Leonard came from families that had multi-generational legacies of cottaging – such kin knew what 'family' at the cottage meant, and their presence was made real in the cottage furnishings.

The term "object" does not really seem to capture some examples of the materialization of 'family' at the cottage. Some examples of such hard-to-describe "objects" were the boards, door frames, or walls on which the physical growth of 'family' members was recorded annually, often over more than one generation. Frances told the story of the only visit of her ninety-year-old mother-in-law to the family cottage, which had been in Frances' family for three generations and was now owned by her and her husband. She explained that there was a wall there on which were recorded the measurements of everyone's height and date all through childhood. Each child's growth was noted on his or her annual return to the cottage. As she was the oldest person ever to visit the cottage and, as Frances said, she "absolutely adored the experience," the nonagenarian had her name, age, date of her visit, and her height – as "she was so short" – added to the 'family' wall. This wall and others I was shown were not only visual records of 'family' but, as B.C. Haldrup and J. Larsen (2003, 24) argue for family photographs, they also narrate and thereby produce social relations (see also Edwards and Strathern 2000, 162; Hallman and Benbow 2007).

Simple things such as board games (like the Scrabble game that is missing the ten-point "z"), jigsaw puzzles (including the one everyone has done many times over and which never fails to incite speculation about which 'family' member lost the piece in the middle of the sky and when), the curtains Mom/Grandma made many years ago that are now tattered and faded (but which nobody can be convinced should be replaced), or the battered baking tins that she always used to make muffins and cakes – all are examples of some of the objects that carry a dense patina of 'family' relations. The "z-less" Scrabble game is not just another board game; the puzzle with the missing piece is not deemed flawed and destined for the garbage. Rather, the actions and stories that these valued objects evoke knit relations together when they sit down to play the game, do the puzzle, eat the muffins, or close the curtains to turn their attention inward to 'family.'

Sally noted that her father was absolutely "homicidal" about the cedar strip canoe that had been his father's most treasured possession. For Sam, it was not just a canoe; rather, it was his tangible link to the original cottage owned by his parents, and a materialization of the memories and times that he had shared with his parents. Sally stressed that she always told her friends when they came to the cottage that they "must not in any way touch the canoe because that is the one thing that is sacred." It was her father's alone to take out onto the lake.

Neil listed several things he had kept from earlier cottages that had been in his family, things which he had proudly installed in his Haliburton cottage to make tangible ties across generations: his mother's canvas canoe that he had had refinished and was soon going "to launch again" at his cottage; the deck chairs from his mother's cottage, which had been around the bay from where he now owned one; the wooden water skis that he had learned to ski on at his grandparent's cottage; old oil lamps that were used by his grandparents and were still lit on his family's winter visits to their cottage. He was particularly pleased that his daughter had asked when her grandparents' cottage was sold that a lamp be kept and then rehung in their cottage in Haliburton.

'Family' members themselves can, after death, inhabit a material form that ensures their ongoing presence at the cottage; however ephemeral its materiality may be, the spirit that it embodies invariably endures. More than one cottager has had or wished to have his or her ashes scattered at their cottage. So common is this practice that websites that advise on funerary practices in Ontario offer advice on what to consider when contemplating scattering ashes at the cottage.[14]

Sam told the story of his and his brother's efforts to keep alive the family spirit at what had been their original cottage by scattering their parents' ashes there. His parents had owned a cottage on a Haliburton lake for several years when he and his brother were growing up. After he and his brother had moved on to start their own lives, and for reasons Sam never fully understood, his parents sold the cottage. Memories of that place and the times spent there were especially treasured by him. He returned to the same lake annually with his own family, and eventually purchased property and built a cottage there. It was where he planned to spend extended periods of time once he retired. Even his parents, after having sold their cottage, continued to rent one on the lake for several years, affirming for him that their connection to the place paralleled his own. The return of his parents' ashes to their original cottage property symbolized a return to the place where home and 'family' were one, a place for Sam that retained a lifelong pull on his emotions. Standing in the water on the beach in front of their former property, Sam recounted, he and his brother emptied the urns. He observed that they were very lucky that the current owners were not home. They were somewhat dismayed, however, that the ashes did not spread when they poured them out, but rather sank to the bottom in a large lump. Unsure of whether they should stir them up to dissipate them, he and his brother proceeded to play a game of catch with the empty urns. He remembers having a lot of fun that day, and thinking that his parents would have taken pleasure in their frivolity, as they had all enjoyed similar games years ago, albeit using something other than a funerary urn. In reality, however, nobody but Sam and his brother and their 'families,' whom they regaled with this story, would know that this was the final resting place of their parents/in-laws/grandparents. As such, it would become a 'family' secret.

That cottagers also shared 'family' secrets at the cottage is crucial: these secrets mostly glued 'families' together. While some secrets are heartwarming, humorous, or even mildly embarrassing, as Sam's daughters and wife found his tale of scattering their grandparents' ashes, the more pejorative sense of the phrase 'family secrets' held somewhat darker elements that challenged what 'family' was assumed to represent. Ultimately, such secrets chafed at 'family' values, revealing the tensions of 'family.'

'Family' Secrets

It generally took until the latter part of an interview or research visit before cottagers began to reveal a few secrets about life and 'family' at the cottage. That it was generally women who told me these stories is a point I will return to in the next chapter. Demanding significant amounts of "kin work," generally done by women, 'family' could be stressful (Di Leonardo 1987). Gillis (1996a, 16) stated frankly that "family times" like those spent together at the cottage "tend to be anxiously anticipated and fondly remembered, but, as events they are often experienced as stressful and frustrating."

While 'family' reflects an interplay between the biological and the social, I came to understand that biology sometimes could be more important. Shared biology could garner a privileged measure of social capital for 'family' members, implying that genetic material could "hardwire" someone to be receptive to the cottage experience. It also suggested the virtue of bonds that extended through time – something valued by 'family' and which non-biological kin clearly could not claim (Edwards and Strathern 2000, 156). In-laws, potential or established, could thus prove problematic to 'family.' Some in-laws who had been married into the 'family' for several years, even decades, remained under scrutiny if their commitment to the cottage was anything short of obvious and unfailing. Comments like "our daughter-in-law tolerates the cottage"; "she's not a cottager at all"; "my wife is not enamoured with [my parent's cottage]"; "our son-in-law is not comfortable here"; "my brother's spouse has a little bit of trouble with the family cottage"; and "it depends on who you marry ... they might not want to come here" indicate the delicate nature of such relationships. Frances emphasized the tentativeness of her father's role at the cottage that had passed down through her mother's lineage beginning in the 1930s. She said, "He's *just* the son-in-law ... and his first time up here was 1946" – suggesting that he was still viewed as outside of the inner circle, even though he had been coming up to the cottage for nearly seventy years. There was always hope that signs of a full conversion to the cottage experience would become evident in such individuals, at which point blood bonds could cease to play a role.

For one Haliburton cottage 'family,' all new relationships of their off-spring were put to the cottage litmus test. Any single 'family' member's new romantic interests who did not demonstrate a love of the cottage, or at least real potential to develop it, were troubling. Newcomers who came from a cottaging background had a distinct advantage, but even their on-going commitment and passion was thoroughly interrogated. All 'family' members were entitled to make an assessment of such relationships, and blind adherence to what these judgments determined was taken as a 'family' pact. By implication, anyone who continued on in a relationship with someone who failed the test put a severe strain on 'familial' ties. As the father of one 'family' said, "If you do not love the cottage, you do not belong in our family."

Those who might be considered of dubious influence in the 'familial' context had their own views of the tensions in the 'family' that they married into. Too much 'family' could prove to be suffocating. Isabelle, for instance, who had married into her husband's 'family' cottage enclave, was grateful that even though they saw everyone regularly, her in-laws were not "on each other's backs all the time."

Edwards and Strathern (2000 153, 155) noted that in the English village Alltown it was possible for a "relative ... to cease to belong ... [leaving] the family sphere." The same seemed to be true for 'family' members. Gwen and her husband turned over the ownership of the cottage where their children had spent their summers since they were small to their two adult daughters. Gwen commented, "We have a son also; he had a cottage next door. He sold it. He is not interested in cottage life, which is funny." It would seem that Gwen's son had stepped outside of the 'family.' Becky's brother had "gotten away from [the cottage, as] he liked to do more city things." Marnie noted that their son had moved out to British Columbia and had established a life there. He had bought himself a boat big enough to live in, what he called "his cottage." The Haliburton family cottage exerted no pull on him. He had not been there for many years. Gwen, Marnie, and Becky could not offer any real explanation of why the men had lost interest in the 'family' cottage over the years, why they had stepped out of the 'family.'

Gwen's son still came to the cottage periodically. He had come up the previous summer and, as she said, had had a "great time with his dad in the water," reminiscent of his childhood when he loved to swim and water ski. There was a tone of hope in her comments that her son would potentially find his way back into the fold of 'family.' He could, as Edwards and Strathern (2000, 160) suggested for various disowned or forgotten kin in Alltown, be "resurrected." Gwen's son had both the biological links that played a big role in the Alltown resurrections but also, from his mother's point of view, the memories of the joys of his childhood at the cottage. To her, these memories and the ongoing pleasures of the cottage should have socialized him as 'family.' Clearly, he saw things differently.

Marnie was resigned to the fact that her son was not coming back to Ontario and was not interested in assuming any responsibility for the 'family' cottage. She also felt that her daughter, who still lived in Ontario, was wary of taking it on. She noted that her daughter "sees the writing on the wall. She's watched us over all these years and she's a smart kid, she knows better than to get involved with a cottage and its responsibilities."

'Family' who took their leave did not always do so peacefully. One might presume that siblings who had been raised at the cottage would share a vision of what a cottage ought to be. There are at least two broad understandings of what a cottager should be, embodied in the categories I introduced in Chapter 2: the traditionalists and the socialites. As for the cottage, one conception envisions a modest dwelling, making a minimal impact on the environment, suggesting little landscaping and tree clearance, requiring minimal technologies beyond basic electricity and a septic system. Cottage toys are kept to a minimum. Most critically, time spent there is to be peaceful, restful, and restorative.

The other type of cottage is a renovated or even new structure that functions as a party place, with fast boats, all the latest motorized water toys, a good stereo system, internet connection, and lots of visitors. Lana lamented the transition that had taken place in her husband's family cottage once it passed, by default, into the hands of Garry's younger brother, Sheridan, following their parents' death. She said that by the time they had "their young children and it would have been nice to have a family cottage, Sheridan was a young adult and it was a party cottage."

Cheney (2002) documents the story of two brothers who inherited the family cottage – a fairly modest structure – and found themselves in vicious legal battles, fighting for their respective visions of what the cottage was to be, extremes that reflected the two ideal types I describe above. They had obviously shared the same childhood experience at the cottage but as adults had differing visions of life there. Their fight left 'family' irreparably fragmented. Several cottagers told stories of their similar struggles. Some speculated that such battles, or even more modest ones, could possibly be spurred on by devilish 'in-laws', a group that could typically be seen to disrupt and challenge all that had been inculcated into 'family' as they grew up together. As Robyn reckoned,

> Somebody has to take the responsibility for things. And usually it's not so bad if there is one who is single. But if you have three who are married … I think it's the spouse[s].

Some cottagers who had adolescent children expressed considerable anxiety about how many teenagers reject the cottage as a place they want to be. Life in the city can be perceived as being a lot more exciting than life at the cottage, which can seem too distant from where the action is. As Deborah said of her youngest daughter, who for a period of time had resisted coming to the cottage on a regular basis,

> [She] loved the cottage growing up. But she had always said, "I want to live in New York City." She had no idea, I don't think, of what New York City was but she'd heard that it was quite a happening place. When we started building the cottage for the first couple of years, she thought that she was a city girl and that she would want to be there, or California, to surf and all that. It was just the appeal of the "busyness."

Many parents with children of this age saw any distancing from the 'family' at the cottage as something that just had to be waited out. Like Gwen, they had unfailing faith that once their adolescent children aged into their twenties, they would be "resurrected" back into the 'family'. Deborah contentedly concluded her story of her daughter with the comment, "She has come full circle … come back to where her heart is." Such a statement hints at the assumption that it was natural for her daughter to want to be at the cottage. Her grandparents had originally owned a small resort in the region, and her father grew up in Haliburton, but had moved away to Toronto as a young adult. This young girl's connections to cottage life in Haliburton went back two generations, and had been established when she was a baby. It seemed her mother, Deborah, assumed her daughter's emotional centre – her heart – was thus pre-programmed when it came to knowing where she belonged.

Generational differences also flared up in other ways, putting strain on 'family' ties. Ava felt that her grandsons did not understand the ethos of the cottage, as they showed little willingness to pitch in and help with the things that needed doing, and every year appeared only to be interested in the new toys that they could get – and then store – at her rather small cottage. One year it was a water tube, another year it was a kayak, then wakeboards, and now they wanted a PWC but nobody had volunteered to spend the money – yet. She wondered what had happened to simple pleasures at the cottage.

Ava attributed some of these tensions and misplaced priorities to her son-in-law who was a staunch Republican American. The cottage and the 'familial' context that her daughter knew so well did not help to ameliorate the tensions that blew up around politics when they gathered at the cottage, as Ava's views leaned decidedly left. She said, "At least [her daughters] have a history, but their husbands don't have that history. It's almost more than I can handle sometimes and I just make up an excuse to return home to [the city] for a few days." A further irritant was that her daughters and their families were not prepared to make do with the limited space in the cottage, and suggested that Ava's husband, who had built the original cottage from logs on the property, add on to it to give everyone more room. She found it highly symbolic that nobody wanted to share space at the cottage. She saw the intimate sharing of space as a metaphor for what the cottage stood for, a principle she thought her daughters would respect, having spent their childhood summers there. Ava found that everyone's desire to "do their own thing" and a refusal to see life at the cottage as a collective experience put strain on 'familial' relations.

'Familial' tensions, however, did not always need to be inflamed by in-laws. Ava found herself caught in conflicts between her daughters. One of them had recently divorced, moved back to live with her parents, and was somewhat depressed. Her younger sister – the one now living in the United States – did not want her sister coming up there while she and her family were there "on vacation." She did not want their holiday tainted by her negative presence, and she wanted her mother to communicate this message.

Garry's older brother had not been to the 'family' cottage for many years after he and his father had a falling out there. For him, the place was symbolic of these painful memories. He never went back, even after his parents' deaths, as the 'family' cottage was just assumed to belong to their younger brother – whom he and Garry saw as the favoured child – even before their parents died. Garry and his wife, Lana, upon observing who was obviously going to inherit his parent's cottage, had gone ahead and acquired their own cottage, still on the same lake, but some distance – physically and metaphorically – from what had become his younger brother Sheridan's property.

Others tiptoed around how time and maintenance costs were going to be dispersed among siblings who had inherited the 'family' cottage. Richard and Michael talked of the year-long negotiation process with siblings, and in Michael's case, with his own adult children about who was going to spend which weeks at the cottage each summer. Memories were long as individual family members informally kept track of who got the cottage when, to ensure they got their turn at what were considered the best weeks in the summer.

At times, 'family' had to hunker down to protect themselves from barbed comments from relatives who did not appreciate or understand their strong desire to be at the cottage. Over the first two years of owning their cottage, Vicky coached her sisters to stop inviting them to family events in the city. If it was a summer weekend, Vicky told them that they would not come, as they wanted to be at their cottage. She noted, however, that their absence never went unnoticed and was regularly remarked upon.

Journalist Peter Cheney quoted an estate lawyer with ample experience dealing with the settling of wills that included cottages: "The fight over the cottage conjures up memories of who used to get the biggest piece of cake and who [M]om loved best" (2002, F1). Those who inherit cottages stand to pay considerable capital gains taxes based on the appreciated value of the cottage from the time it was first acquired by those who then willed it to their children/descendants. Cottagers get around this in various ways: for instance, by selling the cottage to their children before their deaths or at least before they become too frail to spend much time there. Sometimes this is done for a nominal value, but sometimes ageing parents realize that they need the revenue from the cottage to support them in their final years, and thus need to sell the cottage at something approaching market value – which is often more than their children can afford. Or, just to complicate things, one sibling can afford a share, but others cannot, a scenario that can cause tension among siblings or between siblings and parents, never mind husbands and wives, if one partner – often the in-law – does not want to invest a significant amount of money in something of which they as a couple will only have partial ownership. Other 'families' turn the property into a 'family' trust, in which various members are partners.

All of these arrangements are outside the issue of how maintenance and upkeep costs are to be managed. Tensions can flare up over not only what are priorities for repair but how they will be done and by whom. As Ben explained, he really only owned "one-sixth of every blade of grass" on the property, but he was the one who spent the most time at the cottage and invested much emotional energy worrying about how he and his brothers were going to manage all the attendant expenses. This imbalance was the source of some tension with his brothers – and he did not even want to think about what would happen when he passed on. Should his two children inherit his fraction? Would they be able to contribute financially to its upkeep? Would they want to if they each only had a one-twelfth interest in the property? How much time would they actually get to spend there? Would they even want to spend time there? Ben's dilemmas were not unique.

Ultimately, though some 'family' members may find it impossible to accept, cottages are commodities (Kopytoff 1986, 85). They have an exchange value, the specifics of which are determined by the real estate market. Several cottagers were simply resigned to the reality that their cottages would inevitably be sold at some point in the future. Such resignation was met sometimes matter-of-factly, but more often with a true sadness and sense of loss. For some it meant the dissipation of 'family' and the loss of all that had been invested in developing life at the cottage and all that it symbolized.

But some 'family' cottages were never fully commoditized. For Sam, his original 'family' cottage could be described as an "inalienable possession" (A. Weiner 1992). The scattering of his parents' ashes in front of it demonstrated his feeling that his 'family' continued to have some rights of ownership to it, even though it had legally passed out of their hands many years ago. It was a place redolent in memories that could not be erased by a deed of sale. The act of making it the final resting place of his parents made the 'familial' bond to this place all the more indelible.

In the next chapter, I continue to explore the tensions between the values that hold 'families' together and the secrets that can undermine this connection as they play out at the cottage. I reflect on those who were both wives and mothers, seen to be the centre around which 'family' life at the cottage revolved, and on their not uncommon deep-seated ambivalence to that positioning – a sentiment that many kept secreted away in the interest of ensuring continued "good times" at the cottage for their children and husbands. Fathers and husbands, meanwhile, were literally and metaphorically working at the cottage to keep its infrastructure stable, and in the process struggling to find a physical and emotional place for themselves in the complexity of the domestic and generational spaces there. All was clearly not unquestionably rewarding at the cottage.

7

Gender at the Cottage

When I began this research, I did not anticipate writing about gender roles and identities at the cottage. But it became clear early on that, in talking about what people did at the cottage, those I interviewed categorized various activities on the basis of gender. Despite having encountered a couple of cottages owned by homosexual couples or single men, and having heard stories of single women who had owned them before they were married, cottage life was very much understood as the domain of families structured around heterosexual married couples. At the cottage, men (fathers) did certain things and women (mothers) did others. While there were overlaps and exceptions to this categorization, such separation was still considered the norm. For those with longer histories as cottagers on Haliburton lakes, these areas of responsibility were remembered from their own childhoods or their own lives as young married couples in the 1950s and '60s. The Haliburton cottage experience in the immediate postwar era can be seen as part of the modernist project of building the postwar family, an entity that reached and retains its most idealized character in the 'family' I discussed in the previous chapter. This kind of modern 'family' was structured around assumed hetero-normative gender roles and identities, all of which the cottage experience in large measure reinforced, if not enhanced.

Rebuilding the Family in the Postwar Era

In the immediate post-World War II era, two related themes were widespread in Canadian public discourse: one was the rebuilding of the Canadian family and the other was the question of what was the ideal structure and nature of that family (Gölz 1993). Some saw the Canadian family as still carrying the scars of Depression poverty, which had resulted in a declining birth rate, the conceptualization of children as a "burden," and what sociologist Annalee Gölz (1993, 12) described as "the subversion of the unemployed male breadwinner's traditional familial authority." Additionally, the topsy-turvy social realities of the World War II era had seen women temporarily enter the workforce in unprecedented large numbers. As the war effort ended and men arrived home in large numbers to take up new forms of employment, many women were displaced to resume their more traditional and assumedly preferred roles of home-makers and caregivers for children.[1] There was a sense that Canadian society had to regain its stability in the face of the "perceived relaxation of social morals and a concomitant rise in illegitimacy, and the increase in hasty and unstable marriages" (ibid., 13) that for some had characterized the war years.

Initiatives like the 1944 Family Allowance Act in Canada were an at-tempt to re-stabilize and nurture the "ideal" Canadian family, asserting what Gölz (1993, 17) calls the "hegemony of familialism." By default, this act reasserted quite powerfully that the real place for women was in the home, raising children, while men resumed their appropriate role as the main breadwinner in the family (ibid., 28). The massive expansion of suburbs in Canada both isolated women in the home and, in some measure, established clear demarcations between work and non-work for men who now found themselves commuting farther to their places of employment (Rutherdale 1999; Strong-Boag 1991, 1995).

The revitalized postwar Canadian "modern family" was not the family of the Victorian era, particularly with respect to the role of the father. In the 1950s, fathers were to play a new role. Marriages of the 1950s were understood to be companionate partnerships, meaning, in theory, that men played a more obvious role in the domestic lives and spaces of their families. Fatherhood was to be seen as part of family life (Rutherdale 1999, 353; Strong-Boag 1991, 475). Fathers were supposed "to be warm and nur-turing parents," as Steven Gelber (1997, 94) noted, which would lead to what Gölz (1993, 27) described as the "close affectionate relationships, personal ties and happiness of belonging and being loved" in the family. This presumption fuelled, at least in part, the emergence of what Margaret

Marsh called "masculine domesticity," referring to "the adoption of family-
and-home-centred practices among fathers" (quoted in Gelber 1999, 352).[2]
Marsh identified three structural factors necessary for "the emergence of
masculine domesticity": sufficient family incomes for a middle-class standard of living; work schedules that allowed fathers to return home daily at
consistent times; and sufficient family living space to permit recreational
spaces both within and outside the home (Marsh 1988, 167; see also
Rutherdale 1999, 352). Christopher Dummitt (1998, 12) has suggested that
outdoor cooking, specifically barbecuing done on the suburban home
patio, was one key example of a "recreational space" and activity dominated
by men. He suggests that such activities "linked ... cooking to symbols of
virile masculinity and manly leisure." The physical location of this cookery
is a key point here.

Skilfully being able to cook hamburgers and hot dogs on the patio
barbecue was not the only example of masculine domesticity. Fathers in
the 1950s were expected to take on a role as "pals ... [as] hockey or baseball coaches" (Owram 1996, 86; see also Gelber 1997, 69), unlike the more
austere and distant patriarchal roles of their early-twentieth-century
fathers. Regardless of these niche roles being filled by fathers, the transition
into the female domestic space of the postwar home was not always an
easy one. For the newly domesticated father, most comfort seemed to be
found in spaces separate, or even completely removed, from the central
domestic arena. Fathers could be found most contentedly located in spaces
external to the main living spaces of the family home: basement workshops, patios, the lawn (an expanse that could always be guaranteed to
need mowing), the hockey arena, the baseball diamond, or, even more
distantly, organizing life in the campground or at the cottage. Gelber (1997,
77) would argue that following the earlier "disappearance of the [in-home]
library, men still seem to want a room of their own, [which leads to the]
setting aside [of] some territory for themselves." Such masculine spaces,
he insisted, "permitted men to be both a part of the house and apart from
it, sharing the home with their families while retaining spatial and functional autonomy" (ibid., 69). I suggest below, however, that identifying
the cottage as a primarily masculine space – even if it did fill the roles that
Gelber enumerated – does not capture its gendered complexity.

According to one Canadian psychiatrist of the period, the suburbs were
spaces of "watered-down maleness," where a man's "traditional function

of ruler and protector [had been] usurped" (quoted in Strong-Boag 1995, 48; see also Dummitt 2007b, 78). In what can be read as a resistance to this depleted masculinity, men took part in the "great do-it-yourself boom of the 1950s" (Gelber 1999, 5; 1997). In this context, household chores for men frequently became hobbies, and vice versa. Through the 1950s, a man's workshop, located somewhat externally to the living space of the home, either in the basement or garage, became "command central" (Gelber 1997, 94-102). For some men, the honing of such skills was preparation for taking on a cottage as a do-it-yourself project, even if the latter was on a much grander scale than many home improvements.

In keeping with the externality of the domestic spaces claimed as their own by middle-class fathers of the 1950s, and a measure of their commercial and financial success as breadwinners, were the vacations and holidays away from home (Rutherdale 1998, 316). Fred Bodsworth, a 1950s magazine columnist, posited that automobile camping was clearly an opportunity for men to show their prowess in "things domestic'" (quoted in Rutherdale 1999, 354). Starting in the 1950s, the privileging of such capacities among middle-class men had become "like sobriety and fidelity ... an expected quality in a good husband" (Gelber 1997, 98). These activities, Bodsworth charged, put "the male back in the role of provider and protector" (quoted in Rutherdale 1999, 354). Building and developing a waterfront cottage can be seen as an expression of the "masculine domesticity" that Marsh (quoted in Gelber 1999, 352) argued had come to shape men's/fathers' roles within the home. Work on or at a cottage required a significant degree of brute physical labour and at least a modest, but preferably a significant execution of manual skill – something many cottagers rarely utilized in their largely white-collar jobs. Middle-class Haliburton cottages provided and continue to provide powerful statements of a man's claim to a domain of domestic space.

"I Built It with My Own Hands"

What fuelled the desire of middle-class men in the 1950s onward to take on the project of building or at least acquiring a cottage in a location such as Haliburton? Roberta observed that men were a very necessary presence at the cottage: "Every cottage needed a man, to hammer this and hammer that." As a result, the role of men at the cottage seemed to evolve into one that required that they tax their physical capacities and manual skills in the construction or development of a basic cottage in the relative wilderness of the waterfronts of Haliburton lakes. This pattern continued in the latter decades of the twentieth century as a newer generation took on these modest cottages, frequently expanding and upgrading them. And even if these later structures are sturdier or professionally built, they are unrelenting in their demand for maintenance and upkeep. As everyone I interviewed agreed, "a cottage is work." In Tim Ingold's (2000, 195-97) terms, a cottage is a "taskscape," a place where the interlocking of all labours and practices inscribe the place with sociality and meaning.

Acquiring a Haliburton cottage required middle-class men to spend most weekends from May to September there, as well as much of their annual vacation. Such dedication was expanded throughout the year if the cottage was winterized, which meant that the same journey had to be made more frequently and that attention had to be paid to a whole new set of maintenance issues distinct from but just as laborious as those undertaken in the spring and summer. Some of the tasks were digging outhouses, clearing land, wiring cottages, building steps down steep rocky embankments, often lacking the real tools and expertise needed to do the job. Today, men at the cottage regularly tackle a similar roster of jobs, only slightly enhanced – some would say hampered – by more sophisticated tools and upgraded expectations of what the outcomes should be. And while some of these projects were long completed, I was assured by all those I interviewed that no cottage was without unrelenting demands for upkeep, if not redevelopment. These stories became the subject of myth. One Haliburton cottager aptly documented his father's legacy at the cottage:

> My father's ... levels of productivity reached mythical heights. He would wake up before 6 a.m., down a cup of strong coffee, and then build. He plumbed. He laid wire. He painted. He sanded. He built the pumphouse. He built the outhouse. He built the dock ... He did not build the cottage itself, but he has modified and added so much to it that it would take a team of forensic archaeologists to determine the original structure ... the truth is that [our cottage is] the scene of an epic battle. It's where my father wages his never-ending battle against Mother Nature and her evil henchmen. Entropy. (Schatzker 2005, 89-90)

Men I interviewed expressed similar sentiments about what occupied their time at the cottage.

> A cottage is work. Many of these things require physical work of a scope and intensity that would not be acceptable in a city job. Oddly, many relish this because of the deep satisfaction that comes with physical exertion and the ability to say, "I built that with my own hands."

> My house in the city always has something that needs fixing. I hire people to do that. But at the cottage, I want to do everything myself, building docks, fixing septic pumps, putting up storm windows.

> There's always something else to be fixed. You don't think about anything else, you're out in the fresh air. Cottaging is not for the weak.

These labours and obligations were what many men wanted to talk to me about – they are what make the cottage a meaningful and somewhat ironically highly desirable place to be.

"Turn It On; Turn It Off"

From what male cottagers told me, it was clear that the ever-pervasive work of a cottage offers its own powerful rewards, pleasures, and enjoyment. To the "eternal putterer," as one cottager described himself, there was nothing more enticing than "banging nails into things and mixing concrete" while he was at the cottage. Some found such work therapeutic, as they could take full control over its eventual success or failure, unlike some of the work they did in their professional lives. As Neil said, "its direct purpose is obvious," a statement that offers a window into what comprised the paid employment of some I met. For others, tasks such as the sanding of the cottage exterior or the dock took on a zen-like quality. Aaron observed, "It transports you to another zone ... makes you forget everything ... just what you want at the cottage."

To these men, these labours were as satisfying as any moments of leisure squeezed in once a summer day's chores were done. However, the labours were and still are guaranteed to generate considerable sweat, perhaps even a few tears, and not a little colourful language, along with many durable and even satisfying memories. In addition to the regular maintenance of the cottage, many men talked of building their cottages and/or completing significant renovations or redesigns of the original structures they had purchased or inherited. Many undertook these major projects as rank amateurs. They practised what could be labelled "trial-and-error" construction and maintenance. Sean noted that "watching the cottage go up" was a memory he treasured deeply. This pleasure, however, paled in comparison to his satisfaction that his first major construction project "actually ... did not fall down."

The cottages of those I interviewed were typically seasonal properties on lakefronts and were thus subject to the vagaries of such environs. In many cases, they needed to be battened down in the fall to withstand the cold, winds, and snows of winter, and then opened up again in the spring – activities which demanded significant amounts of physical labour and, as Garry suggested, perseverance. He remembered a scenario that had repeated itself annually at his family's cottage when he was growing up. He rolled his eyes as he recalled the hours spent trying to coax the water pump to life to get water flowing to the cottage after every spring:

> There was a pipe on the pump near the water that had wires running down to it from the fuse box on the cottage. Of course there was no switch on the pump, just the fuse in the fuse box to turn it on and off. Dad would be priming the pump, yelling out to me to "turn it on, turn it off, turn it on, turn it off." I remember spending days flipping the switch back and forth, back and forth. Then there was the plumbing under the cottage. The cottage is built on sand, up on blocks and, of course, over time it sank, crushing the copper pipes that were under it. And every once in a while we wouldn't get all the water out of the pipes in the fall, and they'd burst. Then somebody would have to go under the cottage in the spring to repair them. It was usually Dad. Thank goodness he was all skin and bones.

Year-round properties did not escape the regime of regular maintenance and seasonal transition activities. There was a wide array of jobs to be done – bringing in the dock, putting the boat away, ensuring every fall that the plumbing system was ready for the winter. In addition to these tasks, there was the ongoing maintenance of the cottage structure, storage sheds, docks, septic systems, roadways, boats, and other cottage toys. One had to keep an eye on the vegetation or forest that surrounded the cottage to make certain that it did not encroach too closely and that any hazardous trees that might fall victim to the next windstorm or heavy snowfall would not fall on any structures or vital power lines. These jobs were separate and additional to any upgrades and improvements undertaken by cottagers to the original structure.

Very few of the men I interviewed had any professional skills as carpenters, plumbers, electricians, or other such tradesmen.[3] Rather, most had learned some of the basic skills of these professions by puttering in a home workshop, developing their skills doing renovations to their house in the city, but eventually dedicating all of their DIY skill to their cottage. But like the complete neophytes to such labours, even those who were do-it-yourselfers learned at the cottage on a largely trial-and-error basis. Cottage work often presented challenges that were not regularly encountered in modest home renovations orchestrated from a well-organized workshop: uneven ground, large protrusions of Precambrian granite just where you needed to dig, difficult access routes, or unruly vegetation growth were just a few obstacles that could hamper smooth construction progress.

Several cottagers had experienced – some would say endured – the tutelage of their fathers, who were themselves frequently neophytes when they first undertook to build or develop a cottage. As one cottager acknowledged of his father, he "had made it up as he went along." Many recognized that this strategy had resulted in their inherited cottages being very unique constructions, whose maintenance and future could only be secured through the careful training of the next generation in the structure's "quirkiness." It was imperative, then, that sons or sons-in-law – as it was always assumed that this knowledge would be passed on patrilineally – took the time and demonstrated the patience to learn, as one cottager said, about "how the place worked." This seemed to ensure that male cottagers were forevermore destined to labour at the cottage. Those who had purchased the products of the labour of such handymen-by-default grappled with the complexities of trying to sort out how things worked at the cottage without the aid of a tutor or an instruction manual. These inevitably frustrating realities had prompted some to acquire a professionally built cottage, but they still amounted to a minority among those I came to know.

Most male cottagers continued the tradition laid down by their fathers (or in a few cases, their grandfathers) as they laboured to accomplish the same physical competencies as these ancestral figures. More than one cottager I interviewed marvelled at the genius and manual skill demonstrated by his father in the original construction of the cottage, often done with limited resources and only the most basic tools. Still, some also noted the obvious absence of skill demonstrated by their fathers, as they puzzled over just how structural, plumbing, and electrical elements of their cottages had been cobbled or, as one said, "jerry-rigged" together. Disentangling and improving these jobs often gave later generations a great sense of pride, as it enhanced their masculine identity as problem-solvers, as well as their obvious greater skill at manual labour, outside of their professional success in their "real" careers. As their knowledge and skill advanced while they worked to improve, rebuild, or simply stabilize their inherited cottages, these late-twentieth-century men grew more confident in using more sophisticated and more modern (and usually more expensive) tools and technologies. For Michael, the fact that Minden had the largest Home Hardware store in Ontario was a source of pride and adventure for him. Wandering the aisles imagining how all the tools, gadgets, and reference materials could be of use to him in maintaining his cottage had become a favourite rainy-day pastime. Such resources were well beyond anything his father, who had originally built the family cottage, could ever have imagined might be accessible to a Haliburton cottager.

These later generations also had much more information at their fingertips to assist them in cottage repairs and maintenance, like the numerous columns and articles that are a regular feature of *Cottage Life*. These improved technologies and access to more sophisticated knowledge fulfilled the modernist assumption that things such as life at the cottage would continue to progress and develop aided by such resources. Many would argue that this was evident in the continual development and expansion of the once-basic cottages erected on many lakes in Haliburton (see Dummitt 2007a, 12-13). Some of these structures did not look like cottages anymore, but rather elaborate suburban houses. Yet while such "progress" might afford increased creature comforts, some would argue that it has undermined the essence of what life at the cottage is about.

"Envisioning Swims, Fishing Trips and Holiday Fun"

The cottage development begun in 1952 in South Bay on Haliburton Lake exemplifies many of the early experiences of the cottagers I met. South Bay was typical of cottage development in Haliburton in this period: a block of lakeshore land subdivided into lots, with a small basic cottage erected on each lot. On South Bay, the development was spearheaded by two businessmen who acquired the land from a local family with a long history in the area's lumbering industry; on other lakes, it was often a local farmer who sold the land directly to cottagers. Still other cottages were constructed on Crown land that was released for sale.

The South Bay cottagers I interviewed talked about the legendary mobs of would-be cottagers eager to put down a deposit on the cottage lots being offered for sale on Haliburton Lake in the fall of 1952. Ads in Toronto newspapers offered 400 cottage lots for sale in the first major recreational development on this somewhat isolated, but very picturesque, lake in Haliburton County. I heard stories of money literally being thrown at the salesmen who set up promotional booths in the fall of 1952 at venues like the Toronto Sportsmen Show to market these properties. Cheques were being tossed at them faster than they could tally them. A small deposit would hold a single lot and the choice of one of four basic frame cottages. The full price of the package was $2,500, which could be paid off in monthly instalments over five years. The development sold out quickly. Many enthusiastic buyers were, as local newspaper reports suggested, "envisioning swims, fishing trips and holiday fun" in their "spare time" at the cottage (Honeyford 1953, 25).

These Torontonians were buying their piece of paradise sight unseen, many without any real sense of where the lake was even located. They got their first chance to see their intended investment on a rainy weekend in May of 1953. The real estate company chartered a train from Toronto's Union Station and several buses to take people up to Haliburton Lake, and then a flotilla of small boats to ferry these would-be cottagers to their chosen lots. It must have taken a leap of faith to see these properties as sites of recreation, due to their rugged terrain, dense bush covering, and the inclement weather of the day. Nevertheless, few were deterred. Some, the tales suggest, horse-traded lots among themselves while out on the water, but I heard no stories of abandoning the purchase altogether.

Information distributed to the prospective buyers and retained in the personal archives of some South Bay cottagers outlined the construction details of the cottages, along with the extras, such as log siding and picture windows that could be acquired for additional costs. It also listed other amenities such as electrical wiring, plumbing, and painting that would need to be done by the cottager himself in his anticipated "spare time." It was clear from the very beginning that access to leisure time at the cottage on Haliburton Lake would cost these new cottage owners more than dollars. From its earliest days, the experience was expected to extract from them their physical labour. It was also seemingly presumed that the cottager, who was always of course referred to as male, would have a working knowledge of such things as wiring, plumbing, electricity, masonry, and painting.

What was somewhat distinctive about the South Bay development was that there had been limited recreational development on the lake prior to 1952, possibly due to the poor road access into the lake relative to other Haliburton lakes. Increased cottage development on the lake, however, did not immediately open up improved access. Several of those whose families acquired cottages in this early development regaled me with stories of their childhood memories of the trials and tribulations of regularly getting stuck in axle-deep mud on the one-lane access road on many trips up to the cottage, and requiring the assistance of a local farmer to pull them out. To some, he clearly made a good living, as his rescue services were constantly in demand.

The South Bay development was a large one: four hundred cottage lots were on the block at once. Some of these properties might well have been considered somewhat less than desirable, as they were, as the advertisements said, "high" – meaning that there was a steep, rocky, and tree-covered embankment to be navigated to get down to the lake. This topography required cottagers to construct navigable paths or steps down the hill to get to the water. A compensatory virtue was that the cottages were to be built near the top of these embankments, which would eventually provide relatively easy vehicular access.

Furthermore, as with many parts of the county, the Haliburton Lake area had been logged, and many of the "beach" and waterfront areas were generously littered with dead-fall remnants. Because of the en masse development on the lake, a strong sense of community developed as everyone was facing the same challenges in making their cottages habitable and their lakeshores accessible.

This community spirit was also found on many other Haliburton lakes during this period, as frequently several lots would become available for cottage development at one time, meaning that many neophyte cottagers were learning basic construction skills simultaneously. As Allen noted, when he first built his cottage, everyone in his bay was doing the same thing. They helped each other figure out how to do things and pitched in with the physical job of construction. Many were erecting structures from scratch on very limited budgets; others were wrestling with prefabricated units from Eaton's catalogue, packages that often seemed like complicated jigsaw puzzles. These shared activities sowed the seeds of a strong sense of community with one's neighbours on the lake; many valued this history of community-building, and lamented what they saw as its erosion over the last decade.

The original South Bay cottages seemingly offered their new owners something better: at least they did not have to build one from scratch. But the cottages that came with these properties were, at best, modest structures. They had only partial internal partitions rather than full walls between rooms; no kitchen cupboards and counters; no indoor plumbing, which meant that water had to be ferried up the hill from the lake in pails; no outhouses dug – a project that was known to require the use of dynamite to blast out large boulders – and often very few windows. Many of the lots had been cleared only enough to erect the cottage; parking and driveways had to be constructed, along with access routes to the water. Additionally, there was work to be done on the lakeshore to reduce the hazards for swimming and boating. Garry told me that his joyous childhood memories at the cottage were significantly tempered by the never-ending list of jobs – moving logs, fixing steps, shifting boulders, digging trenches – his father left to him and his brother each week. His sister, it seemed, was never expected to assist in these tasks, but instead was to help her mother with more standard domestic duties. In any case, such labours not only helped build the cottage and its amenities but also could be imagined as part of the larger project of rebuilding the family in the postwar period – even if it was not always a harmonious undertaking: tempers flared, frustrations mounted, bodies ached, and patience was

tested in the process. Moreover, it can be argued that these labours countered the tensions of the "watered-down maleness" associated with modernity, which I have found continues now in the discourse of many of the
male Haliburton cottagers I came to know.

Real Men Do Real Work at the Cottage

Christopher Dummitt (2007a, 5) posits that in Canada's postwar era,
"masculinity was equated with modernity," while in some contexts, "para-
doxically ... being modern was also antithetical to being masculine." Tina
Loo (2006, 32-33) suggests for an earlier generation that Canadian men
had an established history of being rather intractable "middle-class
victims" of modernity, a group that could potentially be aided by an
"intense engagement" with the outdoors. Modernity, she continues, had
"taken a ... toll on middle-class men, rendering them overly rational,
soft, a breed prone to nervous exhaustion and incapable of being men"
(ibid., 32).[4] Dummitt (2007b, 78) argues in concert that for middle-class
men in the postwar period, "modernist values and institutions created
a sense of alienation for many," which fostered an interest in demonstrating
skills, capacities, and values associated with a more "primal masculinity"
– something seen as undermined by "the enervating nothingness of
white-collar work" and the banality of the "feminine spaces" of suburban
living. Such an overt expression of masculinity in the modern world was
simultaneously about risk taking and risk management (Dummitt 2007a,
2007b). Work and life at the cottage demanded a careful negotiation between these modern and primal masculinities and between taking and
managing risks.

A particularly Canadian "primal masculinity" had long been infused
into national discourse. Colloquially, the nation's citizens – assumed to be
male – were labelled as "hewers of wood and drawers of water," an identity
grounded in what, at a more scholarly level, Harold Innis (1962) called
the nation's "staples economy."[5] How could the Canadian postwar rational,
technologically adept, often white-collar modern male position himself
within such taken-for-granted national rhetorics? Links could be made
between mega-projects of the era, like the building of the St. Lawrence
Seaway, and the development of a rather modest and somewhat rustic
cottage. The former boldly demonstrated that the natural environment could
be successfully managed, if not controlled, through modern technologies

(Dummitt 2007a, 9), and at a much more micro level, cottage development suggested that nature could be managed and made more accessible and amenable to individual citizens, albeit with much humbler technologies. In the latter, the risks of the wilderness could be tamed, even while being taunted. For example, while Haliburton lakes provided enticing places for family recreation with their pristine waters, this downplayed their fundamentally hazardous character; popular imaginings clashed, as Stevens (2008b, 53) notes, with the "fallibility of cottagers in the face of natural phenomena." Newspapers in the early 1950s documented the high number of drownings during the cottaging season in Ontario:

> Particularly on long weekends, newspapers printed death tolls cataloguing infants who had fallen off of docks, fishermen whose boats had capsized, and youth who perished while swimming ... [some] of these incidents can be chalked up to some combination of alcohol, technological failure, and human stupidity. (ibid.)

Fifty years later, cottagers had gotten smarter about managing risk – while still having fun – in and around Haliburton lakes, and the overall number of drownings in Ontario had steadily dropped, but it was still a long way from zero. Between the late 1980s and 2004, deaths by drowning dropped by 50 percent but still averaged about 140 per year, the vast majority of which happened in lakes and rivers in cottage country (Iltan 2010; Lifesaving Society 2008, 7, 9).

For cottagers in Haliburton, the cottage facilitated a resonance with this Canadian "primal masculinity." It reconnected men with the experience of manual labour, something guaranteed to produce a sweat, and which, fifty years later, my cottagers affirmed constituted "real work." Corroborating such disconnections, one cottager suggested, "Nobody ever breaks a sweat sitting in front of a computer." In the same tradition, Michael Kimmel and Michael Kaufman (1994, 259) noted for men in the 1980s and early 1990s that physical labour was something over which men had autonomy, something "fewer and fewer men experience ... [in the] increas[ing] bureaucratization [and more recently technologization] of office work." Such labours reflected what more than one woman cottager called the never-ending list of projects that their husbands readily undertook at the cottage, which, as these women admitted, were also what kept them (i.e., their wives) sane at the cottage. As Martha said, "If he does not have a project on the go, if he is not fixing, repairing, or building something, he is not happy." Such busyness led to the frustration of another cottager who was "driven crazy" by her husband who refused to "sit down and enjoy his cottage." His daughter remembered that he had to always be "building, painting, hammering," which, based on what I was told, meant that he was enjoying his cottage.

Furthermore, the need to continually invest such do-it-yourself labour at the cottage exemplifies what Gelber called the transfer of "the ideology of the workplace" into the domestic space. These efforts thus became – and I argue they remain today – a "form of productive leisure" (1999, 2, 15). They made a contribution to the capitalist economy in the postwar period. At their most abstract, these efforts were – and are – about increasing individual capital and assets, even if, in their lived experience, they are understood to be about much more. As Veronica Strong-Boag (1991, 475) argued about life in the Canadian suburb in the immediate postwar period, the cottage contributed to the security and renewal of middle-class family life. Those who headed these families were to be rational, authoritative, efficient, modern men who believed in the virtues of science, technology, progress, and capitalism. But at the same time they were Canadian, rooted in an anti-modernist primal persona, capable of manly acts of physical labour – "real work" – things that happened well outside of a white-collar city office, at places such as the cottage. As such, these Canadian men expressed a more conflicted relationship with modernism than did American men of the period. To Dummitt (2007a, 14; 2007b, 98), these ambiguities were at the "centre of modernity" in Canada. This draws to mind a point I have raised throughout this book: that the Ontario cottage experience, even if sometimes conceptualized as something anti-modern, was at its heart a profoundly modern experience.

The cottage's postmodern twenty-first-century expression retains much of this ambiguity even if, in many cases, one has to look long and hard for anything pre- or anti-modern in the physical manifestation of many Haliburton cottages today. Instead, as I have already suggested, the social and cultural meanings that such structures retain embody the powerful resonances of something more traditional, more fundamental, more "real," if not something pre-modern. One key way in which the cottages that I visited were invested with these meanings was through the labours of the men who took responsibility for them. Ingold's (2000) idea of the "taskscape" captures this process. A taskscape gathers its meaning from the bodily performance of "an ensemble of tasks" performed in series or in parallel; in the legacy of previous – and the anticipation of future – generations doing the same; and with the hands-on assistance of others, affirming the "mutually interlocking" character of such labours across time and space. These elements describe precisely the work of men at their cottage and incorporate – as opposed to merely inscribe – social, cultural, and personal values and meanings into the very being of the cottage and what people experience there. Returning to Heidegger, such labours of men are some of the most vital "constitutive acts of dwelling" for a Haliburton cottage (Ingold 2000, 193-95; see also Connerton 1989, 72-73; see Chapter 2 of this book). Thus today, as it was in the immediate post-war era, the Haliburton cottage provides a forum for middle-class men to express what it means for them to be a "good" Canadian father.

Being a Good Canadian Father

As a place to negotiate the tensions between modern and primal/anti-modern masculinities, the cottage also offered an arena for the expression of Marsh's "masculine domesticity" (quoted in Gelber 1999, 352). It allowed men a venue in which to demonstrate true "family-and-home-centred practices." Men could see themselves as taking an active part in their family's life. They could – and can – see themselves as being "good fathers." In the summer of 2007, one of the lots from the 1952 South Bay development, with a somewhat upgraded original cottage, was advertised for sale at $399,000.[6] Such an inflated value would have been hard to imagine by even the most enthusiastic buyer in 1952. Regardless, those I interviewed who either themselves or whose parents purchased cottages in South Bay – and on many of the other lakes I visited – were not necessarily primarily motivated at the time by the idea that they were making a sound financial investment for their family's future, as there was little thought about what these properties might someday be worth at resale. For the men I talked to, the acquisition of these properties was a deeper kind of investment in their family's future well-being.

All the male cottagers I interviewed would argue that their ongoing improvements at the cottage were fundamentally intended to enhance their family's experience there or to nurture 'family' at the cottage. In the same breath, they recognized the imperative to do regular maintenance, simply to ensure the cottage's usability and, more laterally, to secure the multi-faceted investment it represented. For many, this work meant the steady creep of upgrades, a trajectory that began with indoor plumbing and running water. And if such modern amenities were installed as do-it-yourself projects, the net result of that investment was even greater – assuming that the skill level of the cottager was such that the work was done competently and produced a functioning and durable outcome. Gelber (1997, 100) cautions that such projects are not necessarily always cheaper, as amateurs can make costly mistakes. Undertaking these projects as labours of love was the true essence of a "real cottage/cottager" – in other words, the resourceful Haliburton cottager – situating them, as many interviewees commented, in contrast to cottages and cottagers in Muskoka. Cottages in Muskoka were understood to have been built and maintained by hired labour (the truth is, many middle-class cottagers in Muskoka have struggled or are struggling to keep their cottages); as such, they became "just something you could just consume," as Sean said.[7] They were not Heidegger's "dwellings," as many imagined their own cottage to be.[8]

Men's labour at the cottage was at least in part about creating a venue to turn family into 'family.' These original purchasers would reap the social and cultural capital generated from both their initiative to purchase and their later labours to improve the cottage life of their families. But by default their descendants have reaped the benefits of what became sound, if ongoing, financial investments.[9] In all of this, they were acting out the role of a "good" father who imagined a secure future for his family and whose legacy would instill in them what it meant to be Canadian. Men's labours at the cottage affirmed an ideology that championed self-reliance, stability, perseverance, and competence; both risk taking and risk management; the investment of labour to assure meaningful return; and the simultaneous recognition of the value of both community and personal independence. It offered them an opportunity to reassert the "traditional male control of the physical environment ... in a way that [was imagined to] evoke pre-industrial manual competence" by demonstrating a wide array of skills (Gelber 1997, 68). These domestic skills were rigidly seen to be possessed by men, as women were largely deemed to be "limited ... to helping their ... husbands and acting as an appreciative audience to their triumphs" (ibid.).

I turn my attention now to those who, some assumed, happily looked on appreciatively from the sidelines, admiring their husbands' handiwork and accomplishments at the cottage – the lives and experiences of women at the Haliburton cottage. In fact, many women were not always so blissfully happy at the cottage and, it turns out, were far from passive sideline observers. While some were absolutely passionate about the experience from the beginning, some openly admitted that there were periods when they merely tolerated life at the cottage. There was far from unanimous agreement with Neil, whose childhood summers were spent at a cottage with his mother and who boldly stated that the cottage presented "a pretty damn good life" for women. In contrast to their husbands and many of their children in later life, some women I spoke to much preferred to look forward than to look back when it came to thinking about the cottage. A few readily admitted that they awaited the day when they would be free of the burden and responsibility of their cottage. These women and others who had grown to appreciate their cottage experiences acknowledged that their relationship to their cottage was one filled with deep ambivalence. Marnie captured these sentiments when she emphatically stated, "Cottages are for men and kids ... they are not a place for women."

"Cottages Are for Men and Kids"

Strong-Boag (1991, 486-87, 491-92) argues that women "forge[d] ... the moral basis for postwar Canada," positing that they did so in the ubiquitous and uniform spaces that came to constitute the Canadian suburbs in the 1950s and '60s. I would argue that women extended this project to the middle-class cottage throughout the first decades of the postwar era. Women worked to change suburban real estate developments into humane spaces, fighting for improved public transport, schools, libraries, playgrounds, shopping facilities, sidewalks, garbage collection and sewers, and founding along the way parent-teacher groups and other community organizations and advocacy groups while their husbands were away at the office (ibid., 495-96). So if their hard work and diligence began to transform the suburbs from corporate investments into places more suitable, even more humane, in which to raise a family, why did some women agree to leave them for the summer? Why relocate to spend as much time as possible with one's children at a place that frequently lacked basic amenities such as running water, indoor toilets, laundry facilities, and access to shops and services, and where you were just as likely to be greeted by a black bear as another human being when you stepped out your door? And if the cottage needed a significant investment of manual labour simply to make it habitable, and was also a place where women, it was presumed, were largely "limited ... to helping their ... husbands and acting as an appreciative audience to their triumphs" (Gelber 1997, 68), why would women want to go there?[10] What were the rewards for them? As I found out, they were not always straightforward.

Davina Chaplin (1999, 189) observed that British men and women who owned second homes in France interacted quite differently with such places. She noted, "For men, it is the context in which they connect with different aspects of the self." Men saw the cottage as a place where they could express a more masculine self, somehow a more "real" self, articulated through physical labour and manual accomplishments. They could also make a statement about their investment in their families. For women, Chaplin noted, such places were where they "tend[ed] to experience and represent the home as a space that symbolizes interactive growth or development, for themselves, their partners and their children." I argue that this "interactive growth or development" was a central element of what made the cottage a morally rewarding place for women – one tempered, however, with more than a little resentment. The cottage experience, they felt, instilled in their children what they saw as good middle-class Canadian values: independence, resourcefulness, and confidence. Betty felt it made her children "responsible ... yet gave them freedom," and her children had turned out "all right as adults," so she concluded that spending time at the cottage must have been good for them.

The cottage experience built on long-established Canadian ideas that for children "contact with nature was ... a prerequisite for physical, emotional, and spiritual health" (Wall 2009, 33). But it was not always a place that gave women personal satisfaction and reward – although it is important to note that I met some women who would argue emphatically that they loved their cottage. The Haliburton cottage, certainly for women who began their cottage experience as young married mothers in the immediate postwar decade, was only inadvertently a place where they themselves grew and developed. As Marnie emphatically stated, "Did I have a choice? Did I have a choice to spend my entire summer at the cottage, with only my kids to talk to most of the week?" Describing herself as "the most unlikely cottager," she said, "There are people who should never, ever try to be a cottager and I'm fairly convinced I was one of them." But as she said, "I adapted."

Marnie had no natal family history of life at the cottage, and so she saw herself as "someone ill-equipped to be a cottager." But she knew when she married Norman that he was keen to acquire a cottage in Haliburton. He and a cottage were, as she said, "a package deal." They acquired their Haliburton cottage lot very shortly after they married. Supporting those who would argue that women's leisure is shaped by "patriarchal capitalist ideology" and as such is "closely monitored and regulated," Marnie's only option was to adapt, though she remained skeptical of what she personally stood to gain from the experience (Woodward and Green 1988, 131). Women's responses to, and memories of, the cottage were complex and often ambivalent, and in many cases changed over time. Many concurred with Marnie: cottages were places for "men and kids." Life at the cottage was, for those I met, mainly a rewarding experience. And for both men and women who had spent their childhood summers at the cottage, these were treasured periods of their lives. As Roberta said of her childhood memories, "barefoot and fancy-free was me."

But was the cottage *good* for women? Many of the women acknowledged that they generally did most of the packing, grocery shopping, cooking, and cleaning at the cottage. Feminist leisure and recreation analysts have long argued that for women

> holidays and outings away from home are only a relative freedom from the workaday surroundings and routines of daily life since much of women's lives is compounded by the preparation and planning of holidays ... caring and cleaning roles continued on holiday, often under less convenient and more stressful conditions. (Wimbush and Talbot 1988, xix)

Rosemary Deem (1986, 63) summed this point up aptly:

> Holidays are not necessarily leisure for women ... but may be an extension of their normal domestic and childcare responsibilities; nor are they necessarily a rest from tensions and conflicts within households or families.

These sentiments capture what many women told me about their experiences at the cottage. And thus it would appear that my feminist colleagues were right when they emphatically pointed out when I launched this research that "cottages are just another form of domestic labour ... another fridge to fill ... another toilet to clean." It is worth noting that some of the women did *not* for many years have "another [flush] toilet to clean," as all they had was an outhouse at the cottage. Proper outhouse maintenance, however, demanded skills and knowledge long lost to the modern housewife. Odoriferous visits to such edifices were generally memories best forgotten. Women conducted strong lobby efforts in their families to get indoor plumbing and running water at the cottage as soon as possible, not only for the improvement it represented over an outhouse, but simply because it made cooking, laundry, and cleaning much easier.

Sandra insisted on the installation of a pump to bring water up to the cottage as soon as possible – "I had diapers to soak," she said. Lily resented having to trudge up the hill to their original cottage parking spot, particularly after she started working and visits to the cottage became weekend excursions, precipitating a great deal more packing and unpacking. So a new driveway down to the cottage was built. Lily also refused to think about an island cottage, even if it was her husband's dream retreat. As she said, "You would have to transport all those diapers, in the car, into a boat, out to the cottage ... and then you are leaving and it's pouring rain and you have little children ... forget it!"

Strong-Boag (1995, 61) noted that women of the postwar period "recognized that [domestic] expectations of cleanliness and tidiness grew with each technological addition" of such things as vacuum cleaners and washing machines (see also Cowan 1983). Efforts to even minimally meet these emerging standards dogged some women at the cottage – even if none of these advanced aids would have provided any assistance, as many cottages were off the electric grid in their early years.

Other women readily acquiesced to the reality that a clean cottage was a relative concept, and found pleasure in the liberation it offered from such expectations. A couple of women who took this view expressed amazement that anyone would upgrade a cottage to include such things as carpets, hardwood floors, multiple bathrooms, even big windows, which are found in many cottages today. To them, such things represented nothing more than an increase in the time and labour required to be invested in cleaning, all the while provoking higher standards and expectations of what routine cottage housekeeping should entail. As Isabelle noted, apart from a thorough clean in the spring, housekeeping at her cottage over the summer meant "doing a little bit at a time, and only worrying about the cobwebs when guests from the city were coming." A real cottage, Gwen noted, was "a place where you could keep your sandals on when you went in, for the sand could be dealt with by a quick sweep at the end of each day." Deidre said, "Nobody minds a little sand scattered around."

But despite the potential release from housekeeping standards that the cottage might offer, some women did not like living without what they saw as reasonable standards of cleanliness and comforts of amenities that their house in the city/suburb allowed. Several others listed an array of female relatives – aunts, mothers, mothers-in-law, sisters-in-law – who were known for only begrudgingly visiting the cottage, or happily shipping their children off to a relative's cottage for extended periods to avoid the experience themselves. Kristina, Ben's wife, had no affection for his family's much-loved cottage. She spent time there under duress. She had grown up in a rural area and had lived with outdoor plumbing as a child and she saw no reason to revisit it. Even in the eyes of some children now grown to adults themselves, it took a veritable saint of a woman to dedicate her summers to life at the cottage with only them for company.

"God Bless Mother"

Many of those I interviewed had memories of spending the entire summer at the cottage, either as children or as mothers. Trevor's comments captured the essence of the stories many told me:

> The car would be packed to leave for the cottage on the afternoon school ended in June, and not return until late in the afternoon on the Monday of Labour Day in September. Somehow we would be ready for school on Tuesday morning. I do not know how my mother did it ... Dad would come up every Friday and leave again Sunday night, or sometimes very early Monday morning.

Several cottagers lamented the shift in this pattern that had progressively happened in recent decades as many more women began to work full-time, thereby reducing time at the cottage – with the exception of a couple of weeks during the summer – to a weekend experience. Ava felt that such sporadic residence at the cottage undermined both the commitment to it that children developed and, at a broader level, the sense of community on a lake. Yet the demise of full-time summer residence for mothers and children at the cottage did not necessarily garner a sense of loss among women. Such a commitment came at a personal cost to them, as Marnie suggested above. But these early residence patterns did infuse the cottage with a powerful female force that is often overlooked.

If cottage country in Ontario should be seen as an extension of the metropolitan urban space, a geography that includes the suburbs, then in the 1950s and '60s, a series of absences at the cottage, varying only in scale, were what reinforced this link (Luka 2006; see also Halseth 1998, 2004). Canadian suburbs were expanding rapidly at the time when many of those I interviewed, or their parents, acquired their cottages.[11] As others have suggested, the former came to be seen as female spaces, in contrast to the male spaces of the city and the hinterlands beyond the suburbs (see Dummitt 2007a, 2007b; Strong-Boag 1991, 1995).[12] However, I would argue that at a more subtle level, even if located in this "hinterland beyond the suburb," the cottage shared many of the attributes of suburbs as a female space. Many women spent far more time at the cottage than their husbands did. Just as men vacated the suburbs daily – and sometimes for a week at a time if they travelled with their jobs – so were many consistently absent from the cottage from Monday to Friday, with the exception of their two or three weeks of annual vacation. Men at the cottage were, in fact, the same "weekend husbands" who populated the suburbs of the era (Strong-Boag 1995, 56). And according to Marnie, it was "always on Monday morning" after her "weekend husband" had left that things went wrong: the boat motor would start to leak oil and gas everywhere, the woodpile collapsed, a window in the cottage would get broken. Remembering the litany of such incidents, she declared, "Cottaging is not a rosy picture," but it did teach her to use coping skills she didn't know she had – even if they were ones she had never desired to cultivate.

If women felt that the communication and transportation systems and other public services in the suburbs were limited, what must they have felt when they arrived at the cottage? For many years, the only phone available was at a local marina, reachable only by boat, sometimes a trip of some length. As for limited transportation systems, even such basic infrastructure as a road into the cottage was frequently absent, never mind the poor state of the main highways that linked the city with the cottage (see Pcholkina 2006, 34; Stevens 2008a). Even if the cottage did have direct road access, none of the families I met had two cars during this period. The only available vehicle for many women remained a small boat with duly small motors. Some women learned how to drive that boat before they ever learned how to drive a car, as the former was the only way they could leave the cottage property during the week.

Times at the cottage were often lonely and isolated for some women. The density of cottages varied but on some Haliburton lakes there were only limited pockets of cottage development. Those who spent the summer at the cottage with their children had limited opportunity to connect with other adults during the week. Marnie and her neighbour in the next bay bought "cowbells because the sound carried so well. If either of us or our children heard the bell, they knew we needed assistance right away ... and to come over in the boat ... we were here with the youngsters by ourselves." She recounted stories of seeing bears walk by her kitchen window at the cottage, yet remembered being less wary of these four-legged intruders than of "strangers on two legs." She recounted an incident of two men arriving in some strange boat who seemed only too happy to hang around once they landed at her cottage. She admitted that she was never quite sure what they were doing there, and harboured anxieties that they might return with some untoward intentions when she was there with only her children.

Some who stayed at the cottage for the summer on a Haliburton lake had more extensive and consistent social networks, particularly where there was a greater density of cottages. The South Bay development on Haliburton Lake, for example, had a small commercial centre with such conveniences as a laundromat, marina, and coffee shop; the latter provided, Marianne reminisced, the "best pies and buns in the world." Women and children would gather there on Thursdays to call their husbands with the week's grocery list and do the laundry – which, Marianne recalled, seemed to "take all day." Garry, who had spent his childhood summers on the lake, told me, "It was a big social event; we always got to have ice cream; it was great." His mother may not have agreed.

At times, preteen children were sent off for a day to give their mothers peace and quiet. One mother talked of dropping her children off on a small island a few hundred yards offshore from her cottage. She would pack them a lunch and give them a watch. She required that they stand out on a certain point at designated times during the day so she could see them. She could hear them on the island but they were comfortably separate from her for the day. Another recounted how pleased she was when her son would spend endless hours out on a raft his father had built for him in the sheltered bay in front of the cottage.

Other women had somewhat more positive memories of these times. Ava said, "The best times here were when my kids were small, before they were teenagers." In those years, the children were still filled with the wonder and adventure of life at the cottage and, she admitted, were also still fairly compliant to what she felt was the best way to spend their time there. Adolescents and the cottage were not necessarily a harmonious mix and such tensions made the lives of women somewhat fraught as their children grew older.

Children sent off on day-long hikes treasured such experiences. They saw them as their time to escape the watchful eye of a parent and imagine worlds of fantasy and adventure. For them, such excursions were the stuff of powerful memories. These experiences, their mothers claimed, taught their children the desirable qualities of independence and self-reliance. Marnie, despite her ambivalence about the experience, summed it up: "I think there's nothing better than a cottage for kids; they had to be able to be self-sufficient or they couldn't enjoy the place."

Outside analysts would argue that Marnie had internalized well the expectation of married women of the period that the "care and well-being" and ultimately the happiness of male partners and children was their responsibility (Woodward and Green 1988, 133). Even if fathers were supposed to take a more central role in their children's lives, this played out only in certain arenas. The primary responsibility for familial nurturance remained with women – as it does today in most cases. Many women stressed the "high value they placed on family-centredness" and found then, as they do now, the cottage an excellent place to foster this, even if some secretly resented what it cost them personally (Strong-Boag 1995, 52). But I learned that not all women made such responsibilities an absolute priority all of the time.

Garry laughingly told me about his mother "heading back to Toronto with his father" one Sunday night. "I guess she had had enough of us ...

and I know she missed life in the city." She did not come back until the following Friday when she and his father returned. Garry and his brother, nine and twelve, respectively, spent a memorable week at the cottage by themselves. Their life at their cottage was interconnected with others' on the same bay. He felt quite comfortable knowing that there were other mothers he could call on if he needed help. For a couple of nights that week, he set up his pup tent close to road access into the marina. Everyone checked in on him regularly. He cooked his meals over a fire, and now remembered these repasts as the best he had ever eaten. He even invited his friends to join him. Garry concluded that his mother "would have been hauled off by the Children's Aid Society today; but it really was a great time for us."

While not part of the popular rhetoric about the cottage, the desire some women expressed to escape from its closeted experience slipped out more often than one might expect. One cottager remembered her mother's heartfelt declaration that her favourite day of the summer was Labour Day in September when she and her family returned to the city. That, she said, was the day she "escaped from her prison, the cottage." Such stories capture the essence of Delores's heartfelt sentiments about her mother's experience at the cottage. No wonder, Delores noted, her mother dreaded rainy days; but even then she "put a raincoat on us" and sent Delores and her siblings outside. Delores said, "[Mom even convinced] us that it would be fun, and it was." Delores concluded her reflections on what it must have been like for her mother day-in and day-out at the cottage with only her children for company with an emphatic, "God bless Mother."

"Do We Have Ketchup at Home?"
In the era before washers and dryers were installed in cottages – which many of those I interviewed still did not have and never intended to acquire – the need to do laundry was a recurring theme in any discussion of the household tasks that occupied women's lives at the cottage. Whether it was dealing with soiled diapers when you had no indoor plumbing, or washing sheets in the lake and then getting them dry before the rain came, or negotiating a scrub board in the lake while keeping your toddlers who played nearby from falling in, or, for those who had the luxury, toting a week's worth of laundry in the boat to the nearest public laundromat, many of the women had stories about trying to keep a family in clean clothes and

bed linen. These women exhibited a significant degree of embarrassment with respect to what is now known about the environmental damage that arises from the washing of diapers, hair, bodies, boats, or cars in the lake. But as Sandra said, "Everyone did it. We had no choice" (see also Stevens 2008b). From those who had more recently become cottagers, I heard stories about trips to local towns timed in relation to the need to do laundry, or about timing the lengths of one's stay at the cottage to coincide with the length of time a family could last without doing laundry.

Ava, who had been a cottager since the early 1960s, described how, in early years there, she had rigged up a wringer washer in the woods close to the lake once they got electricity at the cottage. She had acquired a more modern, up-to-date washing machine and dryer at their house in the city, freeing up the now outdated technology for the cottage. She cheerfully noted that this arrangement was a significant improvement over doing the family wash in the lake. In addition, unlike in the city, she could continue to do the laundry outdoors, even if it meant her more modern washing machine sat idle in the city all summer. I was told one story about an old ironing board that had been found at a friend's cottage. It was a point of amusement that there had ever been a time when anyone would bother to iron clothes at the cottage; it took enough effort simply to get things clean.

Doing basic household tasks outdoors once electricity arrived was a point of pleasure for some cottagers. I was told that bread, cakes, cookies, and pies prepared outdoors and baked in a woodstove oven always tasted best. Some women rigged up outdoor workspaces to cook, bake, and make jams, preserves, and pickles. Such spaces were pleasant to work in, not the least because they were a lot cooler than a small cottage with a wood-stove blazing.

Later generations of women, particularly those who travelled to the cottage most frequently on weekends, lamented having to keep two refrigerators stocked over the summer – one at home and one at the cottage. When it came time to pack up for each trip to the cottage, Isabelle was left trying to remember, "Do we have ketchup at the cottage? Is there jam there? And what about mustard? Should I bring the butter?" And while some women were pleased when they stopped spending the entire summer at the cottage, and others had never even known such a pattern, they all lamented the relentless packing and unpacking of clothes, laundry, food, toys, and miscellanea that every trip to the cottage demanded. Lily said,

"I just hate carting everything back and forth, back and forth." But I also learned that it was more than these traditional arenas of female domestic responsibility that kept women busy. Some cottagers had stories of their grandmothers, mothers, or themselves making forays into what would generally be seen as domains of male labour at the cottage.

"Our Other Son"

Marnie and Norman called their daughter "our other son." One evening their daughter came to the cottage with some male friends, who announced as they arrived in the boat, "We've brought your son here." Apparently, the boat's motor had sheared a pin at the other end of the lake. So their daughter "upped the motor, took the pin out, put in a new one, and away they went, just like she would always have done." Marnie felt that as only boys were her daughter's friends at the cottage and she had only a brother, she had become "one of the lads." As she grew into a young adult, she continued to show interest – and more ability than her brother – in repairing things at the cottage. But she still had doubts about assuming full responsibility for the cottage. Marnie noted that her daughter had seen what life at the cottage meant for Marnie, and thus was reluctant to commit to assuming responsibility for the cottage as her parents aged. As Marnie said, "She has seen the cost ... she is smart."

Just as Strong-Boag (1985, 48) noted of women in the suburbs in the postwar era that "expediency demand[ed] that they control finances and fix drains," women at the cottage took on roles and tasks normally presumed to be the prerogative of men. Garry remembers his mother, when she was at least six months' pregnant with his younger brother, building stone stairs down the steep embankment to the lake. As he said, there had been "sort of a trail down to the water but Mom decided to build a switchback trail with steps down the bank ... Dad had cut the trail but she did all the stair work ... they've come into disrepair now ... but it was really a neat setup ... she built the first one right as you stepped out of the cottage ... we then had a nice trail down to the lake." She also laid the tiles in the kitchen one summer, using "a hot plate to melt the glue ... and then they were there forever more."

Alice staked a 50 percent claim to all of the work – from design, to acquisition of materials, to the physical labours of construction, whatever they involved – that she and Leonard had done at their cottage. In her mind, "it was all truly a joint effort." Every project was something they both worked on, and thus they shared in all the tears of frustration and joys of accomplishment. Meanwhile, Trudy's grandmother had taken her grandchildren of both genders into her husband's workshop at the cottage and had them building small sailboats and bird houses to refine their carpentry skills, skills which she herself used around the cottage. These wide-ranging contributions and more independently undertaken projects such as the building of steps, laying of tiles, and fixing of motors positioned these women in the male spaces of labour at the cottage. Some women may not have spent as much time in these spaces taking charge of the wide array of tasks that men did, but many proudly admitted to not simply standing on the sidelines as "an appreciative audience" of their husband's labours.[13] But other women did take full charge of renovations and development of the cottage. Vicky took evening courses during the winter on carpentry and plumbing to develop her skills to do the necessary repairs on their small cottage that she and her husband had purchased.

Women frequently reminded me of the labour needed at the cottage simply to keep everyone fed. Laura admitted that she did not care if her guests were male or female: if she was feeding them, they could help with something at the cottage. If their labour was not useful in the kitchen, then she would find a job for them outside. Everyone knew that this was her rule. She said, "There are lots of great times at the cottage for everyone, but there is no free food."

Several women acknowledged that men regularly did take charge of a popular method of food preparation at the cottage – barbecuing – which was a pattern that had begun in the postwar era (Dummitt 1998). However, Gwen echoed others when she was quick to point out that it "was the women who got everything ready." The location of men's cookery maintained the exclusion of men from the place where the vast majority of food preparation went on – the kitchen – which remained among those women I met a resolutely female space, even at the cottage. Gwen and others noted that men did sometimes enter the kitchen to wash the dishes and do the cleanup, but with more than a hint of cynicism, she noted that such a division of labour had "likely resulted in dishwashers" being installed at many cottages in recent years. Deborah, on the other hand, reaped the benefit of her husband's cooking skills when they were at the cottage, abilities that extended well beyond the barbecue.

The idea of the cottage as a largely male domain was further countered by the stories I heard of single women buying cottages during the 1950s and '60s cottage boom in Haliburton. One did it as an investment, as she could afford a cottage but not a house in the city; one did it to ensure that she was close to her parents, who owned a cottage on the same bay; others were trying to recapture a childhood experience that they had had at a family cottage elsewhere that had subsequently been sold. None of these women were married at the time of purchase but all were professionally employed. All had previous experience at a cottage prior to their purchase in Haliburton. They kept these cottages through much of their married life. A male relative – a father, an uncle, and eventually a husband – by default took on much of the responsibility for the maintenance and up-keep over the years. But none of these women lost their deep sense of personal ownership of these places. Women were fiercely proprietary over them. Neil's mother, a career woman and an amateur pilot who loved the outdoors, bought a cottage in Haliburton as a young woman near where her brother had purchased one. Her family had once worked and cottaged on Georgian Bay. She had insisted that an equal amount of time be spent every summer at both her cottage and his father's family cottage. When the difficult decision was eventually made to sell his mother's cottage, as his parents could not afford to maintain and cover the expenses of both properties, Neil remembered his mother "crying all the way home" after their last visit. Ironically, Neil and his wife, Stephanie, had ended up buying their own cottage just around the bay from where his mother's cottage had been. Neil insisted that he had not set out to buy a cottage in this location, or even in Haliburton, but "nothing else they looked at felt right." He knew it was the right cottage for him even before he went inside. His wife agreed.

Stephanie's deep attachment to her cottage – and she emphatically called it "her" cottage – was representative of the attitudes of some of the younger women I interviewed. Neil noted of his wife, "If her friends are looking for her, and they cannot find her, they know where she will be – at her cottage. She cannot get here enough and often comes up on her own mid-week, if I am away." Neil and Stephanie's children were young adults at the time. She did not feel a need to be around every day to attend to them and her employment schedule was flexible. If she felt like it, she hopped in her car for the ninety-minute drive up to the cottage. The upgraded roads made the trip very easy compared to how it was for those who had travelled the route in the 1960s or earlier. In keeping with their desire to maintain some separation between their home and their cottage, Neil and Stephanie had not expanded or redesigned the original 1950s cottage they purchased. It had been upgraded by previous owners, and had a fully developed basement, electricity, and a telephone. There was no television, which they resolutely determined would never be brought to the cottage. Its décor was "cozy and cottagey," as Neil said, making it "very comfortable." It had a large rock garden that demanded, happily, much of Stephanie's attention – a form of labour that she classed as leisure, not work. Neil also noted that things like the grocery stores in the town of Haliburton were much improved from his childhood memories. Thus, for Stephanie, it was an easy transition to the cottage, a place she frequently chose to come on her own, or with just her son. There was a separation and a peace she sought there, but it was not one she was confined to, as an earlier generation of women had experienced. Spending time there was her real choice, unlike the "choice" Marnie made. Stephanie's decision was made unquestioningly and without any pressure from her family or society at large. Going to the cottage was all about leaving work and the busyness of home behind; it was a luxurious indulgence in leisure, even if she might end up cleaning out the fridge on rainy days.

Gendered Realities of Work as Leisure/Leisure as Work

All those I interviewed would affirm that a cottage is work. But in the end, such affirmations challenged what might be defined as work. Sociologists, anthropologists, psychologists, and leisure theorists have long debated the distinctions between work and leisure. Concepts such as "serious leisure" (Stebbins 1997) and "productive leisure" (Gelber 1999, 20) highlight that such activities are undertaken not only for superficial experiences of distraction and fun. Gelber argued that leisure activities capture the "ideology of the workplace," reconnecting the home – in this case, the second home – to the world of paid industrial (and now what some would call "post-industrial") work. Chris Rojek (2010, 188) would argue that the idea of leisure is integrally linked to affirming the values and virtues of labour as defined by the capitalist system, rather than a pathway to "being free." To him, leisure is grounded in rewarding the accomplishments of the individual to boost "personal prestige." It is well established that leisure activities embed dominant ideologies and, in fact, are often seen to be more enjoyable if they are obviously compatible with the same "beliefs and values generated by ... day-to-day work" (Breer and Locke quoted in Gelber 1999, 15). Leisure can be seen as the payback for work, a balance sheet that gets muddied if work is also perceived as leisure. As Jacob said, "You really have to work for your relaxation at the cottage."

Serious leisure encompasses leisure activities described by those who engage in them "as satisfying or rewarding"; such practices are still "fun to do" even though frequently they require "special training to enjoy" them (Stebbins 1997, 18, 21). In the minds of many cottagers, that special training could incorporate the knowledge passed on from previous generations about how the septic pump could be mobilized into action, or it could simply include, as I have discussed, what it meant to *be* at the cottage. Casual leisure, that which has been described as nurturing feelings of "pleasure and enjoyment" and is primarily done for its "hedonic reward," was surprisingly minimized for many adults and even some children who lamented the labours they felt had burdened them in their younger years at the cottage (Stebbins, ibid.). Jacob and his sister (now young adults) bemoaned all that their mother had made them do each weekend when they arrived at the cottage when they were much younger: unpack and pack the car, cut the lawn, help with jobs such as sanding and painting, prepare the bonfire they so enjoyed – the list went on. In response to their carping, their mother challenged them to "stop such talk ... everyone will think all you did at the cottage was work." When reminded, they had to agree that such a representation was not entirely accurate, but not completely false, either.

In the first decade of the twenty-first century, the work/leisure discussion expanded to engage discussions of work as leisure in the post-industrialized world. Suzan Lewis (2003, 344) argued that for a group of mid-career, middle-class professionals whose careers mirrored those of many cottagers I came to know, their paid "work is what [they] choose to spend their time on and enjoy doing." Such work for these professionals is not the antithesis of leisure; rather, it is "increasingly interesting, absorbing and challenging" (343). This may not be what drives all professionals in the post-industrial world, but it does highlight the desire – some would say, pressure – to not leave work behind at the end of the day. The internet and portable technologies that allow one to remain permanently linked to one's place of employment have made their way to the cottage. High speed internet now serves most corners of Haliburton.

For some, the transportation of one's office/professional responsibilities to the cottage is the "wrong" kind of work to do at the cottage. As twenty-something Jacob, who came from a three-generation familial tradition of cottaging emphatically said, "If I walked down on the dock and saw someone on his dock with a laptop or his Blackberry, I'd think, what are you doing? Turn it off!" But his sentiments belie a reality that had gone on for many years at the cottage. Several of the women who were teachers acknowledged that August was a busy time for them at the cottage, as they had spent many hours beginning to prepare lessons for the upcoming school term. It offered them time to think about what they were going to do when school resumed in September. Ava and Deidre both found summers at the cottage an excellent time and place to study and write as they worked their way through university as mature students. Some of the men cottagers who were Protestant ministers – incidentally, the same profession Ava eventually took up – found the cottage a place to catch up on their theological reading and reflection. Some might argue that the cottage is the perfect place for such labours, and could not imagine calling them work. These individuals, I was told, were often called on to work professionally at the cottage, as they were urged by their neighbours to conduct Sunday church services. In the eyes of their children, such work allowed them more direct access to their fathers, which clarified for them that doing such reading – and Sunday preaching – at the cottage was definitely not work.

So, can the labours at the cottage actually be called work? Was it leisure? Susan Shaw (1985, 20-22) suggested that leisure among a group of Canadian white-collar workers – a category that includes the vast majority of the cottagers I met – was characterized by enjoyment, freedom of choice, relaxation, intrinsic motivation, and the lack of evaluation. For the men I met, the work that they did at the cottage could well be classified as leisure, based on these criteria. As Steven said, "Work at the cottage is part of the fun; figuring out how to fix something ... how to do it with little money ... that is better than bringing someone in to do it ... that is what is fun." He continued, "I am happy at the cottage when I wake up in the morning and I have some work to do." He adamantly affirmed that at the cottage, he did not "want to play, or to fish," activities he saw as detracting from what he really wanted to do which was, as he said, "to cut grass." To him, the latter was productive; it was something that needed doing. It was thus enjoyable in ways these other activities were not.

But for women, much of the work at the cottage could not be so readily classed as leisure. Stephanie may see cleaning the fridge at the cottage as something that has to be done, but few women who washed diapers in the lake or who were responsible for keeping the fridge stocked with adequate provisions as their family life oscillated between the cottage and their house in the city, would necessarily see it that way. It was women who took charge of doing, or at least organizing, housecleaning at the cottage – just as they did at home. They may incidentally have taken on some new tasks, many falling into the realms of those usually associated with men, but they did this in addition to their regular domestic duties. The bulk of the labour done by the men I met at the cottage had little to do with their labour away from it. Their labours constituted a change, which as the adage suggests, "is as good as a rest." Women got little of the same rest. It is worth noting that not all women cottagers saw these labours as entirely burdensome, but few failed to acknowledge the irony when asked.

The efforts to accomplish female domestic labours at the cottage did become somewhat more leisure-like once things were upgraded. Electricity brought stoves, fridges, and eventually, for some, laundry facilities and dishwashers. Fresh food at least became easier to keep. The arrival of the telephone truncated, usually desirably, women's isolation at the cottage. And in recent years, the expansion of communication technologies brought televisions, as well as high speed internet and cellphones, which have facilitated for some the expansion of professional/paid employment to the cottage. However, this has simply caused the realm of professional labours to become more integrated into cottage life. For several women – and men – I met, such work had never been absent from the cottage in the first place.

But for some women – and some men – this expansion offered too much capacity to stay connected to the working world beyond the cottage. Richard's mother refused to answer the phone if it rang at the cottage. The attitudinal difference between her generation and that of her grandchildren was considerable, as the younger group generally could not wait for wireless access to arrive at the cottage, so they could remain connected to the world outside. Their desires for what the cottage should afford them had out-stripped the incursions of modernity, and sped ahead to the postmodern wired world. Even their father, who deeply treasured his childhood mem-ories of the simple life at the cottage, had begun to see the wired cottage as a place where he could bring his professional work, thus extending the time he was able to spend at his beloved retreat.

In his early writing about the tourist experience and its links to mod-ernity, Dean MacCannell ([1976] 1999) acknowledged the complexities of the relationship between work and leisure. He noted that tourists often observe others at work or simply visit places of work as attractions. I have also argued elsewhere that being a tourist can be a lot of work: planning, organizing, packing, driving, relentless sightseeing, taking and compiling one's photographs, or even the effort needed to communicate all that a trip entailed to a somewhat disinterested listener, can be laborious (J. Harrison 2003). In my initial observations, being a domestic tourist or a cottager similarly seemed to require work, a theme that originally piqued my curi-osity about the phenomenon of the cottage. For the cottagers I interviewed, ambiguities surrounding what was work and what was leisure were real, particularly when looking at how such work/leisure was parcelled out on gender lines. The gendered classification of all that went on at the cottage fuelled the complexities of the understanding of the work/leisure relation-ship at the cottage, and ultimately shaped the enjoyment, the reward, the satisfaction, and the larger ideological and political agendas of what made life at the cottage deeply meaningful, if somewhat "messy." Assumptions about gender, along with those of class, nation, nature, family, belonging and memory, community, bodily discipline, and even race have influenced what has been seen as desirable, pleasing, even beautiful about life at a Haliburton cottage over the last sixty years. I am left wondering if the privileging of such understandings will be the same at the midpoint of the twenty-first century.

8

Privilege at the Cottage

Recently, Penny Caldwell (2010, 15), editor of *Cottage Life* magazine, began a column that took aim at the assumption made by non-cottagers that all cottagers are wealthy; they are not, she insisted. To her, most cottagers are just ordinary people. One has to assume she means members of the middle-class, however she might loosely define such a grouping. It would be hard to make the case that many of those of the lower/working class, that is, those who exist on precarious minimum wage jobs, could afford to own and maintain a cottage, just as it cannot be denied that there are certainly cottage owners who could be classed as a wealthy elite. Caldwell went on to emphasize that the enjoyment of the cottage experience is grounded in an openness to appreciating the beauty and small pleasures that it affords. She posited that all cottagers should be "grateful" for the opportunity they have to experience life at their cottage, yet "proud" of the fact that they value this "profoundly beautiful country ... [with its] vast forests, massive amounts of fresh water, and an extraordinary natural world teeming with wildlife." Her comments lead me to assume that possibly not everyone, maybe not even all Canadians, appreciates such treasures; her statements could also be read to imply that it is desirable, even virtuous, to have such capacity and insight.

The tenor and specific content of this editorial suggest a taken-for-granted assumption about all the good things the cottage is seen to represent. She notes activities such as swimming in the lake, fishing, enjoying wildlife, spending extended time with 'family,' even if to experience these things one must endure long drives and blackfly bites, which, Caldwell acknowledges, cottagers often trumpet as "badge[s] of honour" marking their commitment, tenacity, and unbridled passion for cottage life. Valuing these things, being able to remember one's experience of them in the past and contemplate their recurrence in the future, denotes to her the "privilege" of cottagers. But as Michael Kimmel (1990, 94) has asserted, there is a "painlessness" to such "presumptions of privilege." While it implies something greatly valued, such privilege also suggests something natural, even something one is owed, exemplifying what Stevens (2008a, 49) argued many Ontario cottagers in the postwar era saw owning a cottage to be – a "birthright." I posit that there is nothing natural about intensely enjoying or longing for the experience of the cottage as it was known and desired by those I interviewed. In fact, some cottagers saw their commitment to the cottage as, to quote Betty, "quite insane." Having spent forty years as a cottager, Marnie asserted at the conclusion of our conversation, "No one with any sense owns a cottage. I am absolutely persuaded that there is a sanity gene missing in people who own a cottage."

I would in large measure have agreed with her before I began my research to try to understand what was meaningful about the cottage experience. But listening carefully to those who patiently and enthusiastically tutored me in what their cottage meant to them convinced me that a commitment to owning – or at least regularly experiencing – a Haliburton cottage was much more nuanced than Betty's quip might suggest, and it was fundamentally not without its "presumption" of the "painlessness ... of privilege."

It is obvious that those I interviewed were not driven to own a cottage by some genetic deviation. Nor were they motivated by any primordial programming that spawned their passion for the experience, despite what Ben and Deborah told me. For Ben, coming to the cottage is "like sleeping or eating, it is just natural to think of going there." For her part, Deborah implied that it is somehow programmed into one's genes if the practice has been in one's family for several generations. Even if such notions resonated with many cottagers I came to know, what drove their intense devotion to and love for the experience was much more complicated. It was not simply the potential of "just good times," as one cottager described, that made the cottage so appealing to those Haliburton cottagers I came to know. I suggest that the relationships that Haliburton cottagers have with their cottages are grounded in a dialectic tension between presences and absences, even if these are not located in a genetic coding omission or in atavistic yearnings.

What It Takes to Be Present at the Cottage

Life at the cottage and cottage ownership are about learned behaviours. Simply put, everyone has to be nurtured as to how "to be" at the cottage. Knowing how "to be" at the cottage, sensing what it means "to dwell" there, possessing the expertise to deal with the most prosaic and mundane details about how physical and mechanical things function, as well as having the embodied knowledge and richly symbolic sensorial responses to the natural and social world that envelopes the cottage – these things are repeatedly validated in the discourses that actively promulgate the desirability of the cottage experience in Ontario. If one gets to a cottage – assuming it is an experience that lives up to the mythologies that surround it, or it is simply something one has always known – the potency of the memories of simply 'being there' become a powerful lure to bring one back, time and time again. Caldwell (2010, 15) quotes one cottager whose profound attachment to the cottage stemmed from it being the place "where she remember[ed] the people she loved." Such accretions foster the capacity of the cottager to intuit their enjoyment, if not their passion, for the cottage experience. Simply put, one's discovery of how to be at the cottage becomes layered at the cognitive, emotional, and embodied levels. It occurs over time with repeated return. Many cottagers claimed this process began when they were barely out of the womb; others acknowledged that they learned this through the good fortune of being introduced to the cottage when they were young children; others married into it; still others specifically pursued the experience through the acquisition of a cottage or cottages and then began the process of steadily accumulating the knowledge and cultural capital needed to fulfill their dream of truly being at the cottage.

Once on this path, many cottagers said, they desired to return to indulge in it, willingly investing over the years and often decades significant amounts of financial, temporal, emotional, and psychological energies to secure this opportunity for return. Many felt a significant part of their personal identity was grounded in their self-identification as Haliburton cottagers. It was the "materiality of [their] social identity"; their cottage became an "inalienable possession" (A. Weiner 1992; Miller 1998, 129). Others, however, were somewhat less rapturous about such returns, transposing their commitment to be at the cottage as something that was good for their children and highly desired by their husbands. Regardless, such tenacity is valued, a quality that many insisted was elucidated by the cottage experience, but normally from a slightly less conflicted perspective.

Most of the cottagers I spoke with would have argued that owning a cottage is primarily driven by "habits of the heart" (Bellah et al. 1985), though they would also see it as stemming from a particular rationality because of what it offers (or has the potential to offer) those who are "Canadian," as this is understood within the Ontario zeitgeist. Fundamentally, Haliburton cottagers see the experience (both past and present) of their cottage as something good or rewarding for their 'family' and for themselves. It offers them what they are due; it expresses the "expectations, possibilities, probabilities, and aspirations" of what the "good life" should be (Conley 2008, 371-72). Rewards come in the form of affirmation of a certain economic stability, a strengthened social positioning and an assumed right to leisure (Urry 1995, 130); confidence about one's identity, which is entangled with notions of a pioneering spirit, hard work, dependability, and resilience; an appreciation of, and a connection to – even if completely fictional – the Canadian landscape and what spending time in it offers one at a physical, emotional, and even moral level; clarity about gender roles and, implicitly, sexual identities; a valuing of 'family' and kin connections and a wealth of personal and familial memories and experiences; and a sense of belonging to a place and, for most, a community that was imagined as steadfast and unwavering – if at times falsely so. The cottage experience affirms, if almost by default, a particularly racialized Canadian identity. Cottagers find comfort in knowing that there will be others like them in cottage country. They will find there those who, as Caldwell emphasized, appreciate all the beauty and riches of the Canadian landscape and understand and know what to do there. Additionally, I would argue, cottagers accept, if only at an intuitive level, all that is implicit in ideas of private property, larger discourses of capitalism and labour, and tropes of nationalism as they play out in the practice of cottaging. Such a practice denotes "external goods" that can carry certain "internal goods" – the aesthetic, emotional, and moral values of life at a Haliburton cottage and being a Haliburton cottager (MacIntyre, as quoted in Sayer 2005a, 957-58; see also Sayer 2005b, 111-13).

The strength of Lisa's feelings about what it meant to be a Haliburton cottager was captured in her assertion, "We are the best." Laura championed, as does Caldwell (2010, 15), cottagers as "a hardy group to put up with some of the crazy things" that life in that place demands. These "crazy things" – blackfly bites, for instance, the bane of all who return to the cottage in the early spring – "you suffer for them, might not like them, but you are proud of them all the same." And, in the end, they make a statement about one's resourcefulness, commitment, unfailing labours, patient resilience, and emotional comportment to garner all that is meaningful and beautiful about life at a Haliburton cottage for your family, friends, and yourself. Such values, as Lawler (2005, 797) said of the middle class, signal that that they are "morally worthwhile ... having the right kind of taste." They make a statement about a commitment to a certain kind of labour, which those cottagers I came to know would argue is about nurturing the intangible but vital parts of life – the bonds between family members or friends who are welcomed or found there, simply "the emotional and affective dimensions of life" (ibid., 804). As Aaron says, his cottage is a place that he feels "responsible for," a place – physically, socially, culturally, and emotionally – that needs him to be the right kind of person – dependable, reliable, and hard-working – in order to ensure its continuance.

Those who dedicate themselves to repeating the Haliburton cottage experience negotiate myriad social, cultural, economic, and emotional forces to secure their place at the cottage, to find themselves, as Trevor said, in the "real world." On the one hand, cottagers position themselves within an array of influences that presume both what the experience should be and how they personally, or at least their family, will define it. For example, they can either actively embrace the "cottager's bible" as one of those I interviewed called the magazine *Cottage Life,* or they can ignore it, seeing it as a sacrilegious attempt to commodify something that to them can never fall prey to such forces due to its idiosyncratic and heartfelt character. Members of even the most dedicated Haliburton cottage 'family' "got away," some daring to express hesitancy, even unwillingness, about assuming the responsibility of all that the experience symbolizes and demands – the anxiety about which was often only compounded as each generation passed, as the layers of memory and the moral, emotional, physical, temporal, and financial investment became denser and more weighty. Such responses affirmed that being a passionate Haliburton cottage owner was about making certain choices. They highlight, despite strong assertions that nothing changes at the cottage, that it is a place ever in flux. Thus, at the micro level, the cottage could be seen as a place in motion; a contingent place; a place characterized at many levels by mobility, if not fluidity.

However, at the macro level there are certain constants at work at the Haliburton cottage. Rojek (2010) argues that leisure activities such as cottaging are undertaken to reinforce larger ideological narratives. So while there may be choice, in reality there is only so much choice. To him, leisure activities in countries such as Canada – or, in his specific case, the United Kingdom – profoundly strengthen dominant cultural and moral values, and thereby fundamentally affirm the values of the capitalist system, defining for some such pursuits and the places they occur as reactionary imagined sources of stability and unquestioned identities (see Cresswell 2004, 75-79). Cresswell draws on Harvey (1996) and Massey (1993) in his discussion. The Haliburton cottage experience would support such a positioning. As Holman (2000, 98) noted, the legacy passed on to the Ontario middle class sees "capitalism as the natural order of things; economic competition as an essential part of the human order and private property was an inviolable right." The world at the Haliburton cottage did not happen "on the head of a pin" (ibid., 27) but was greatly influenced by these realities – including the global market system and the social hierarchies of race, gender, and class and colonial histories – that play out in Canada.

Haliburton cottaging can be seen to reinforce such notions as the value of hard work (sometimes redefined as play), the need to affirm one's social position, and what it means to be 'family,' and to validate individual accomplishment, resiliency, and resourcefulness. It thus fundamentally affirms a central pillar of the capitalist system: the value of private property in the Canadian economic, political, and social matrix. While public boat access to Ontario lakes cannot legally be prevented, it is growing ever more difficult to find public land on many Haliburton lakes, as more and more is sold off for cottage development. Even some cottagers found the disappearance of this resource troubling, just as in times past generations of other non-cottagers might have found the development of the cottages by those who now own them equally disconcerting and exclusionary.

Cottagers extended a sense of metaphorical ownership beyond their own cottage to talk of "their lake," over which, through lake plans and covenants, they attempted to assert control. Of particular concern were the social behaviours of fellow cottagers on the lake; there was a significant degree of disquiet that things were changing in Haliburton cottage country in ways many found discomforting. Such unease stemmed largely from the sense that those now arriving in Haliburton would not be schooled in what many took to be the central tenets of "the cultural codes" of Haliburton cottagers. Simply put, they did not know what was truly meaningful about the experience of a Haliburton cottage. They were not "real cottagers."

There is a sense that those who really understand how special this experience is, how Canadian, how meaningful, how authentic – a term I do not use lightly – will keep all that it symbolizes alive; they will respect its traditions and richness. Leonard, who bought his cottage over fifty years ago, asserted to me that even though the physical character of his family's cottage has been altered, expanded, or even completely remodelled over the years, "its place in the family has not." However, many are asking: Will it always be so? Will the much-desired multi-generational legacy of the cottagers who have invested so much in their Haliburton cottage come to be? And for those who have achieved in part that goal with multiple generations now arriving at the cottage, how long will this legacy continue? Will the Ontario middle class still be present at the Haliburton cottage in another sixty years? Such musings prompt another question: Who will then be the Canadian middle class? And will that middle class continue to be interested in owning a cottage in Haliburton? Will they make the same choices about how and where to invest their financial, emotional, social, and personal resources to affirm their sense of what it means to be "Canadian"? Will a Haliburton cottage continue to have the capacity to validate what those I interviewed seemed to hold so dear?

But other factors are currently at play here that may have a dramatic impact on who can venture to cottage country regularly in the future. Oil prices in the spring of 2011 hit their highest level in Canadian history. It will therefore cost more to travel to the cottage. Additionally, such increases have the capacity to affect the cost of many other things in everyday, and certainly cottage, life. Will such realities take a toll on who can afford to marshal the resources to either newly acquire a cottage or, at the very least, maintain one they own or inherited, be it something quite modest or creeping into "monster" cottage territory? Is it possible to conceive that the idea of retreating to nature, to own a property on a rock- and tree-lined lakeshore, and to understand this as a restorative, therapeutic, and intensely enjoyable leisure experience, will become less trenchantly validated in the Ontario zeitgeist? Will a retreat to the world outside of the city no longer be seen as a fundamentally Canadian desire, a practice that has strong roots in the cultural traditions of Western Europe? Over 80 percent of Canada's population now lives in cities and seems quite happy there. An ever-increasing number of Canadians do not have those Western European roots. Fewer and fewer of us have familial histories outside of the urban environs. Could cottage country ever become a ghost of its former self? It is true that all manner of destinations, from Hawaii to Niagara Falls and to Las Vegas, have reinvented themselves to attract new audiences. Would a similar reimagining of a plethora of privately owned cottages in a place like Haliburton be conceivable?

Reports produced in the spring of 2011 by leading real estate companies insisted that the demand for cottages was strong and had rebounded from any negative impact of the 2008-09 global economic crisis; and yet by the spring of 2012 that rebound had stalled.[1] Just what will Haliburton cottage country look like in 2050, one hundred years on from the period in which cottage expansion in the region really took off? There are no crystal balls, but if the racial and cultural profile of the Greater Toronto Area (GTA) continues to change the way it has in the last thirty years, one could predict that it might have some impact on what happens in cottage country. Presently, such "new" populations are largely not found in Haliburton cottage country; their absence is glaring, given that they will form an increasingly significant component of the Canadian population in the next half-century. The demographics of the GTA have changed dramatically over the past few decades, a fact that has not gone unnoticed by those in the business of affirming the central place of the Canadian landscape in the national psyche. What will be the impact of such absences on cottage life in Haliburton?

Who and What Are Absent at the Haliburton Cottage?

In 2010, Parks Canada launched *Camping 101*, weekend experiences and seminars on how to successfully spend time in Canada's national parks. One program, offered in Banff National Park in partnership with a local Alberta social service agency, was, ironically enough, named *Authentic*

Canada.[2] This initiative is specifically aimed at "new Canadians" who find the idea of spending a weekend living and sleeping in the woods more than a little daunting, if not completely alien. The title of this program speaks volumes about the assumption of what it means to be a "real" Canadian. It implies that to be Canadian, you must enjoy and seek out such experiences as often as you can. It says that urban spaces are not the "real" Canada.

Parks Canada began such initiatives in response to changing national demographics documenting that, since 1995, Canada's national parks had experienced a 22 percent drop in visitation while the national population had increased by almost the same amount (Alphonso and Paul 2010). In May 2011, publicity around these initiatives heightened, as that year marked the hundredth anniversary of a national parks service in Canada, the first of its kind in the world (Allemang 2011).[3] Newspapers, television, and online blogs and articles noted that while this was a time for celebration, it was also a time for concern based on the above statistics. Are Canadians losing interest in such archetypal icons of our national identity?[4]

Why would such matters be of relevance to a discussion about Haliburton cottaging? Cottaging is not camping. To all those I interviewed, the former is a much richer if not simply a more comfortable experience. Most critically, cottaging to them has the capacity to generate experiences and memories that resonate at a deeply affective level, grounding one in a very particular landscape and place. But the average age of cottage owners in the early years of the twenty-first century is fifty-two years (Kremarik 2002). It is a population that soon will need revitalization. It seems obvious from the outside that new blood will need to be infused to maintain the vitality of life at the Haliburton cottage. And that new blood will have to make a strong commitment to the cottage experience to ensure its future. But in the first decade of the twenty-first century even those who have long histories at, and a passionate commitment to, the cottage are spending less time there on an annual basis,[5] and many are uncertain if the often globally dispersed or financially less stable next generation will be able to make the necessary commitment to life at the family's Haliburton cottage. And then there is the large sector of Canadian society who will simply never be able to afford to acquire a cottage.

Ava's neighbour built a very expensive and elaborate cottage, yet comes but a few weekends a year. This scenario is far from unique. One might predict that the attention to maintaining a property that is used so little might wane after a few years. Who will be the next purchasers of such cottages? These places are expensive and can be complex to maintain.

In the spring of 2011, even a minimally desirable waterfront property in Haliburton was priced at over $250,000.[6] I also heard stories of cottages with as many as ten bathrooms and seven bedrooms being built with greater frequency in Haliburton. Such places veered beyond the affordability realm of those whom Caldwell (2010) called "ordinary people," and discarded any real sense of what a Haliburton cottage had been understood to symbolize. However, acquiring any cottage property is not merely about having the necessary financial resources; it is about understanding and desiring the lifestyle, and the cultural and social behaviours that it presumes. It means knowing all that you need to know to even begin to enjoy – and, more importantly, passionately desire to repeat – the experience and invest all the necessary resources to ensure its realization. Some of this knowledge, specifically that revolving around cottage maintenance, can be purchased, even if to many cottagers I came to know this would be a rather non-Haliburton thing to do.

There were also basic things one had to know to ensure one's survival at the cottage. The need for such knowledge is affirmed in studies confirming that a higher percentage of those who have been in Canada for a relatively short time die by drowning in lakes than do those who have been long-time residents (Iltan 2010). As one source said, many "newly" arrived Canadians "want to embrace the Canadian experience, but don't have the knowledge to do so safely" (ibid.). But will learning the basics of water safety translate into a desire to acquire a cottage to ensure unlimited opportunities to enjoy the experience of a refreshing swim? As those I interviewed assured me, the chance to jump in the lake at the cottage as many times as you want when the heat gets intense on a summer's day does not happen in isolation. Swimming, picnics and family gatherings are the rewards one receives for having invested significant time, energy and resources in getting to the cottage and keeping it standing and fully functioning. And if these people do arrive in cottage country in large numbers will they feel welcome there? Or will it feel like a rather alien place? And if they do come, how might they change the place, the experience? It was noted that South Asian campers who participated in the Parks Canada programs quickly began to tweak their experience in ways more amenable to their own cultural values. These adjustments included such things as the food they cooked and how many family members needed to gather to rank the experience as a good one (see Alphonso and Paul 2010, A6).

There are other groups that are not necessarily obviously present in Haliburton cottage country. Presumptions of the normative heterosexual family predominate at the cottage. But what if one does not fit that norm? Where does the homosexual 'family' find a place? If one accepts the trope of feeling at home in, desiring to be in, moving to reside (even if only seasonally) in a place deemed representative of the iconic Canadian landscape, can one feel comfortable there outside of these norms?[7] What about other types of bodies that do not necessarily fit well in cottage country, a key one being the disabled body? Can the cottage ever readily accommodate such bodies, if so much about life at the cottage is about performing taken-for-granted disciplined bodily practices: swimming, driving a boat, physical labour, hiking, walking, and simply making do in a more cramped living space? If one can do all of these things, then a certain humility around the privilege to be able to do so might well be warranted.

An angry student confronted me when I made a presentation about this research to a GTA university class. She had scowled at me through my entire talk. When I opened the class up to questions at the end, she was the first to raise her hand. She then castigated me over why I had not considered studying those who went camping for annual vacations, as her family had done during her childhood, up until the time of her parents' divorce when the capacity for any holiday ended abruptly. She emphatically indicated that she was more than a little weary of the presumptions that "everyone can afford a cottage, that everyone wants a cottage." It was an opportunity available to a small percentage of the population yet, as she stated, "everyone talks about it like it is something that everyone has." What she said was entirely accurate. Those who have access to this practice were in her eyes a "privileged group," and yet they were held out to be the norm. The cottagers I spoke with would not necessarily disagree with her. Many saw themselves as Caldwell (2010) sees her readers – as unwittingly fortunate to have had a parent (or grandparent or other relative) who had the security and the foresight to acquire a cottage property when such things were more affordable, and to have had 'family' willingly invest the resources, time, and effort needed to retain it. Others had made a significant financial and personal commitment to acquire a cottage to secure for themselves all they felt, or had come to understand, were the virtues of the experience. Yet over time, being at the cottage has come to be interpreted as a function of what Douglas Porteous (1996, 21) proposed drives humans more than anything else: the desire to simply "seek happiness"; or, to encapsulate what Jeremy Coote (1992, 246) claims, people are always, even if unconsciously, preoccupied with enhancing the aesthetic quality of their lives.

Contrary to such imaginings, as Luka (2006, 307) has suggested (and I strongly agree), the cottage is far from a "benign landscape of leisure." It is a complex social, cultural, and political – thus implicitly exclusionary – practice. Acknowledging this reality has the capacity to open the door to welcome others who are not, but potentially desire to be, at the cottage. Change is swirling around life at the cottage, and if such broader and more nuanced understandings can be absorbed into all that the cottage is, they have the potential to reimagine what it means to be a "real" cottager and, ultimately, a "real Canadian."

Notes

Chapter 1: An Introduction to the Cottage

1 In the seven years that I worked on this research project, my work was featured in three newspapers and one magazine article, I did three radio interviews on regional radio, and I was asked to give four talks to general public audiences. Such media attention far outstrips what I have experienced for my other scholarly work over the past fifteen years, even if much of it has been on topics of broad public interest (see J. Harrison 2001, 2003).

2 This number corresponds to the same percentage of Canadians who owned a summer residence of some type in the rest of the country. Luka (2006, 9) calculated that 8.2 percent of the Ontario population in 2003 owned a cottage, based on Statistics Canada data. His calculations suggest an average of 7.5 percent in the years 1997 to 2003. My calculations included data collected in the period 2003 to 2006. These percentages remain consistent with an increasing population.

3 When I use the term "cottagers" throughout this manuscript, unless otherwise noted, I am referring to those whom I or my research assistant interviewed, or cottagers with whom I had numerous casual conversations during my time spent in Haliburton. What I say about Haliburton cottaging here may well apply to other enclaves of similar cottagers, but I do not assume such extensions.

4 These cottages were located on lakes adjacent to Highway 35, a main access route through the region. This highway had been improved and upgraded in the 1930s as part of a government make-work project. Those who had spent time at these cottages in the pre-World War II era noted that their grandparents used these properties in part as subsistence plots. Their grandfathers fished in the summer and froze their catch for transport back to the city in the fall. Their grandmothers planted large gardens and picked wild berries and canned, pickled, or preserved all the produce to take back to the city for winter consumption.

5 Several individuals of British ancestry emphatically pointed out to me during the course of this research that the Oxford English Dictionary defines "cottaging" as "to

use or frequent public toilets for homosexual sex." The verb does not appear in North American dictionaries. However, it is commonly used in Ontario (only) to describe the practice of spending time at a recreational cottage.

6 Other areas that developed in a similar manner for a similar population were Georgian Bay and the Thousand Islands (see C. Campbell 2005 for a history of cottaging in Georgian Bay and du Prey and Farr 2004 for a similar overview of the Thousand Islands).

7 See http://www12.statcan.ca/.

8 However, it did experience a steady growth in the two decades that followed, reaching nearly 15 percent in the early to mid-1980s. See http://www12.statcan.ca/ and http://www.statcan.gc.ca/pub/62-557-x/62-557-x1996001-eng.pdf .

9 See Canada Facts and Figures 2011 – Immigration Overview – Permanent and temporary residents. http://www.cic.gc.ca, p. 20.

10 As I discuss in Chapter 6, 'family' is a more expansive collective than what is assumed to be the hetero-normative nuclear Canadian family. It could include more than just those with shared biology.

11 See http://haliburton-tourism.com/index.shtml.

12 Ibid.

13 See http://en.wikipedia.org/wiki/Haliburton_County_Ontario.

14 Archaeological investigations done farther north in what is now Algonquin Park, and the burial mounds located to the south of what is now Peterborough (see Map 3, p. 14), show that these peoples may not, however, have been the first who moved through the region. Such evidence suggests that the Hopewellian peoples, whose territories eventually covered the expanse of lands east of the Mississippi River from Mexico to Ontario, likely flourished in this area at least 2,000 years ago (Reynolds 1973, 2-10). Archaeologists are undecided on what was the eventual fate of these peoples.

15 These reserves were created at Rama on Lake Couchiching, on Rice Lake, Chemong Lake, and near Sarnia.

16 The French colony of Quebec, which fell to the British in 1759, was the other key force along this central access route. Having never abandoned its French language, culture, and national identity, the province of Quebec has had a more ambiguous political, social, and economic role within the nation-state than Ontario.

17 The British lost their more southerly American colonies in 1776.

18 Many things worked against the success of the Canada Land Company, including bad management and a lack of understanding of what they had really undertaken. But the final blow came when the government implemented a "new national policy of Free Land Grants" to those who fulfilled its conditions. "The only people who would buy land from the company wanted well-laid-out properties in villages, within communities and with access to roads" (Barnes 2002, 20-21). Those who took up the

grants, it turned out, were "isolated with no access to schools, churches, stores," and lacked the volume of labour needed to work their land (Cummings 1962, 77).

19 There has always been some mining in the Haliburton region but in relation to the lumber industry such operations were relatively modest (see Proulx 1997). There is current discussion on reopening a uranium mine in the area (Gorrie 2009). Many non-locals with an interest in the region (i.e., cottagers) vehemently oppose this action. Local residents who know all too well the vagaries of the economy in the area are far more supportive of this idea, as it will bring stable employment to the area.

20 See http://www12.statcan.ca/census-recensement/index-eng.cfm.

21 See http://www.algonquinhighlands.ca/.

22 The Municipality of Highlands East sits on the eastern side of Haliburton County and was incorporated as of January 1, 2001. Highlands East is comprised of the former Townships of Bicroft, Cardiff, Glamorgan, and Monmouth. It has a permanent population of approximately 2,700 and a seasonal population of roughly 13,000 with a total of 4,300 households. http://www.highlandseast.ca.

23 See http://www.mindenhills.ca/.

24 The United Townships of Dysart, Guilford, Dudley, and Harburn were incorporated on 7 January 1867, and the first by-law was passed on 13 July 1867. The Municipality of Dysart et al. has grown to encompass the townships of Harcourt, Bruton, Havelock, Eyre, and Clyde, an area of 1,473.87 square kilometres. Its official name is the Corporation of the United Townships of Dysart, Dudley, Harcourt, Guilford, Harburn, Bruton, Havelock, Eyre and Clyde; however, it is known as the Municipality of Dysart et al. See http://www.dysartetal.ca/frameo.asp. (See Map 3, p. 14.)

25 The provincial rate was 6.4 percent; the rate in Haliburton 7.5 percent. See http://www.statcan.gc.ca/tables-tableaux/sum-som/l01/cst01/labor36b-eng.htm. In the 2011 census, no specific data is available for Haliburton but the Muskoka-Kawartha region (which includes Haliburton) reported an unemployment rate of 8.6 percent; the provincial average in 2011 was reported at 7.4 percent.

26 By 1925, the Royal Kushog Hotel on Head Lake was the largest tourist resort in the region. "It had, for a number of years, a special train to and from Toronto for the use of its guests. It boasted a few fishing lodges on other lakes, running water, and electricity, tennis, lawn bowling and even had its own orchestra. It later burned down and the location was used for a municipal high school" (Reynolds 1973, 168). In the 1930s, another large resort development was constructed on Elephant Lake in the northeastern part of the county. In 2012, it was still operating.

27 In 1939, the Highlands of Haliburton County Tourist Association was formed to "promote civic, economic and social welfare to the people of Haliburton County, and to encourage ways of bettering tourist traffic and business development." It continued until 1953, when the Chamber of Commerce was formed (Reynolds 1973, 170).

28 See http://www.lbkglaw.com/cottages.html, which offers advice from a legal point of view about how the very complex issue of inheritance and succession of the family cottage could be handled.

29 Luka (2006, 166-71ff) argues that there is a generic notion of cottage country, which, broadly, I would not dispute. For Luka, "cottage country is a generic settlement category"; in other words, a lake and the potential experiences to be had there have to meet a set of criteria to satisfy cottagers' desires to be at a cottage. What I identify here as an understanding of what constitutes "the quintessentially Canadian experience" corroborates this point. However, as I suggest throughout this book, this assumption is complicated. The particularities of individual families, their cottages, the community on their lake, the physical attributes of their lake, and its history of cottage development were highlighted equally as things that made the cottage and the experiences there decidedly unique. Simply put, cottaging in Haliburton, while generic at one level, was not understood to be like cottaging elsewhere, and the experiences at the cottages of those I interviewed could not be confused with the experiences elsewhere.

30 Perkins and Thorns (2006, 77) highlight some of these absences and their need to be addressed.

31 "You Sold the Cottage" (M. Gane). From the album *This Is the Ice Age*, 1981 Polygram Distribution.

32 See J. Harrison (2008b) for a detailed description of the methodologies I used.

33 Some cottage associations changed their name to the latter monikers as their tax rates rose through the 1990s and early 2000s. This change held significant symbolic meaning as it asserted the cottagers' legal ownership and their subsequent demand for a say in governance and environmental and economic development in their corner of cottage country.

34 By 2010, many more of these groups had adopted websites to communicate with their members.

35 See J. Harrison (2008b) and Pcholkina (2006) for a more detailed discussion of the research methods used here. The interpretation of the materials gathered from all of these interviews and presented here is entirely mine and thus I speak exclusively in the first person when referring to our research. This usage is in no way intended to ignore the valuable contribution made to this research by my assistant's work.

36 I also interviewed the executive director of the Federation of Ontario Cottagers and an individual who had been involved extensively in *Cottage Life TV* for several years. Their interviews gave broad contextual information and some specific reflections on cottaging in Haliburton.

37 One family had American citizenship. Their paternal grandfather was Canadian and had brought his family every summer to a cottage in Haliburton, after he moved to find work in the United States. The next generation of his family had continued this

practice and declared themselves as having a strong affinity – especially politically and socially – to "all things Canadian." Haliburton was where the parents of the family I met intended to spend at least 5 to 6 months of each year once they retired. Another cottager was living in the United States for employment reasons, but remained very connected to Haliburton, returning every summer with his family. He remained a Canadian citizen.

38 Over 50 percent were between forty and sixty, another 45 percent between sixty and seventy-five, and the remainder were between thirty and forty years old.

39 The middle class at one time did have a place in Muskoka, but progressively those who do not own a "gold-plated vacation home" have felt less welcome there. See Reinhart (2004, A11).

40 One Haliburton cottager told me in amazement of a story he had heard about a casual Saturday morning shopping trip of a new Muskoka cottager that had included "the purchase of two personal watercraft, a ski boat, a sailboat, two canoes, and a runabout!"

41 There had been regular dances held at Haliburton Lake at one time in the community centre, but these places were a long way from the dance halls in Muskoka, such as Dunn's Pavilion, where big-name acts used to come to play on a Saturday evening. See http://www.thekee.com.

42 Anonymous "Operation Haliburton" *Toronto Star* advertisement, 1953.

43 See "Canadian Recreational Property Buyers Looking to Renters to Make Dream of Ownership a Reality." http://www.royallepage.ca.

44 See http://www.foca.on.ca/Taxation and http://www.wraft.com/.

45 Newspaper and other media increasingly suggest that the middle-class experience in Canada continues in a position of instability as the distribution of incomes in the country becomes increasingly polarized, leaving those in the middle "flatlined," an economic position that will increasingly disadvantage this group (Grant 2008).

46 See Löfgren (1999, 143) for a discussion of these factors in cottage developments in other international locations.

47 See http://www.statcan.gc.ca/ for reports on the increased wealth of Canadian families from 1999-2005.

48 The developments add further nuance to Halseth's (1998, 2004) and Hall and Müller's (2004) categorization of such recreational landscapes as elite.

49 Hirsch makes the important point that positional and material goods can be the same thing, depending on how they are viewed (quoted in Walter 1982, 296).

50 Howland (2007, D1) quoted a spokesperson for Credit Canada who claimed "many people are house-poor because they want the Canadian dream of home ownership." Thirty percent of pre-tax household income on shelter costs is deemed manageable; in Toronto in 2007, based on average income, this figure was estimated to be an unaffordable 45 percent.

51 Martin (2009, 27-32) outlines how one couple in their thirties could plan to buy a cottage if they did so with another couple and if they planned carefully and cut back on expenses for the next seven years.

Chapter 2: The Cottage

1 My use of the concept of a cottage aesthetic has direct links to the tourist aesthetic that I suggest helped shape the touristic experiences of another group of middle-class Canadian tourists. As I have argued that cottagers can be seen as domestic tourists, it makes sense that an aesthetic sense can then be understood as part of what makes their time at the cottage meaningful to them. The cottage aesthetic incorporates many of the elements that I suggested were part of the tourist aesthetic, varying only in emphasis and degree (see J. Harrison 2003, 92-138).

2 Featherstone's (1996) discussion of the "aestheticization of everyday life" and the emergent middle class in the nineteenth century suggests that these two aesthetic responses need not be understood as being in isolation from each other.

3 See also Halseth (1998) and Stevens (2008a, 2008b).

4 See S. McKay (1996) for a humorous depiction of the journey to the cottage.

5 Stevens (2008a, 29-34) points out that travel by train was not always a pleasant experience, and in particular "it could involve delays and inconveniences that were beyond travelers' own control" (ibid., 32). See Pcholkina (2006) for a discussion of the realities of moving around cottage country without a car, and what these realities symbolize.

6 This is the time it took Deidre and Roger to travel with their family from Alberta every year to spend a month at their family cottage. Roger had agreed that his family would make this annual trek when he had accepted a transfer to the west.

7 After they took early retirement Howard and Emily moved to Gravenhurst from Toronto to allow them to be close to their new cottage.

8 It took Sam Thompson about thirteen hours to drive from Chicago and about ten hours for his daughter to drive from Philadelphia. It used to take Delores's family six hours to get to the cottage from Ottawa.

9 Stephens (2008a) notes that once automobiles became owned widely in Ontario, cottagers began to come from areas outside of the GTA. Many of the cottagers I spoke with did come from the GTA, and the vast majority of traffic that heads to cottage country on the weekend moves out of the GTA (see also Luka 2006).

10 Cottagers who are now permanent residents are not included here.

11 I discuss varying notions of time at the cottage in Chapter 4.

12 Obrador Pons (2003, 49) would argue that as tourists, cottagers are "dwelling" in the world as part of their very mobility back and forth to the cottage, since by doing so they are seeking to be "amidst-the-world."

13 See Obrador Pons (2003) for a discussion of these ideas in relation to tourists who move on less predictable journeys.

14 David Harvey (1993, 11) and others critique Heidegger's romanticization of peasant life as inappropriate for "a highly industrialized, modernist and capitalist world" (see also Cresswell 2004, 60, 71ff; Harvey 1996, 299-316).

15 I am drawing on the Oxford English Dictionary definition of a socialite: "a person who is fond of social activities and entertainment."

16 These developments are limited in Haliburton to date. But there is a fear that when any large block of land comes up for sale on a lake – such as those occupied already by small resorts – they could be zoned for such developments, a point I return to below. They are becoming more common in Muskoka. See Pasternak (2008).

17 McCracken develops this concept in reference to North American homes, based on research done in the mid-1980s.

18 Examples of such shops include: Cottage Chic, http://www.cottagechicstore.com/, Muskoka Teak, http://www.muskokateak.com/, and Lockside Trading Company, http://www.lockside.com/.

19 See Luka (2006, 179ff) for a discussion of these structures and their assault on "the aesthetic subtlety associated with the built-form in cottage country."

20 My research assistant noticed a booth at the *Cottage Life* show in the spring of 2009 that was selling air fresheners specifically designed to combat such smells, particularly those that overwhelmed one on the first visit back to the cottage in the spring. Obviously, Joan was not alone in finding them offensive.

21 I acknowledge the arguments of Robert Sack, Edward Casey, and J.E. Malpas that "place is primary to the construction of meaning and society" (quoted in Cresswell 2004, 32). But as Cresswell (2004, 33) suggests, rather than seeing this position as oppositional to the thinking of scholars such as David Harvey, it is more productive to see it as one that acknowledges that place is "a kind of necessary social construction," as it is impossible to conceive of any human action without positioning it in a 'place.' See Cresswell (2004) for a discussion of the complexities of place as it has emerged in human geography and beyond.

22 I use "place" here as a shorthand for the triad space/place/landscape, but I do so acknowledging that there are recognized conventions as to what is meant by the other two parts of the triad, space and landscape. I take space as the more abstract concept, what Cresswell (2004, 8, 10) calls a "realm without meaning" until people attribute meaning to it, thereby converting it to place. I define landscape as that "topography ... that can be seen" and the "way it is seen"; it is the "physical, visual form" of place (Cresswell 2004, 10; Relph 1976, 30; Sack 1992, 2). Mitchell's (2002, 2) more complicated description of landscape as something that is "a focus for the formation of [national] identity" can be seen in Chapter 3 of this book to be at play in how cottagers see the Canadian landscape and their place in it (see also Wylie 2007).

23 In contrast, many cottagers would characterize their home in the city as a "thinned out place" (Sack 1997, 9; see also Williams and Kaltenborn 1999).

24   Such a cottage structure was defined in Regulation 747 of the Ontario Public Lands Act in the 1950s as "a building in which facilities are provided for cooking and for shelter for one or more persons living therein, as a single and non-profit housekeeping unit." E-mail communication, Neil Hayward, Ministry of Natural Resources, 17 April 2009.

25   Public spaces in the county, such as Buttermilk Falls, the Haliburton Forest, the Hawk Lake Log Chute, and the whitewater kayaking course on the Gull River, were also part of the cottage landscape for many I spoke to.

26   The indigenous and industrial history I highlighted in Chapter 1 were, for most cottagers, not part of that texture.

27   Nora (1989, 8-9) distinguishes between memory and history, seeing the latter as "the reconstruction, always problematic, and incomplete of what is no longer ... a production of intellectual and secular production, [that] calls for analysis and criticism ... is always prosaic, [thus] releas[ing the sacred] ... belong[ing] to everyone and to no one, whence its claim to universal authority ... [bound] ... strictly to temporal continuities, to progressions and to relations between things ... [It] can only conceive the relative."

28   The annual return to the cottage had elements of the newly rediscovered books that Walter Benjamin (1970, 66-67) recorded as he unpacked his library. Each volume pulled from the crates triggered memories or images of where he acquired it, where he read it, how he came to purchase it. Once again surrounded by his library, as he said, memories crowded in. See also Cruikshank (2005) for a rich description of layered memories of time and place in a different context.

29   Tuan (1977, 198) would identify these as the "museum and societies for the preservation of the past," which are intended to cultivate "a sense of place," whereas the cottage as imagined by many cottagers, and promulgated by magazines such as *Cottage Life* and a whole array of other forms of media representation, could be classed as what he sees as the more informal "shrine or monument," both of which indicate that one is "rooted in a place."

30   Bordo (2003, 171-76) draws on the work of Pierre Nora (1989), John Mulvaney (1991), and Henri Bergson (1968) in the development of his idea of a "keeping place."

Chapter 3: Community, Nature, Modernity, and Nationalism at the Cottage

1   See Gordon (2006, 66-71).

2   Lears (1981, xv) suggests that anti-modernists were seeking liberation from "Weber's concept of rationalization of Western culture, the drive for control of outer and inner life."

3   There were many parallels to suburban development in some of the postwar cottage development in Haliburton. The development on South Bay, Haliburton Lake has many of the characteristics of a new suburb. But I agree with Stevens (2008a, 29) that

little has been written that explores this link directly. See also Stevens (2008a, 47) regarding the link between the suburbs and the inward focus on the nuclear family.

4 Anonymous, "Travel in special trains to see cottage sites," *Globe and Mail,* 4 May 1953.

5 See Luka (2006), Pcholkina (2006), and Stevens (2008a, 2008b; 2010) for more thorough discussions about ideas of nature in cottage country.

6 See also Williams (1973).

7 Many of these cuts were initiated by the Mike Harris provincial government in the 1990s. See "The Top Ten Things Wrong with Environmental Protection Under the Common Sense Revolution." http://www.cela.ca. Since the 1970s, the provincial government has implemented various strategies to try to ensure that cottagers minimize their impact on their local environment. It was concluded in the 1990s that the only way such initiatives could be successful, particularly considering the staff reductions at the provincial government level, was through the local volunteer stewardship programs. See http://www.lakeplan.com for a history of the lake plan process in Ontario.

8 See http://www.lakeplan.com/.

9 This turn of phrase strongly links to the notion of glacial time at the cottage. It suggests some notion of a primordial or even just historical moment when we were all closer to nature, which implies somehow that this is our natural state, which we should all want to return to.

10 See Pcholkina (2006) and Stevens (2008a, 2008b) for a discussion of the extent of the ambiguity that surrounds the relationship of cottagers and nature/the environment.

11 See "Lake Partner Program: Ministry of the Environment." http://www.ene.gov.on.ca.

12 See Luka (2006), Pcholkina (2006), and Stevens (2008a, 2008b).

13 There is much literature on the social construction of nature and an increasing attention to this subject with specific reference to cottage country. See for example Cronon (1995), Evernden (1993), A. Wilson (1991), and Wynn (2006), and especially Luka (2006), Pcholkina (2006), and Stevens (2008a, 2008b, 2009).

14 My point here is closely related to Stevens's (quoting Parkins) that cottagers saw themselves as "*in* nature but not *of* it" (2008b, 12; italics in original). I see my discussion here as simply an enhancement of the more in-depth attention that Stevens has given to cottagers' attitudes to nature and the environment (see 2008a, 2008b, 2010; see also Luka 2006).

15 Stevens (2008a, 24) quotes a 1954 *Toronto Star* article that encouraged "making a game out of identifying birds, insects, trees and wildflowers, etc." as a way of teaching (what I might call disciplining) children "to become young naturalists."

16 These animals would fall into the category of what Stevens (2008a, 39-42) would call "good animals." See also Luka (2006, 278).

17 Bears at the dump are, in fact, far from passive. Attendants at the dump regularly warn cottagers to be wary of those that frequent the place, particularly mother bears

with cubs. Cottagers at the dump are advised not to linger out of their cars once they have deposited their refuse.

18 Organizations such as the Federation of Ontario Cottagers Association (FOCA), local cottage associations, and the publishers of *Cottage Life* magazine encourage cottagers to temper their desire to plant a lawn, and try to encourage those who already have to let it return to its natural state. See *Cottage Life* on natural gardening at the cottage. http://www.cottagelife.com. *Cottage Life* and Fisheries and Oceans have also published materials on developing and maintaining a healthy shoreline and building "waterfront friendly docks." See Ford (n.d.) and Burn (n.d.), respectively. See also Steed (2005) on developing lake plans.

19 See J. Harrison (2010) for a more elaborated discussion of this subject.

20 The latter never dissipated despite the French defeat by the British on the Plains of Abraham in 1759 and the strong hold that the Montreal-based Anglophone minority held on the economic and political dimensions of the province, which was greatly aided and abetted socially and culturally by the control the Catholic Church held over the Quebec peasantry. The Quiet Revolution in the 1960s eventually challenged both of these masters (see Gagnon and Montcalm 1990).

21 One tragic event that brought these debates into the popular media was the crash of Air India 182 in 1985 off the coast of Ireland. The flight originated in Canada and many of those on board were Indo-Canadians. Many have suggested that if it had been a planeload of white Canadian citizens, the public, legal, and government response to the crash would have been very different. There was a sense that many of those who perished in the crash were not "real" Canadians (see www.cbc.ca).

22 See http://www12.statcan.gc.ca.

23 See www.cic.gc.ca/english/resources/statistics/facts2011.

24 Some of the Group did travel to western Canada – specifically to the Rocky Mountains – and to the most northerly regions of the country, but with the exception of the mystical works of Lawren Harris, these artists are best known for their images of the landscapes of Ontario.

25 The Canada First movement, which was launched in 1869 shortly after Confederation, envisioned the nation as "a Northern country inhabited by the descendants of Northern races" (Haliburton quoted in Berger 1970, 53).

26 Robert Grant Haliburton was one of the founding members of the Canada First movement. See Berger (1970, 49-77). However, he is not the person for whom the region under discussion is named. Thomas Chandler Haliburton, first chairman of the Canada Land and Emigration Company – the corporation that sold land in the region to newly arrived settlers – gave his name to the region.

27 To further make his point, Wolfe (1977, 27) talks about the design and scale of the cottages of the immediate post-World War II era, details that describe the early cottages in Haliburton as having many parallels to the first log dwellings built by many early agricultural immigrant settlers. In the published version of these comments

in 1977, Wolfe noted that the desire to own a cottage was fuelled by many additional factors, which my research supports.

28 See http://www.blackcreek.ca/v2/museum/history.dot.

29 As much of the excellent work done by cultural geographers such as Luka (2006) and Halseth (1998) has shown and my research would corroborate, cottagers prefer a heavily mediated relationship with "nature" or "wilderness" at the cottage. Earlier generations – those tough, strong, and hardy – had laboured to tame or mediate this iconic landscape in order to survive.

Chapter 4: Time and Order at the Cottage

1 See http://www.lbkglaw.com/cottages.html#children. Keeping the cottage in the family is presented as something unquestionably desired. A few cottagers I interviewed, however, admitted that they doubted their children would keep the cottage when they inherited it, due to their lifestyle choices or distant geographical homes.

2 A search on Google produces a lengthy list of sites and contacts offering advice on cottage succession planning. See also Balfe (1999) and Walmsley (2002).

3 Clearly opening up the cottage is the source of much more interest and enthusiasm than is closing it up. In the index to *Cottage Life* magazine, the former generated thirty-two articles and columns, closing up rituals only thirteen.

4 This variation parallels that described by Luka (2008, 77).

5 This pattern varied for several of those I interviewed whose fathers were teachers or ministers, professions that allowed them the opportunity to be at the cottage full-time during July and August with their families. It also varied for those whose fathers had worked shift work that afforded them the opportunity to come to the cottage mid-week, rather than on weekends. Such work also limited one father to one-day visits to the cottage as he was not given two consecutive days off from his place of employment. He and his wife arranged their days off and their vacations so that at least one of them could be at the cottage with their children for the bulk of the summer.

6 Until recently, banks would not give mortgages for cottages. But 1950s developers did offer purchasers the opportunity to pay off the cottages in instalments. After he married, Paul managed to buy a house in the city and at one time owned three small cottages on this lake. His daughter admitted to me that she was never quite sure how her parents managed to accomplish this as they had only ever held jobs that paid modest wages, and her father had been laid off at various points in his working life. Her mother told me that they just "managed their pennies well." Paul was not the only cottager we talked to who bought a cottage before he bought a house.

7 To Harvey (1989, 240), the increased mobility of capital around the globe, facilitated by ever expanding technological connectedness beginning in the 1970s, hastened "the turnover time of capital." He argues that "the history of capitalism has been characterized by [the] speed-up in the pace of life."

8   This concept was discussed in Chapter 2.

9   The calculation of market value is what many cottagers and rate-payers take exception to. This action was taken, government officials argued, to address historic discrepancies in the system.

10 Some modest relief was offered rate-payers in the form of a phasing in of new tax assessment, but the end result is the same: the increased taxes have to be paid. See www.wraft.com.

11 See Lawrence (2008).

12 The Waterfront Ratepayers After Fair Taxation (WRAFT) and the Coalition After Property Tax Reform (CAPTR) were lobby groups specifically focused on fighting these increases. See www.captr.org.

13 In the late 1970s, about 6 percent of Canadians owned vacation properties; by 1999 it had risen to 7 percent or about 823,000, but between 1999 and 2005 this figure rose to over 1 million, a dramatic increase in a short period of time (Hayes 2009).

14 In the 2006 census, Canada's population was just over 31 million.

15 A 1000-square-foot cottage on the same lake in the spring of 2009 was listed in real estate ads at $350,000.

16 Increased annual costs have prompted some cottagers to think about renting their cottage for a few weeks each summer. The headline on a 2009 issue of *Cottage Life* read "Save the Cottage, Your Survival Guide to Renting." The story begins by raising the point many cottagers find uncomfortable: the idea of letting strangers into their "sacred space," their cottage, their "family homestead." There is actually a long tradition of those who rent out their cottages and those who rent in cottage country, and some families have rented the same cottage for years, thereby establishing a sense of ownership of the property. One cottager told me that when her friend's young daughter heard that the cottage they had rented for a week each summer for twelve years was to be sold to new owners, she was inconsolable, sobbing for hours. Rent collected can help to defray costs such as increased taxes and allow the cottage to remain in the family; it can also be viewed as an altruistic act, as renting lets others share the joys of the experience (Hayes 2009, 119).

17 See the website for the Canadian Retirement Information Centre for details at www.canretire.com. Diversionary strategies have less impact on cottages that were first purchased decades ago. Their effectiveness depends entirely on the amount of discretionary funds that the current owners have when they begin to address this issue in their will. See http://www.dkinsurance.com; http://www.lbkglaw.com/cottages.html#capital; and Cottage Succession Planning at http://www.professional referrals.ca.

18 *Cottage Life* magazine began publishing in 1988. In 2009, it had over 68,000 subscribers. See http://www.cottagelife.com. *Cottage Life TV* was sponsored by *Cottage Life* magazine, and ran on various networks for eleven years beginning in the early

1990s. See http://tonyarmstrong.com/tawork/cltv/. A new *Cottage Life* television channel is being launched in 2013. See http://cottagelife.com/65839/blogs/editors-note -harbingers-of-spring. The *Cottage Life* shows are trade fairs organized by *Cottage Life* magazine. They are held twice a year in Toronto. At the Spring 2009 show there were 475 exhibitors ranging from real estate agents; condominium developers; boat, hot-tub, deck, dock, sauna, composting toilet, septic system, and alternative energy dealers; to builders; to clothing, food, art, and book sellers. The Spring Show was first held in 1994, the first Fall Show in 2004. See http://cottagelife.com/shows/ show-about-us.

19 See Lakeshore Capacity Assessment Handbook, May 2010. http://www.ene.gov.on.ca/ stdprodconsume/groups/lr/@ene/@resources/documents/resource/std01_079878. pdf.

20 Conversation with Bev Clark, Coordinator of the Lake Partner Program, Dorset Environmental Science Centre, Environmental Monitoring and Reporting Branch, 26 May 2005.

21 See http://www.kennisis.ca/.

22 The original document outlined other kinds of more formal implementation strategies, such as working with the local municipality to implement improved by-laws concerning shoreline protection, zoning, and development; enforcement of existing by-laws about boathouses, backlot development, and cottage location; and active participation in government water quality management (see for example Garrah 2006, 2007).

23 See http://www.dragandsprucelakes.ca/.

Chapter 5: The Cottage Body

1 Thrift (1994, 193) and Knowles (2008, 168) embed their discussion of these ideas in the experience of mobility, or, as Knowles says, "never [being] at rest." This mobility captures the experience of the cottager as someone who moves in and out of the "emotional [experience], bodily practices, [and] physical character of [two different] places": the cottage and "the city/home." Knowles specifically centres her discussion on "rural racism" and how "whiteness" is constituted in rural England through the "co-mingl[ing]" of "ordinary (people) and ... vernacular (places)." Such notions resonate with my discussion of life at a Haliburton cottage as I came to understand it through my research.

2 Turner is critiquing Foucault in this conceptualization. See also Coleman and Kohn (2007, 6) for a similar critique of Foucault's notion of the body.

3 See also Csordas (1994, 6) on this point. The first insights were offered on this idea by Mauss (1935) who "argued that the body is at the same time the original tool with which humans shape their world, and the original substance out of which the human is shaped" (quoted in Csordas 1994, 6).

4 This greater acceptance may have to do with the fact that snowmobiles are not ridden solely on the frozen lakes but also often on trails some distance from any actual cottages. Moreover, there are fewer cottagers around in the winter to hear the noise. Snowmobiles also serve a practical purpose, as they allow those who have water access cottages to get to their properties more readily in winter.

5 See http://www.haliburtonholidays.com/summer/kayaking.asp and http://www.trailsandtours.com/.

6 Proper canoeing skills – which in particular included knowledge of the J-stroke – were something that some cottagers learned if they went to summer camp or, less frequently, took canoeing lessons. Such techniques are not absolutely necessary to move a canoe down the lake, if one is not interested in doing so efficiently. During my research, I heard experienced canoe trippers – that is, those who learned "proper" canoeing strokes and regularly went on extended canoe trips – disparage the clumsy paddling skills of many cottagers. Cottagers, on the other hand, told me that all they cared about was being able, as one of them said, "to doodle around the lake," as they were never in a hurry to get anywhere when they took out the canoe.

7 However, PFDs did not prevent drownings or accidents in and around the water (Lifesaving Society, 2003; Stevens 2008b). PFDs are only one dimension of increased efforts by the state to enhance boat and water safety of cottagers.

8 The Lifesaving Society's *Drowning Report: A Profile of Drownings and Water-Related Deaths in Ontario* (2003, 3, 14), drawing on data from the period 1996-2000, indicated that "not wearing a PFD is the number one problem contributing to Ontario drownings," and 69 percent of those who drowned in Ontario in this period knew how to swim.

9 See also Urry (1995,198) for a discussion of these issues in another recreational context.

10 See V. Turner (1982, 55-59) for a full list of what "flow" entails.

11 Roger's water skiing experience could emerge as an experience of "flow," as it results "from ... a structured activity" and/or his "ability to make flow occur." Csikszentmihalyi (1990, 71-73) also suggests, however, that occurrences such as "friends [at] a dinner party ... [where everyone] begin[s] to make jokes and tell stories, and pretty soon all are having fun and feeling good about one another" could produce an experience of flow.

12 See http://www.cottagedreams.org. The founder and director of Cottage Dreams owns a cottage in Haliburton, which is how I connected with her in the course of my research.

13 This pattern is well-documented and consistent. During the course of my research, I spoke with a real estate developer who had built condominium developments in centres adjacent to cottage country for such individuals who find they have to move from their cottage once they reach a certain age, but who either do not want to return to living in the GTA or now lack the resources to do so.

14 The riders of PWCs who "play" in such manners most likely include a far wider demographic than those between the ages of fifteen and twenty-five. See http://boating.ncf.ca/newsspivak.html for details of a failed effort to significantly limit the use of PWCs on lakes. The 2003 Lifesaving Society report, however, did conclude that "young adults 18 to 24 years of age [had] the highest water-related death rate at 1.8 deaths per year per 100,000 population (1996-2000). [This rate was] 38 percent higher than for all age groups combined. Alcohol consumption and not wearing PFDs continue to be significant problems with these 'young risk-takers.'" Most of those who drown can actually swim, and nine out of ten of those who drowned in this age group were men (Lifesaving Society 2003, 10-11).

15 Works of fiction about the cottage often have sexual lust and desire and their ultimate satisfaction – often as acts of transgression – as central themes. Examples include *Summer Gone* (David MacFarlane), *The Ladies' Lending Library* (Janice Kulyk Keefer), and *Wilderness Tips* (Margaret Atwood). It would appear that the cottage was for some not just a "good place for kids."

16 Transport Canada, an agency of the federal government, decreed that all boaters in Canada must hold a valid Pleasure Craft Operator's Card or the equivalent ("proof of competency") to operate a pleasure craft fitted with a motor. These cards are good for life. The law came into effect 15 September 2009. See http://www.tc.gc.ca/eng/menu.htm. There has been a significant heightening of attention to matters of water safety in recent years. Both Canadian and Ontario laws are aimed at addressing preventing the mixing of boats and alcohol. The efforts of Canadian musician Loreena McKennitt, whose fiancé died in a boating accident in 1998, have aided in raising the public profile of water safety. She launched the Cook-Rees Memorial Fund for Water Search and Safety to raise awareness of the need to wear PFDs and the need for increased vigilance on the water and respect for its capacity to claim lives. See http://www.cookreesfund.com/home001En.html. See Stevens (2008b) for a historical reflection on tragic deaths in lakes in cottage country.

17 In statistics gathered between 1996 and 2000, 49 percent of all recreational boating deaths involved alcohol (Lifesaving Society 2003, 18).

18 See http://www.ofah.org for a discussion of this controversial decision.

19 See http://www.cbc.ca/news/background/health/hantavirus.html.

20 I was contacted by a Trent University alumnus of non-Caucasian ancestry whose family had purchased a cottage in Muskoka shortly after they immigrated to Canada, as they were told it was what "Canadians did." At first, they knew little of the experience but they have since grown to love it and see it as a central part of their family life. For an alternative view, see also Jiménez (2006).

21 Ironically, Brand and her companions were travelling to one of Ontario's historic sites that commemorates a terminus on the Underground Railroad for fugitive slaves and free blacks fleeing oppression in the United States in the nineteenth century. See Brand (1997, 73-77); see also Panelli et al. (2009).

22 His thoughts on this subject were most articulate on the class issues that were emerging in cottage country, as he saw it as a place that was now well out of reach for those but the most affluent. He seemed to assume that if visible minorities had the resources they would find their way to a Haliburton cottage.

23 Perry (2001) found in his study of white American college students that being "rational" was a central characteristic that described those who identified as white.

24 The vast majority of the remaining group had American ancestors – an ancestry that does not in any way preclude distant ancestral links to the United Kingdom, Ireland, and Western Europe. Based on phenotypic observation, it is fairly safe to say that all of those in this group most likely had links to the racial and cultural stocks of these latter regions. I interviewed one individual who was from Africa and who was obviously of non-white ancestry. She was married to a man of long-standing WASP ancestry. Another individual was of South Asian ancestry, originally from India. By his own admission, he found the whole cottage experience somewhat curious, but was willing to indulge his wife and his in-laws in their love of it, as long as he had access to a television while there. He valued the sense of family that times at the cottage generated.

25 See Canada Facts and Figures 2011 – Immigration Overview – Permanent and temporary residents. http://www.cic.gc.ca, p. 20.

26 See "Recent Immigrants in Metropolitan Areas: Toronto – A Comparative Profile Based on the 2001 Census." http://www.cic.gc.ca.

Chapter 6: Family at the Cottage

1 See Chapter 1, note 10.

2 The analysis in Conway's book and his policy recommendations are directed towards addressing the changing nature of the family, the needs of Canadian children, the need to improve the lives of women who happen to be mothers, and to offer support to men who find themselves conflicted regarding their role in the family and society at large.

3 It seemed obvious that among those I interviewed, there were two homosexual couples who owned a cottage in Haliburton. I did not, however, ask specifically about sexuality during my interviews; thus, I cannot make any broad assumptions here.

4 The recognition of what has been called the "helicopter parent," the description of the cellphone as "the world's longest umbilical cord," and the return of adult children to live at home highlight the complexities of what such hyper-individualism actually means as a lived experience in the first decade of the twenty-first century (see Gardner 2006; Tyler 2007). However, this discussion is beyond my focus here.

5 There has been wide critical discussion of this position. See for example Chodorow and Contrato (1982), Gillis (1996a), Stacey (1996), and Struening (2002).

6 Feminists have pointed out the flaws in the blanket assumption of family as a place of nurturance. One has only to look at the statistics on neglect, abuse, and other

forms of domestic violence inflicted on spouses and children throughout history (see Collier, Rosaldo, and Yanagisako [1992] 2001, 18; Conway 2003).

7 Edwards and Strathern (2000, 160) suggest that these same qualities are what Alltown residents identified as what was meant by "closeness" among those recognized as family.

8 A shore lunch was a long-established tradition among recreational fishermen and canoeists. It consisted of freshly caught and filleted fish from the morning's catch, often over an open fire.

9 In a short-sheeted bed, the sheets are folded midway up the bed, not allowing the person entering the bed to fully recline.

10 One distinct difference between these French family homes and Ontario cottages is that the former were often the original rural/peasant base of these families. Chevalier borrows heavily from Annette Weiner (1985) in her discussion of these houses. By extension, I do the same.

11 Such attachment counters Luka's (2006) argument that cottagers see themselves as attached to a generic cottage country, rather than specific locations there. As I noted earlier, I found many cottagers knew very little about other lakes in Haliburton, which contrasted to the intimate knowledge they had of "their lake."

12 There are countless examples of these stories in *Cottage Life* magazine. Other sources include MacGregor (2002, 2005) and Gordon (1989, 2006).

13 See also Stevens (2008a, 47). This pattern contrasts with what Chevalier (1999, 93) noted for the movement of furnishings from French country residences. Furniture was never moved from the country residence to family members' urban homes and vice versa.

14 See http://www.funeralhome.on.ca/burial_cremation.htm or http://www.just cremation.com/askdirector.html.

Chapter 7: Gender at the Cottage

1 While women did leave the workforce, their departure was not as immediate or as permanent as is often represented. Joan Sangster (1995, 125) argues that in the period 1945-70, though "the dominant image of married women in the popular media may have focused on their domestic roles and assumed a middle-class lifestyle and a male breadwinner, many women faced a different story (see also Sangster 2010; Strong-Boag 1991, 479). Many of the women I met fit this media image, although several had professional careers, mostly in the education and health care fields. A few others were office workers and bank tellers.

2 Gelber (1997, 73) distinguishes between "domestic masculinity" and Marsh's (1988) "masculine domesticity." To Gelber, domestic masculinity includes those things "that had been the purview of professional [male] craftsmen, [and] therefore retained the aura of pre-industrial vocational masculinity." He emphasizes "the idea of domestic masculinity [as] the creation of a male sphere inside the house" (ibid.). However, I

agree with Rutherdale (1999, 370-71n2) that such distinctions are more often limiting than helpful.

3 One cottager was a high school tech teacher; he taught carpentry and woodworking skills in the GTA. The fine craftsmanship in his cottage and all of its infrastructure evidenced his superior skills in this regard.

4 Loo (2006, 33) goes on to argue that a hunting expedition in the Canadian woods was "the most effective way to restore bourgeois masculinity to its former strength and glory" (see also Jessup 2002, 162-63 on the perceived restorative capacity of wilderness for the middle class). By the postwar era, middle-class men had adopted other ways of re-engaging with such "primal masculinity" (Dummitt 2007a, 2007b).

5 In Innis's terms, the Canadian economy at its most basic was grounded in the extraction of staples, be they fur, fish, or lumber.

6 Ad for Remax Haliburton Highlands Realty Company. *Haliburton Echo,* 19 July 2007, 44.

7 It is important to note that in the first decades of the twenty-first century in Haliburton, cottages are becoming much larger and more elaborate. An increasing number of properties, when they come on the market, are priced over $500,000; some are as high as $2 million. Few of these pricier structures remain what Luka (2006, 272-73) calls an "owner-building." I interviewed some who had redeveloped their cottages to 1600-plus-square-foot structures with all of the amenities of a home in the city. These larger structures were often built by non-local contractors, and are rarely solely maintained by those who own them. As such, they may well be creeping closer to what many I met saw as a "Muskoka cottage." See Archer 2010.

8 See Chapter 2.

9 As such, recreational properties in a capitalist economy have always been understood to be in some measure a worthwhile investment, even if for many years banks would not give mortgages for cottage properties.

10 I would speculate that part of the appreciation of such work was motivated in some measure by how it made women's – that is, mothers' – lives at the cottage more bearable. None lamented the arrival of running water, for example, at the cottage.

11 I do not presume that all of those who purchased Haliburton cottages were suburban dwellers. A small percentage of those interviewed came from small towns in the area around Toronto. Others came from families that had farming backgrounds. However, in the postwar era, none of these families continued to work solely as farmers, a lifestyle that allows little time for weekend trips to the cottage. All had shifted their employment base to paid work either in Toronto or in smaller surrounding communities. Some cottagers did say that either the memories of their parents or their own childhood remembrances of living on a farm had fuelled their parents' desire to acquire a cottage. I heard stories about one Haliburton cottager whose attachment to this legacy fostered her commitment to the idea that the cottage should be a place of work and production, just as the farm had been.

12 See Loo (2006) and Jasen (1995) for discussions of the hinterland as a masculine space.

13 Not all women were so participatory. Ida waited patiently for Leon to finish their new cottage so she could take full charge of the entertaining she wanted to do with friends and family there. She happily read while he laboured.

Chapter 8: Privilege at the Cottage

1 See Royal LePage (2011).

2 See http://4seasonrec.blogspot.com/2010/09/authentic-canada-ccis-parks-canada.html for details.

3 See also "100 Years of Parks Canada," http://www.pc.gc.ca.

4 Any suggestion of lack of interest in Canada's national parks is of concern at multiple levels. Grassroots national public support for the maintenance of these spaces is needed to ensure their preservation and to stop their exploitation for larger economic goals, specifically those of natural resource exploitation. In a parallel manner, some cottagers would argue that their very presence as well as advocacy initiatives have been vital to the protection and health of Haliburton lakes.

5 This reference excludes those who have retired to the cottage. A study of this group is beyond my research here.

6 See Royal LePage Recreational Property Report (2011).

7 See Erickson (2010) for further discussion.

References

Allemang, J. 2011. Parks Canada faces climb of the century. *Globe and Mail,* 13 May. http://www.theglobeandmail.com/.

Alphonso, C., and L. Paul. 2010. Happy campers. *Globe and Mail,* 31 July, A1-A6.

Altmeyer, G. 1976. Three ideas of nature in Canada, 1893-1914. *Journal of Canadian Studies* 11(3): 21-36.

Anastakis, D. 2008. *Car nation: An illustrated history of Canada's transformation behind the wheel.* Toronto: Lorimer.

Anderson, B. [1983] 2006. *Imagined communities: Reflections on the origins and spread of nationalism,* 2nd ed. London: Verso.

Antze, P., and M. Lambek. 1996. Introduction: Forecasting memory. In P. Antze and M. Lambek, eds., *Tense past: Cultural essays in trauma and memory,* xi-xxxviii. New York: Routledge.

Archer, B. 2010. Real estate: After the boom. *Cottage Life* 23(1), 42-44.

Atwood, M. 1991. Wilderness tips. In *Wilderness tips,* 195-223. Toronto: McClelland and Stewart.

Bahloul, J. 1996. *The architecture of memory: A Jewish-Muslim household in colonial Algeria, 1937-1962.* Cambridge: Cambridge University Press.

Baker, R.H. 1930. *History of the provisional county of Haliburton.* Haliburton: Provisional County of Haliburton.

Balfe, J.H. 1999. *Passing it on: The inheritance and use of summer houses.* Montclair, NJ: Pocomo Press.

Bannerji, H. 1993. Popular images of South Asian women. In H. Bannerji, ed., *Returning the gaze: Essays on racism, feminism and politics,* 176-86. Toronto: Sister Vision Press.

Barbour, D. 2011. *Winnipeg Beach: Leisure and courtship in a resort town, 1900-1967.* Winnipeg: University of Manitoba Press.

Barker, K. 2010. Going concern. *Cottage Life* 23(2): 92-100.

Barnes, M. 2002. *The essential Haliburton: Discover highland Ontario.* Ontario: General Store Publishing House.

Baskerville, P. 2002. *Ontario: Image, identity, and power.* New York: Oxford University Press.

Bauer, P. 2006. "My family and I have been ..." Cottage Q & A. *Cottage Life* (May): 30.

Belisle, D. 2011. *Retail nation: Department stores and the making of modern Canada.* Vancouver and Toronto: UBC Press.

Bellah, R., R. Madsen, W. Sullivan, A. Swidler, and S. Tipton. 1985. *Habits of the heart: Individualism and commitment in American life.* Berkeley: University of California Press.

Bender, B. 1993. Introduction – Landscape: Meaning and action. In *Landscape: Politics and perspectives,* 1-18. Oxford: Berg Publishers.

Benjamin, W. 1970. Unpacking my library: A talk about book collecting. In W. Benjamin, ed., *Illuminations,* 59-67. London: Jonathan Cape.

Berger, C. 1970. *The sense of power: Studies in the ideas of Canadian nationalism 1867-1914.* Toronto: University of Toronto Press.

Bergson, H. 1968. *Matière et mémoire.* Paris: P.U.F.

Billig, M. 1995. *Banal nationalism.* London: Sage Publications.

Bonnett, A. 2000. *White identities: Historical and international perspectives.* Toronto: Pearson Education Limited.

Bordo, J. 2003. The keeping place (arising from an incident on the land). In R. Nelson and M. Olin, eds., *Monuments and memory, made and unmade,* 157-82. Chicago: University of Chicago Press.

Boshkung Lake Millennium Book Committee. 2001. *Boshkung Lake memoirs.* Boshkung Lake Property Owners Association.

Bourdieu, P. 1977. *Outline of a theory of practice.* Cambridge: Cambridge University Press.

–. 1984. *Distinction: A social critique of the judgement of taste.* London: Routledge.

–. 2003 [1971]. The Berber house. In S. Low and D. Lawrence-Zúñiga, eds., *The anthropology of space and place,* 131-41. Oxford: Blackwell.

Bovet, L. 1998. Parler "suisse" sans le savoir. *Québec français* 111 (Fall): 98-100. http://id.erudit.org/iderudit/56296ac.

Brand, D. 1997. *Land to light on.* Toronto: McClelland and Stewart.

Bunce, M. 1994. *The countryside ideal: Anglo-American images of landscape.* London: Routledge.

Burn, M. n.d. *The dock primer.* Toronto and Ottawa: Cottage Life and Fisheries and Oceans Canada.

Caldwell, P. 2006. Neighbour to neighbour. *Cottage Life* 19(5): 11.

–. 2007. One score years ago. *Cottage Life* 20(4): 13.

–. 2010. Tears and jeers. *Cottage Life* 23(5): 15.

Campbell, C. 2003. "Our dear north country": Regional identity and national meaning in Ontario's Georgian Bay. *Journal of Canadian Studies* 37(4): 68-91.

–. 2004. *Shaped by the west wind: Nature and history in Georgian Bay.* Vancouver: UBC Press.

Campbell, M. 2008. Ontario struggles to decide whether or not it exists. *Globe and Mail*, 2 August, A15.

Carsten, J. 2000a. In J. Carsten, ed., *Cultures of relatedness: New approaches to the study of kinship*, 1-36. Cambridge: Cambridge University Press.

–. 2000b. "Knowing where you've come from": Ruptures and continuities of time and kinship in narratives of adoption. *Journal of the Royal Anthropological Institute* 6: 687-704.

–. 2004. *After kinship.* Cambridge: Cambridge University Press.

–. 2007. Introduction: Ghosts of memory. In J. Carsten, ed., *Ghosts of memory: Essays on remembrance and relatedness*, 1-35. Oxford: Blackwell.

Casey, A. 2009. *Lakeland: Journeys into the soul of Canada.* Vancouver: Greystone Books/David Suzuki Foundation.

Chaplin, D. 1999a. Back to the cave or playing away? Gender roles in home-from-home environments. *Journal of Consumer Studies and Home Economics* 23(3): 181-89.

–. 1999b. Consuming work/productive leisure: The consumption patterns of second home environments. *Leisure Studies* 18(1): 41-55.

Cheney, P. 2002. Cottage wars. *Globe and Mail*, 18 May, F1.

Chevalier, S. 1999. The French two-home project: Materialization of family identity. In I. Cieraad, ed., *At home: An anthropology of domestic space*, 83-94. Syracuse, NY: Syracuse University Press.

Chodorow, N., and S. Contrato. 1982. The fantasy of the perfect mother. In B. Thorne and M. Yalom, eds., *Rethinking the family: Some feminist questions*, 54-75. New York: Longman.

Clark, S.D. 1966. *The suburban society.* Toronto: University of Toronto.

Coleman, S., and T. Kohn. 2007. The discipline of leisure: Taking play seriously. In S. Coleman and T. Kohn, eds., *The discipline of leisure: Embodying cultures of recreation*, 1-19. Oxford: Berghahn Books.

Collier, J., M. Rosaldo, and S. Yanagisako. [1992] 2001. Is there a family? New anthropological views. In B. Fox, ed., *Family patterns, gender relations*, 2nd ed., 11-21. Oxford: Oxford University Press.

Collins, P. 2008. The practice of discipline and the discipline of practice. In N. Dyck, ed., *Exploring regimes of discipline: The dynamics of restraint*, 135-55. Oxford: Berghahn Books.

Comacchio, C. 2000. "The history of us": Social science, history and the relations of family in Canada. *Labour/Le Travail* 46: 167-220.

Comaroff, J. 1985. *Body of power, spirit of resistance: The culture and history of a South African people.* Chicago: University of Chicago Press.

Conley, D. 2008. Reading class between the lines (of this volume): A reflection on why we should stick to folk concepts of social class. In A. Lareau and D.

Conley, eds., *Social class: How does it work?* 366-73. New York: Russell Sage Foundation.

Connerton, P. 1989. *How societies remember*. Cambridge: Cambridge University Press.

Connor, W. 1993. Beyond reason: The nature of the ethnonational bond. *Ethnic and Racial Studies* 16(3): 373-89.

Conway, J. 2003. *The Canadian family in crisis*. 5th ed. Toronto: James Lorimer and Company.

Coote, J. 1992. Marvels of everyday vision: The anthropology of aesthetics and the cattle-keeping Nilotes. In J. Coote and A. Shelton, eds., *Anthropology, art and aesthetics* 245-73. Oxford: Clarendon Press.

Coppock, J., ed. 1977. *Second homes: Curse or blessing?* Oxford: Pergamon Press.

Courchene, T. 2008. Fiscalamity! Ontario: From heartland to have-not. *Policy Options* (June): 46-54.

Cowan, R. 1983. *More work for mother: The ironies of household technology from the open hearth to the microwave*. New York: Basic Books.

Crang, M., and N. Thrift. 2000. Introduction. In N. Thrift and M. Crang, eds., *Thinking space*, 1-30. London: Routledge.

Cresswell, T. 2004. *Place: A short introduction*. Oxford: Blackwell.

Cronon, W., ed. 1995. *Uncommon ground: Toward reinventing nature*. New York: W.W. Norton.

Cross, A.W. 1992. *The summer house: A tradition of leisure*. Toronto: Harper Perennial.

Crouch, D., and L. Desforges. 2003. The sensuous body in the tourist encounter: Introduction to the power of the body in tourist studies. *Tourist Studies* 3(1): 5-22.

Cruikshank, J. 2005. *Do glaciers listen? Local knowledge, colonial encounters, and social imagination*. Vancouver: UBC Press.

Csikszentmihalyi, M. 1975. *Beyond boredom and anxiety*. San Francisco: Jossye-Bass Publishers.

–. 1990. *Flow: The psychology of optimal experience*. New York: Harper and Row.

Csordas, T. 1994. Introduction: The body as representation and being-in-the-world. In T. Csordas, ed., *Embodiment and experience: The existential ground of culture and self*, 1-24. Cambridge: Cambridge University Press.

Cummings, H.R. 1962. *Early days in Haliburton*. Toronto: Ryerson Press.

Curry-Stevens, A. 2008. Building the case for the study of the middle class: Shifting our gaze from margins to centre. *International Journal of Social Welfare* 17(4): 379-89.

Deem, R. 1986. *All work and no play? A study of women and leisure*. Philadelphia: Open University Press.

Di Leonardo, M. 1987. The female world of cards and holidays: Women, families, and the work of kinship. *Signs* 12(3): 440-53.

Dramstad, W., J.D. Olson, and R. Forman. 1996. *Landscape ecology principles in landscape architecture and land-use planning*. Cambridge, MA/Washington, DC: Harvard University Graduate School of Design/Island Press.

du Prey, P. de la Ruffinière, and D. Farr. 2004. *Ah, wilderness! Resort architecture in the Thousand Islands*. Kingston: Agnes Etherington Art Centre.

Dudley, K.M. 1999. (Dis)locating the middle class. *Anthropology Newsletter* 40(4): 1-4.

Dummitt, C. 1998. Finding a place for father: Selling the barbecue in postwar Canada. *Journal of the Canadian Historical Association* 9(1): 209-23.

–. 2007a. Introduction. In *The manly modern: Masculinity in postwar Canada*, 1-27. Vancouver: UBC Press.

–. 2007b. In the mountains. In *The manly modern: Masculinity in postwar Canada*, 77-99. Vancouver: UBC Press.

Dunk, T. 1991. *It's a working man's town: Male working class culture in northwestern Ontario*. Montreal: McGill-Queen's Press.

Dyck, N. 2000. Parent, kids and coaches: Constructing sport and childhood in Canada. In N. Dyck, ed., *Games, sports and cultures*, 137-61. Oxford: Berg.

–. 2007. Playing like Canadians: Improvising nation and identity through sport. In S. Coleman and T. Kohn, eds. *The discipline of leisure: Embodying cultures of "recreation,"* 109-25. Oxford: Berghahn Books.

–. 2008. Anthropological perspectives on discipline: An introduction to the issues. In N. Dyck, ed., *Exploring regimes of discipline: The dynamics of restraint*, 1-22. Oxford: Berghahn Books.

Dyer, R. 1997. *White*. New York: Routledge.

Eagleton, T. 1990. *The ideology of the aesthetic*. Oxford, UK/Cambridge, MA: Blackwell.

Edwards, J. 2000. *Born and bred: Idioms of kinship and new reproductive technologies in England*. Oxford: Oxford University Press.

Edwards, J., and M. Strathern. 2000. Including our own. In J. Carsten, ed., *Cultures of relatedness: New approaches to the study of kinship*, 149-66. Cambridge: Cambridge University Press.

Ehrenreich, B. 1989. *Fear of falling: The inner life of the middle class*. New York: Pantheon Books.

Erickson, B. 2010. "Fucking close to water": Queering the production of the nation. In Catriona Sandilands and Bruce Erickson, ed., *Queer ecologies: Sex, nature, politics, desire*, 309-30. Bloomington: University of Indiana.

Evernden, N. 1993. *The natural alien*. Toronto: University of Toronto Press.

Featherstone, M. 1996. Postmodernism and the aestheticization of everyday life. In S. Lash and J. Friedman, eds., *Modernity and identity*, 265-89. Oxford: Blackwell.

Ford, R. n.d. *The shore primer: A cottager's guide to a healthy waterfront. Cottage Life* and Fisheries and Oceans Canada.

Frank, R.H. 2007. *Falling behind: How rising inequality harms the middle class.* Berkeley: University of California Press.

Gagnon, A., and M. Montcalm. 1990. *Quebec: Beyond the quiet revolution.* Scarborough: Nelson Canada.

Gardner, R. 2006. In college, you can go home again and again. *New York Times,* 5 November. http://www.nytimes.com.

Garner, S. 2007. *Whiteness: An introduction.* New York: Routledge.

Garrah, K. 2006. *Marketing a lake plan to a cottage community and watershed residents: A review of motivation and behaviour theory and techniques of community based social marketing with a strong emphasis on Kennesis Lake.* http://www.haliburton cooperative.on.ca/.

–. 2007. *Communication and community engagement: Theory and application within a cottage association for the purpose of developing and implementing lake plans and other community based stewardship initiatives.* http://www.haliburtoncooperative.on.ca/.

Gauvreau, M. 2004. Conclusion: The family as pathology, psychology, social science and history construct the nuclear family, 1945-1980. In N. Christie and M. Gauvreau, eds., *Mapping the margins: The family and social discipline in Canada, 1700-1975,* 383-407. Montreal: McGill-Queen's University Press.

Geertz, C. 1973. Religion as a cultural system. In C. Geertz, ed., *The interpretation of cultures,* 87-125. New York: Basic Books.

Gelber, S. 1997. Do-it-yourself: Constructing, repairing and maintaining domestic masculinity. *American Quarterly* 49(1): 66-112.

–. 1999. *Hobbies: Leisure and the culture of work in America.* New York: Columbia University Press.

Giddens, A. 1990. *The consequences of modernity.* Cambridge: Polity Press.

–. 1991. The self: Ontological security and existential anxiety. In A. Giddens, ed., *Modernity and self-identity: Self and society in the late modern age,* 35-69. Stanford, CA: Stanford University Press.

Gillis, J. 1996a. Making time for family: The invention of family time(s) and the re-invention of family history. *Journal of Family History* 21(1): 4-21.

–. 1996b. *A world of their own making: Myth, ritual, and the quest for family values.* New York: Basic Books.

Gölz, A. 1993. Family matters: The Canadian family and the state in the postwar period. *Left History* 1(2): 9-49.

Gordon, C. 1989. *At the cottage: A fearless look at Canada's summer obsession.* Toronto: McClelland and Stewart.

–. 2006. *Still at the cottage.* Toronto: McClelland and Stewart.

Gorrie, P. 2009. Will uranium mining ruin cottage country? http://www.cottagelife.com.

Grant, T. 2008. The rich, the poor, and chasm between. *Globe and Mail,* 1 May. http://www.theglobeandmail.com.

Green, N. 1990. *The spectacle of nature: Landscape and bourgeois culture in nineteenth century France*. Manchester: Manchester University Press.

Gullestad, M. 1990. Doing interpretive analysis in a modern large scale society: The meaning of peace and quiet in Norway. *Social Analysis* 20: 38-61.

–. 1993. Home decoration as popular culture: Constructing homes, genders, and classes in Norway. In T. del Valle, ed., *Gendered anthropology*, 128-61. London: Routledge.

Gunn, C. 1997. *Vacationscape*. Washington, DC: Taylor and Francis.

Halbwachs, M. 1992. *On collective memory*. Trans. L. Coser. Chicago: University of Chicago Press.

Haldrup, B.C., and J. Larsen. 2003. The family gaze. *Tourist Studies* 3(1): 23-46.

Haldrup, M. 2004. Laid-back mobilities: Second-home holidays in time and space. *Tourism Geographies* 6(4): 434-54.

Hall, M., and D. Müller, eds. 2004. *Tourism, mobility and second homes: Between elite landscapes and common ground*. Toronto: Channel View Publications.

Hallman, B., and S.M. Benbow. 2007. *Social and cultural geography* 8(6): 871-88.

Halseth, G. 1998. *Cottage country in transition: A social geography of change and contention in the rural-recreational countryside*. Montreal: McGill-Queen's University Press.

–. 2004. The "cottage privilege": Increasingly elite landscapes of second homes in Canada. In M. Hall and D. Müller, ed., *Tourism, mobility, and second homes: Between elite landscapes and common ground*, 35-54. Toronto: Channel View Publications.

Halseth, G., and M. Rosenberg. 1995. Cottagers in an urban field. *Professional Geographer* 47(2): 148-59.

Harding, L. 2010. Hiking along the Great Divide: Exploring socio-natures in the Canadian Rockies. MA thesis, York University.

Harré, R. 1989. Perfections and imperfections of form: Cults of the body and their aesthetic underpinnings. *International Journal of Moral and Social Studies* 4(3): 183-94.

Harrison, F. 1995. The persistent power of "race" in the cultural and political economy of racism. *Annual Review of Anthropology* 24: 47-74.

Harrison, J. 2001. The tourist aesthetic. *International Sociology* 14(2): 159-72.

–. 2003. *Being a tourist: Finding meaning in pleasure travel*. Vancouver: UBC Press.

–. 2008a. Engaging ethnography: Researching tourists. *Tourist Studies* 8(1): 5-18.

–. 2008b. Shifting positions. *Tourist Studies* 8(1): 41-60.

–. 2010. Belonging at the cottage. In J. Scott and T. Selwyn, eds., *Thinking through tourism*, 71-92. New York: Berg.

–. 2012. "I'm sorry I got emotional": 'Real work and 'real' men at the Canadian cottage. In D. Picard and M. Robinson, eds., *Emotion in Motion: Tourism, Affect and Transformation*, 231-46. London: Ashgate.

Hartigan, J. 1997. Establishing the fact of whiteness. *American Anthropologist* 99(3): 495-505.

–. 2005. *Odd tribes: Toward a cultural analysis of white people.* Durham: Duke University Press.

Harvey, D. 1989. *The condition of postmodernity.* Oxford: Blackwell.

–. 1993. From space to place and back again: Reflections on the condition of post-modernity. In J. Bird, B. Curtis, T. Putnam, G. Robertson, and L. Tickner, eds., *Mapping the futures: Local cultures, global change,* 3-29. London: Routledge.

–. 1996. *Justice, nature, and the geography of difference.* Oxford: Blackwell.

Hayes, D. 2009. The race to rent. *Cottage Life* 22(1): 60-64, 117-19.

Heidegger, M. 1977. Building dwelling thinking. In D.F. Krell, ed., *Martin Heidegger: Basic writings,* 1st ed., 347-63. San Francisco: Harper.

Helmes-Hayes, R. and J. Curtis. 1998. Introduction. In R. Helmes-Hayes and J. Curtis, eds., *The vertical mosaic revisited,* 3-33. Toronto: University of Toronto Press.

Hodgins, B., and J. Benidickson. 1989. *The Temagami experience: Recreation, resources, and aboriginal rights in the northern Ontario wilderness.* Toronto: University of Toronto Press.

Hodgson, J.D. 1992. *Living traditions: The story of Clayton and Phyllis Hodgson.* Self-published.

Holman, A. 2000. *A sense of their duty: Middle class formation in Victorian Ontario towns.* Montreal: McGill-Queen's University Press.

Honeyford, H. 1953. Villagers welcome summer residents. *The Telegram* (Toronto), 4 May, 25.

Hospers, J. 1972. Problems of aesthetics. In P. Edwards, ed., *Encyclopedia of philosophy,* 35-54. New York: MacMillan.

Howes, D., ed. 1991. *The varieties of sensory experience: A sourcebook in the anthropology of the senses.* Toronto: University of Toronto.

Howland, A. 2007. Housing affordability deteriorating: Bank report, more home-owners feel the mortgage squeeze. *Ottawa Citizen,* 13 September, D1.

Ibbitson, J. 2008. *The landing.* Toronto: KCP Fiction.

Illouz, E. 1997. *Consuming the romantic utopia: Love and the cultural contradictions of capitalism.* Berkeley: University of California Press.

Iltan, C. 2010. In a country defined by water, new Canadians at greater risk of drowning. *Globe and Mail,* 15 July. http://www.theglobeandmail.com/.

Ingold, T. 2000. *The perception of the environment: Essays in livelihood, dwelling and skill.* London: Routledge.

Innis, H. 1962. *The fur trade in Canada: An introduction to Canadian economic history.* Toronto: University of Toronto Press.

Irving, J. 1989. *A prayer for Owen Meany.* New York: William and Morrow.

Jaakson, R. 1986. Second-home domestic tourism. *Annals of Tourism Research* 13(3): 367-91.

Jasen, P. 1995. *Wild things: Nature, culture, and tourism in Ontario, 1790-1914.* Toronto: University of Toronto Press.

Jessup, L. The Group of Seven and the tourist landscape. *Journal of Canadian Studies* 37(1): 144-79.

Jiménez, M. 2006. Why they call cottage country the Great White North. *Globe and Mail,* 20 May, F1, F6.

Kaltenborn, B., and T. Bjerke. 2002. Associations between landscape preferences and place-attachment: A study in Roros, southern Norway. *Landscape Research* 27(4), 381-96.

Kedourie, E. 1960. *Nationalism.* London: Hutchinson University Press.

Kendall, F.E. 2006. *Understanding white privilege: Creating pathways to authentic relationships across race.* New York: Routledge.

Kenny, M. 1999. A place for memory: The interface between individual and collective memory. *Comparative Studies in Society and History* 41(3): 420-37.

Kimmel, M. 1990. After fifteen years: The impact of the sociology of masculinity on the masculinity of sociology. In J. Hearn and D.H.J. Morgan, eds., *Men, masculinities and social theory,* 93-109. London: Unwin Hyman.

Kimmel, M., and M. Kaufman. 1994. Weekend warriors: The new men's movement. In H. Brod and M. Kaufman, eds., *Theorizing masculinities,* 259-88. Thousand Oaks, CA: Sage Publications.

Knowles, C. 1996. *Family boundaries: The invention of normality and dangerousness.* Peterborough, ON: Broadview Press.

–. 2005. Making whiteness: British lifestyle migrants in Hong Kong. In C. Alexander and C. Knowles, eds., *Making race matter: Bodies, space and identity,* 90-110. London: Palgrave MacMillan.

–. 2008. The landscape of post-imperial whiteness in rural Britain. *Ethnic and Racial Studies* 31(1): 167-84.

Kopytoff, I. 1986. The cultural biography of things: Commoditization as process. In A. Appadurai, ed., *The social life of things: Commodities in cultural perspective,* 64-94. Cambridge: Cambridge University Press.

Kremarik, F. 2002. A little place in the country: A profile of Canadians who own vacation property. *Canadian Social Trends* (Summer): 12-14.

Kuffert, L.B. 2003. *A great duty: Canadian responses to modern life and mass culture, 1939-1967.* Montreal: McGill-Queen's University Press.

Kuhn, A. 1995. *Family secrets: Acts of memory and imagination.* New York: Verso.

Kulyk Keefer, J. 2007. *The ladies' lending library.* Toronto: Harper Collins.

Lakoff, G. 1987. *Women, fire, and dangerous things: What categories reveal about the mind.* Chicago: University of Chicago.

Lambert, R.S., and P. Pross. 1967. *Renewing nature's wealth: A centennial history.* Canada: Hunter Rose Company.

Lamont, M. 1992. *Money, morals, and manners: The culture of the French and American upper-middle class.* Chicago: University of Chicago Press.

Lamont, M., and V. Molnar. 2002. The study of symbolic boundaries in the social sciences. *Annual Review of Sociology* 28: 167-95.

Langlois, C. 2008. Cottage watch. *Cottage Life* 21(5): 39-44.

Lash, S., and J. Urry. 1994. *Economies of signs and space*. London: Sage Publications.

Latour, B. 1993. *We have never been modern*. Trans. C. Porter. Cambridge, MA: Harvard University Press.

Lawler, S. 2005. Introduction: Class, culture and identity. *Sociology* 39(5): 797-806.

Lawrence, J. 2008. Study predicts dramatic increase in assessment. 30 April. http://www.cottagecountrynow.ca/.

Lears, J. 1981. *No place of grace: Antimodernism and the transformation of American culture 1880-1920*. New York: Pantheon Books.

Leddy, T. 1995. Everyday surface aesthetic qualities: "neat," "messy," "clean," "dirty." *Journal of Aesthetics and Art Criticism* 53(3): 259-68.

Lefebvre, H. [1974] 1993. *The production of space*. Trans. D. Nicholson-Smith. Oxford: Blackwell.

Lehr, J., J. Selwood, and E. Badiuk. 1991. Ethnicity, religion, and class as elements in the evolution of Lake Winnipeg resorts. *Canadian Geographer* 35(1): 46-58.

Levine-Rasky, C., ed. 2002. *Working through whiteness: International perspectives*. Albany: State University of New York Press.

Lewis, S. 2003. The integration of paid work and the rest of life: Is post-industrial work the new leisure? *Leisure Studies* 22(4): 343-55.

Lifesaving Society. 2003. *The drowning report: A profile of drownings and water-related deaths in Ontario*. www.lifesaving.com.

–. 2008. *The drowning report: A profile of Ontario drowning and water-related injuries, 1987-2004*. Toronto: Royal Life Saving Society of Canada.

Lillico, P. 2009. Love in the time of co-ownership. *Cottage Life* 22(4): 41-42, 44.

Löfgren, O. 1999. *On holiday: A history of vacationing*. Berkeley: University of California Press.

Long, C. 2000. The cottager's catalogue. http://www.civilization.ca.

Loo, T. 2006. *States of nature: Conserving Canada's wildlife in the twentieth century*. Vancouver: UBC Press.

Lorinc, J. 2010. Biggest dream on the block. *Cottage Life* 23(1): 39-40, 91, 93-94, 98.

Low, S., and D. Lawrence-Zúñiga, eds. 2003. *The anthropology of space and place*. Oxford: Blackwell.

Lowenthal, D. 1985. *The past is a foreign country*. Cambridge: Cambridge University Press.

–. 1989. Nostalgia tells it like it wasn't. In C. Shaw and M. Case, eds. *The Imagined Past: History and Nostalgia*, 18-32. Manchester: Manchester University Press.

Luka, N. 2006. Placing the "Natural" edges of a metropolitan region through multiple residency: Landscape and urban form in Toronto's "cottage country." PhD diss., University of Toronto.

–. 2008. Waterfront second homes in the central Canada woodlands: Images, social practice, and attachment to multiple residency. *Ethnologica Europea* 37(1-2): 71-87.

Lyon, M.L., and J.M. Barbalet, 1994. Society's body: Emotion and the "somatization" of social theory. In T. Csordas, ed., *Embodiment and experience: The existential ground of culture and self,* 48-66. Cambridge: Cambridge University Press.

MacCannell, D. [1976] 1999. *The tourist: A new theory of the leisure class.* Los Angeles: University of California Press.

MacFarlane, D. 2000. *Summer gone.* Toronto: Vintage Canada.

MacGregor, R. 2002. *Escape: In search of the natural soul of Canada.* Toronto: McClelland and Stewart.

–. 2005. *The weekender: A cottage journal.* Hamilton: Viking Canada.

MacLean, J. 2006. Letter to the editor. *Cottage Life* 19(6): 17.

Macnaghten, P., and J. Urry. 1998. *Contested natures.* London: Sage Publications.

Marcoux, J. 2001. The refurbishment of memory. In D. Miller, ed., *Home possessions,* 69-86. London: Palgrave MacMillan.

Marsh, M. 1988. Suburban men and masculine domesticity, 1870-1915. *American Quarterly* 40(1): 165-86.

Martin, S.E. 2009. Real estate: Can we afford a cottage? *Cottage Life* 22(1): 27-28, 30, 32.

Martin-Roy, S. 2007. La transformation de chalets en résidences permanents dans les milieux périurbains de l'agglomération de Québec. Faculté d'aménagement, d'architecture et des arts visuels, Université de Laval.

Maslow, A. 1964. *Religion, values and peak experiences.* New York: Viking.

Massey, D. 1991. The political place of locality studies. *Environment and Planning A* 23: 267-91.

–. 1993. Power-geometry and a progressive sense of place. In J. Bird, B. Curtis, T. Putnam, G. Robertson, and L. Tickner, eds., *Mapping the futures: Local cultures, global change,* 59-69. London: Routledge.

Mathieson, A., and G. Wall. 1982. *Tourism: Economic, physical and social impacts.* London: Longman.

Mauss, M. [1935] 1975. Techniques of the body. *Economy and Society* 2(1): 70-88.

McCracken, G. 1989. "Homeyness": A cultural account of one constellation of consumer goods and meanings. In E. Hirschman, ed., *Interpretive consumer research,* 168-83. Provo, UT: Association for Consumer Research.

McGregor, G. 1985. *The Wacousta syndrome: Explorations in the Canadian landscape.* Toronto: University of Toronto Press.

McIntyre, N., Williams, D., and McHugh, K. eds. 2006. *Multiple dwelling and tourism: Negotiating place, home, and identity.* Wallingford, Oxfordshire: CABI.

McKay, I. 1994. *The quest of the folk: Antimodernism and cultural selection in twentieth-century Nova Scotia.* Montreal: McGill-Queen's University Press.

McKay, S. 1996. The incredible journey. *Cottage Life* 9(4): 40-43.

Michael, M. 2000. These boots are made for walking ... : Mundane technology, the body, and human-environment relations. *Body and Society* 6(3-4): 107-26.

Miller, D. 1987. *Material culture and mass consumption.* Oxford: Blackwell.

–. 1998. *A theory of shopping.* Ithaca, New York: Cornell University Press.

Mitchell, W.J.T. 2002. *Landscape and power.* 2nd ed. Chicago: University of Chicago Press.

Morphy, H. 1992. From dull to brilliant: The aesthetics of spiritual power among the Yolngu. In J. Coote and A. Shelton, eds., *Anthropology, art, and aesthetics,* 181-208. Oxford: Clarendon Press.

Mulvaney, J. 1991. Past regained, future lost: The Kow Swamp Pleistocene burials. *Antiquity* 65(246): 12-21.

Muro, D. 2005. Nationalism and nostalgia: The case of radical Basque nationalism. *Nations and Nationalism* 4: 571-89.

Myerhoff, B. 1984. Rites and signs of ripening: The intertwining of ritual, time, and growing older. In D. Kertzer and J. Keith, eds., *Age and anthropological theory,* 305-31. Ithaca, New York: Cornell University Press.

Newman, K. 1988. *Falling from grace: The experience of downward mobility in the American middle class.* New York: Vintage Books.

–. 1991. Uncertain seas: Cultural turmoil and the domestic economy. In A. Wolfe, ed., *America at century's end,* 112-30. Berkeley: University of California Press.

Nora, P. 1989. Between memory and history: Les lieux de mémoire. *Representations* 26: 7-24.

Obrador Pons, P. 2003. Being-on-holiday: Tourist dwelling, bodies and place. *Tourist Studies* 3(1): 47-66.

Ondaatje, M. 1987. *In the skin of a lion.* Toronto: McClelland and Stewart.

Osborne, B. 1992. Interpreting a nation's identity: Artists as creators of national consciousness. In A. Baker and G. Biger, eds. *Ideology and landscape in historical perspective,* 230-54. Cambridge: Cambridge University Press.

Owram, D. 1996. *Born at the right time: A history of the baby-boom generation.* Toronto: University of Toronto.

Palmer, B. 2009. *Canada's 1960s: The ironies of identity in a rebellious era.* Toronto: University of Toronto.

Palmer, C. 2003. Touring Churchill's England: Rituals of kingship and belonging. *Annals of Tourism Research* 30(2): 426-45.

Palmer, D. 2010. *When Fenelon Falls.* Toronto: Coach House.

Panelli, R., P. Hubbard, B. Coombes, and S. Suchet-Pearson. 2009. De-centring white ruralities: Ethnic diversity, racialisation, and indigenous countrysides. *Journal of Rural Studies* 25: 355-64.

Paris, L. 2008. *Children's nature: The rise of the American summer camp.* New York: New York University Press.

Pasternak, J. 2008. Getting a slice of the cottage life. *Financial Post*, 21 November. http://www.financialpost.com/.

Pcholkina, S. 2006. Construction and disruption of cottage idylls. MA thesis, Frost Centre for Canadian Studies and Indigenous Studies, Trent University.

Pearson, K. 1991. *Looking at the moon*. Toronto: Penguin Group Canada.

Periäinen, K. 2006. The summer cottage: A dream in the Finnish forest. In N. McIntyre, D. Williams, and K. McHugh, eds., *Multiple dwellings and tourism: Negotiating place, home and identity*. 103-13. Cambridge, MA: CABI.

Perkins, H., and D. Thorns. 2006. Home away from home: The primary/second-home relationship. In N. McIntyre, D. Williams, and K. McHugh, eds., *Multiple dwelling and tourism: Negotiating place, home and identity*, 67-81. Cambridge, MA: CABI.

Perkins, M. 2005. Where are they now? *Minden Times*, 12 August. http://www.mindentimes.ca/.

Perry, P. 2001. White means never having to say you're ethnic: White youth and the construction of "cultureless" identities. *Journal of Contemporary Ethnography* 30(1): 56-91.

Pigg, S. 2012. Ontario cottage country feels drag of eurozone crisis. *Toronto Star*, 16 May. http://www.thestar.com/business/.

Pitkänen, K. 2008. Second-home landscape: the meaning(s) of landscape for second-home tourism in Finnish Lakeland. *Tourism Geographies* 10(2): 169-92.

Plog, S. 2001. Why destination areas rise and fall in popularity: An update of a Cornell Quarterly Classic. *Cornell Hotel and Restaurant Administration Quarterly* 42(3): 13-24.

Popenoe, D. 1988. *Disturbing the nest: Family change and decline in modern societies*. New York: Aldine De Guyter.

Porteous, D. 1996. *Environmental aesthetics: Ideas, politics, and planning*. London: Routledge.

Porter, J. 1965. *The vertical mosaic: An analysis of social class and power in Canada*. Toronto: University of Toronto Press.

Priddle, G., and R. Kreutzwiser. 1977. Evaluating cottage environments in Ontario. In J.T. Coppock, ed., *Second homes: Curse or blessing?* 165-80. Oxford: Pergamon Press.

Proulx, M. 1997. The uranium mining industry of the Bancroft area: An environmental history and heritage assessment. MA thesis, Trent University.

Purdy, A. 1974. *In search of Owen Roblin*. Madeira Park, BC: Harbour Publishing.

Quinn, B. 2004. Dwelling through multiple places: A case study of second home ownership in Ireland. In M. Hall and D. Müller, eds., *Tourism, mobility and second homes: Between elite landscape and common ground*. 113-32. Toronto: Channel View Publications.

Rea, R. 2003. *The earth, the stars, and whisper*. Peterborough: Mapleland Press.

Reinhart, A. 2004. Humble paradise is not for sale. *Globe and Mail*, 31 July, A11.

Relph, T. 1976. *Place and placelessness*. London: Pion Limited.

Reynolds, N. 1973. *In quest of yesterday: Haliburton county*. Lindsay: John Deyell Company.

Richler, M. 1997. *Barney's version*. Toronto: Alfred Knopf.

Robinson, G. 2011. *Providence Island*. Toronto: Dundurn Press.

Rojek, C. 1993. *Ways of escape*. London: Rowman and Littlefield.

–. 2010. *The labour of leisure*. London: Sage.

Rotary Club of Haliburton, and R.J. Curry. 1975. *Haliburton*. Peterborough: Maxwell Review Ltd.

Royal LePage. 2007, 2008, 2009, 2011, 2012. *Recreational property report*. http://www-c.royallepage.ca/info-and-advice/market-reports-and-surveys/.

Rutherdale, R. 1998. Fatherhood and masculine domesticity during the baby boom: Consumption and leisure in advertising and life stories. In L. Chambers and E. Montigny, eds., *Family matters: Papers in post-confederation Canadian family history*, 309-33. Toronto: Canadian Scholars' Press.

–. 1999. Fatherhood, masculinity, and the good life during Canada's baby boom, 1945-1965. *Journal of Family History* 24(3): 351-73.

Sack, R. 1992. *Place, modernity, and the consumer's world: A relational framework for geographical analysis*. Baltimore: Johns Hopkins University Press.

–. 1997. *Homo geographicus: A framework for action, awareness and moral concern*. Baltimore: Johns Hopkins University Press.

Sangster, J. 1995. Doing two jobs: The wage-earning mother, 1945-1970. In J. Parr, ed., *A diversity of women: Ontario, 1945-1970*, 98-134. Toronto: University of Toronto Press.

–. 2010. *Transforming labour: Women and work in post-war Canada*. Toronto: University of Toronto Press.

Satsuka, S. 1997. Re-creation through landscape: Subject production in Canadian cottage country. MA thesis. York University.

Sayer, A. 2005a. Class, moral worth and recognition. *Sociology* 39(5): 947-63.

–. 2005b. *The moral significance of class*. Cambridge: Cambridge University Press.

Scanlan, L. 2004. *Harvest of a quiet eye: The cabin as sanctuary*. Toronto: Viking Canada.

Schatzker, M. 2005. The putterer's apprentice. *Cottage Life* 18(3): 87, 89-90, 146.

Schneider, D. 1968. *American kinship: A cultural account*. Englewood Cliffs, CA: Prentice Hall.

Schroeder, J. 2002. *Visual consumption*. London: Routledge.

Shaw, S. 1985. The meaning of leisure in everyday life. *Leisure Science* 7(1): 1-24.

Sibley, F. 1959. Aesthetic concepts. *The Philosophical Review* 68(4): 421-50.

Sider, G. 1986. *Culture and class in anthropology and history: A Newfoundland illustration*. Cambridge: Cambridge University Press.

Skeggs, B. 2004. *Class, self, culture*. New York: Routledge.

Smith, A.D. 1991. *National identity*. Reno: University of Nevada Press.

Stacey, J. 1996. *In the name of the family: Rethinking family values in the postmodern age.* Boston: Beacon Press.

Stebbins, R. 1997. Casual leisure: A conceptual statement. *Leisure Studies* 16(1): 17-25.

Steed, J. 2005. Cottage consultant cashes in on clean-up consensus. *Toronto Star,* 24 October. http://www.thestar.com/.

Stevens, P. 2008a. Cars and cottages: The automotive transformation of Ontario's summer home tradition. *Ontario History* 100(1): 26-56, 115.

–. 2008b. The nature of cottaging: Summer homes and the environment in postwar Ontario. *Proceedings of the Canadian Historical Association.* 3 June, Vancouver, BC.

–. 2010. Getting away from it all: Family cottaging in postwar Ontario. PhD diss., York University.

Stone, L. 2004. Introduction: The demise and revival of kinship. In R. Parkin and L. Stone, eds., *Kinship and family: An anthropological reader,* 241-56. Oxford: Blackwell.

Strathern, M. 1981. *Kinship at the core: An anthropology of Elmdon, a village in northwest Essex in the nineteen sixties.* Cambridge: Cambridge University Press.

Strong-Boag, V. 1985. Discovering the home: The last 150 years of domestic work in Canada. In P. Bourne, ed., *Women's paid and unpaid work: Historical and contemporary perspectives,* 35-60. Toronto: University of Toronto Press.

–. 1991. Home dreams: Women and the suburban experiment in Canada, 1945-60. *Canadian Historical Review* 72(4): 471-504.

–. 1995. "Their side of the story": Women's voices from Ontario suburbs, 1945-1960. In J. Parr, ed., *A diversity of women: Ontario, 1945-1980,* 46-74. Toronto: University of Toronto.

Struening, K. 2002. *New family values: Liberty, equality, diversity.* New York: Rowman and Littlefield.

Struthers, B. 1996. *Virgin territory.* Hamilton, ON: Wolsak and Wynn.

–. 2005. *In her fifties.* Windsor, ON: Black Moss Press.

–. 2008. *Where night comes closest.* Windsor, ON: Black Moss Press.

Stuber, J. 2006. Talk of class: The discursive repertoires of white working- and upper-middle-class college students. *Journal of Contemporary Ethnography* 35(3): 285-318.

Svenson, S. 2004. The cottage and the city: An interpretation of the Canadian second home experience. In M. Hall and D. Müller, eds., *Tourism, mobility and second homes: Between elite landscape and common ground,* 55-74. Toronto: Channel View Publications.

Teitel, J. 2009. The one that got away: Tales of love and loss through our family archives. *Cottage Life* 22(2): 82-83, 88, 114-15.

Thrift, N. 1994. Inhuman geographies: Landscapes of speed, light and power. In P. Cloke, M. Doel, D. Matless, M. Phillips, and N. Thrift, eds., *Writing the rural: Five cultural geographies,* 191-248. London: Paul Chapman Publishing.

Tillson, T. 2000/2001. Dial "M" for muddle: Unravelling mysteries of bringing 9-1-1 to cottage country. *Cottage Life* 13(6): 29-30.

Tuan, Y. 1974. *Topophilia: A study of environmental perception, attitudes and values.* Englewood Cliffs, CA: Prentice Hall.

–. 1977. *Space and place: The perspective of experience.* Minneapolis: University of Minnesota Press.

Turkel, W. 2007. *The archive of place: Unearthing the pasts of the Chilcotin Plateau.* Vancouver: UBC Press.

Turner, T. 1994. Bodies and anti-bodies: Flesh and fetish in contemporary social theory. In T. Csordas, ed., *Embodiment and experience: The existential ground of culture and self,* 27-47. Cambridge: Cambridge University Press.

Turner, V. 1982. Liminal to liminoid, in play, flow and ritual: An essay in comparative symbology. In V. Turner, ed., *From ritual to theatre: The human seriousness of play,* 20-60. New York: PAJ Publications.

Tyler, K. 2007. The tethered generation. *HR Magazine,* 1 May. http://www.shrm.org.

Urry, J. 1990. The consumption of tourism. *Sociology* 24(1): 23-35.

–. 1995. *Consuming places.* London: Routledge.

Valenius, J. 2004. *Undressing the maid: Gender, sexuality and the body in the construction of the Finnish nation.* Helsinki: Suomalaisen Kirjallisuuden Seura.

Vepsäläinen, M., and K. Pitkänen. 2010. Second home countryside: Representations of the rural in Finnish popular discourses. *Journal of Rural Studies* 26(2): 194-204.

Wall, S. 2009. *The nurture of nature: Childhood, antimodernism, and Ontario summer camps, 1920-55.* Vancouver: UBC Press.

Walmsley, A. 2002. How to succeed at succession. *Cottage Life* 15(2): 54-60.

Warkentin, J. 1966. Southern Ontario: A view from the west. *Canadian Geographer* 10(3): 157-71.

Walter, J.A. 1982. Social limits to tourism. *Leisure Studies* 1(3): 295-304.

Weiner, A. 1992. *Inalienable possessions: The paradox of keeping while giving.* Berkeley: University of California Press.

Weiner, J. 1996. Aesthetics. In A. Barnard and J. Spencer, eds., *Encyclopedia of social and cultural anthropology,* 6-7. London: Routledge.

Whitelaw, A. 2000. "Whiffs of balsam, pine, and spruce: Art museums and the production of a Canadian aesthetic." In J. Berland and S. Hornstein, eds., *Capital culture: A Reader on modernist legacies, state institutions, and the value(s) of art,* 122-37. Montreal: McGill-Queen's University Press.

Williams, D., and B. Kaltenborn. 1999. Leisure places and modernity: The use and meaning of recreational cottages in Norway and the USA. In D. Crouch, ed., *Leisure/ tourism geographies,* 214-30. London: Routledge.

Williams, D., and N. McIntyre. 2001. Where heart and home reside: Changing constructions of place and identity. In *Trends 2000: Shaping the future: The 5th outdoor recreation and tourism trends symposium,* 392-403. Lansing, MI: Department of Parks, Recreation and Tourism Resources, Michigan State University.

Williams, D., and S. Van Patten. 2006. Home *and* away? Creating identities and sustaining places in a multi-centred world. In N. McIntyre, D. Williams, and K. McHugh, eds., *Multiple dwelling and tourism: Negotiating place, home and identity,* 32-50. Cambridge, MA: CABI.

Williams, R. 1973. *The country and the city.* London: Paladin.

Wilson, A. 1991. *The culture of nature: North American landscape from Disney to the Exxon Valdez.* Cambridge, MA: Blackwell.

Wilson, S. 1997. *Explore Haliburton.* Toronto: Boston Mills Press.

Wimbush, E., and M. Talbot. 1988. Introduction. In E. Wimbush and M. Talbot, eds., *Relative freedoms: Women and leisure,* xiii-xxii. Philadelphia: Open University Press.

Wolfe, R. 1951. Summer cottagers in Ontario. *Economic Geography* 27(1): 10-32.

–. 1952. Wasaga Beach: The divorce from the geographic environment. *Canadian Geographer* 1(2): 57-65.

–. 1962. The summer resorts of Ontario in the nineteenth century. *Ontario History* 54(3): 149-60.

–. 1965. About cottages and cottagers. *Landscape* 15(1): 6-8.

–. 1966. Recreation travel: The new migration. *Canadian Geographer* 10(1): 1-14.

–. 1977. Summer cottages in Ontario: Purpose-built for an inessential purpose. In J. Coppock, ed., *Second homes: Curse or blessing?* 17-33. Oxford: Pergamon Press.

Woodward, D., and E. Green. 1988. "Not tonight, dear!" The social control of women's leisure. In E. Wimbush and M. Talbot, eds., *Relative freedoms: Women and leisure,* 131-46. Philadelphia: Open University Press.

Wylie, J. 2007. *Landscape.* London: Routledge.

Wynn, G. 2006. Troubles with nature. In T. Loo, ed., *States of nature: Conserving Canada's wildlife in the twentieth century,* xi-xxi. Vancouver: UBC Press.

–. 2007. Foreword. In *The archive of place: Unearthing the pasts of the Chilcotin Plateau,* ix-xxvi. Vancouver: UBC Press.

Index

cottaging: absences, 243-46; across
Canada, 18-19; as Canadian, 1-2, 67,
86-87, 92, 241; definitions, 247n5; in
film, 25; future of, 243-46; history in
Haliburton, 4-5, 12-13, 15-18, 254n3;
history in Ontario, 4-5; in literature,
18, 19-25; as modern experience, 71-
74; presences, 237-42; as privilege,
235-36, 245-46; purpose of, 15-16;
and sense of community, 68-71, 131,
141, 150, 188
Courchene, T., 88
Cowan, R., 220
Crang, M., 59
creativity at cottage, 140-41
Cresswell, T., 59, 60, 240, 253nn14,21,22
Cronon, W., 255n13
Cross, A.W., 3, 25, 74
Crouch, D., 121
Cruikshank, J., 254n28
Csikszentmihalyi, M., 64, 134, 154, 260n1
Csordas, T., 121, 259n3
cultural values: and post–World War II
immigration, 5; reflected in cottage
aesthetic, 41-42; related to class, 32,
33-38
Cummings, H.R., 10, 11, 248n18
Curry, R.J., 14
Curry-Stevens, A., 32, 33
Curtis, R., 32

Deem, R., 219
demographics: of cottagers in Harrison
research, 27-29, 250n37, 251n38
Depression, 14, 201
Desforges, L., 121
developments: condominiums, 17, 50,
253n16; environmental concerns, 75;
lake plans, 3, 115-17; suburban-like,
30, 34, 73, 209, 254n3; "trophy"
cottages, 34, 36-37, 56-57

Di Leonardo, M., 167, 192
disability, 245
discipline: of cottage body, 121-22; and
moral behaviours, 122-23
Dramstad, W., 74
drownings, 213, 244, 260nn7,8, 261n14
du Prey, P. de la R., 248n6
Dudley, K.M., 35
Dummitt, C., 19, 72, 202, 203, 208, 212-
13, 214, 222, 228, 264n4
dumps, 74, 80, 255n17
Dunk, T., 32
Dunn's Pavilion, Muskoka, 251n41
Dyck, N., 32, 33, 37, 38, 121-23, 131, 151,
157
Dyer, R., 158, 159
Dysart et al. township, 11, 12, 249n24

Eagleton, T., 154
Edwards, J., 169, 170, 190, 192, 193, 194,
263n7
Ehrenreich, B., 32
electricity at cottage: importance to
women, 220, 226, 233, 264n10; mostly accepted, 54, 107
emergency 9-1-1 system, 107-11
England: immigrants from, 10, 87
environment. *See* nature
Erickson, B., 166, 265n7
escape: from city, 71-72, 105, 106, 151;
from cottage (for women), 225; from
time, 104, 106. *See also* liberation
Europe: immigrants from, 5, 32, 162
Evernden, N., 255n13

family: activities together, 180-86;
anchored by cottage, 187-91; centrality to cottage experience, 164; and
cottage inheritance, 17-18, 97-98, 113,
197-98, 257n1, 258n17; definitions
and roles, 164-65, 166-71, 248n10;